DATE DUE

BLACKS IN THE NEW WORLD

August Meier, Series Editor

A list of books in the series appears at the end of this book.

RISE TO BE A PEOPLE

PAUL
CAPTAIN
CUFFEE
1812.

RISE TO BE A PEOPLE

A Biography of Paul Cuffe

LAMONT D. THOMAS

UNIVERSITY OF ILLINOIS PRESS
Urbana and Chicago

Publication of this work was supported in part by a grant from the Andrew W. Mellon Foundation.

Manufactured in the United States of America
C 5 4 3 2 1

This book is printed on acid-free paper.

The jacket illustration and frontispiece graphically illustrate Paul Cuffe's centrality between America and Africa. Off the brig *Traveller*'s bow lies the rocky New England shoreline, to her stern the palm-lined West African coast. John Pole, M.D., of Bristol, England, made the original drawing. Abraham L. Pennock had it engraved by Mason & Mass. Photograph courtesy of the Library of Congress.

Library of Congress Cataloging-in-Publication Data

Thomas, Lamont D. (Lamont Dominick), 1937–
Rise to be a people.

Bibliography: p.
Includes index.
1. Cuffe, Paul, 1759–1817. 2. Afro-Americans—Biography. 3. Afro-Americans—Massachusetts—Biography. 4. Massachusetts—Biography. 5. Back to Africa movement. 6. Civil rights—Massachusetts—History—18th century. 7. Sierra Leone—History—To 1896. I. Title.
E185.97.C96T48 1986 974.4'00496073'0924 [B] 85-16335
ISBN 0-252-01212-7 (alk. paper)

To Margie, for her meticulous research assistance and her stamina as my birthing coach during years of labor on this book,

and

To Byron and Angela, who since learning to talk have increasingly asked, "When will it be finished?"

CONTENTS

PREFACE

TWENTY years ago I met Walter Yates, a visiting scholar at the Hartford Seminary Foundation in Connecticut, who was doing research on black American missionary work in West Africa. During a leisurely dinner one evening we discussed my search for a topic for my master's thesis, to be completed at Trinity College. This Livingstone College (North Carolina) professor told me that at times during his childhood, a black person in the South was referred to as a "bad Cuff" if he showed poor judgment. He guessed that the derogatory label stemmed from Paul Cuffe, an eighteenth-century black Yankee merchant who had urged his black brethren to leave the United States for Africa, presumably abandoning to a life of perpetual slavery those who chose to stay in this country. Yates also assumed that Cuffe had had a decided influence on the American Colonization Society, which eventually led to the establishment of Liberia. Should I wish to test these ideas, Cuffe's letters and other papers were somewhere in a Massachusetts library. As I had briefly taught in Liberia and had thrived on African studies courses in London and Hartford, I decided to accept Yates's challenge. The next morning I began the search that culminated in the writing of this book.

My first stop was the New Bedford Free Public Library, where Cuffe's known papers lay stacked in a large cardboard box; since then they have been carefully preserved and microfilmed. Glenn Weaver, my Trinity College advisor, patiently and enthusiastically directed the initial stage of my research and writing. Two years passed while I resumed teaching at Montclair Academy in New Jersey. Then, in the summer of 1969, I met the late Letitia Brown while we both were on the staff at Carnegie-Mellon University in Pittsburgh. Cuffe had always been one of her heroes, a "one-man civil rights movement," she liked to call him. She strongly encouraged me to pursue publication of my research and arranged a meeting with a friend at a New York publishing house. Good start, I was told, but had I really exhausted all the available sources?

With the goal of speedy publication I resumed full-time research in 1971, beginning at the New York Public Library and the New-York Historical Society. At this point I began to see more clearly the vast array of available historical sources. Liberian expert Svend Holsoe, at the University of Delaware, introduced me to American Colonization Society publications; George Brooks, at Indiana University, cited sources for West African–United States maritime trade; and Sierra Leone historian Christopher Fyfe, at the University of Edinburgh, insisted that any competent biography draw from the wealth of British colonial documents. Later, with Fyfe's invaluable assistance, my wife and I plowed through volumes at the Public Record Office in London. In Edinburgh, George Shepperson emphatically rejected the theory of a "bad Cuff." Probe further, he insisted, and I would find that black American and African scholars had not abandoned the man. In retrospect I realize only bad historiography has hidden the real Paul Cuffe.

The ever-widening search through university, public, private, religious, government, and historical society records in the United States and England repeatedly proved the limitations of existing historical interpretations. Henry Noble Sherwood's pioneering work on Cuffe in the *Journal of Negro History* (1923) set an enviable example for future researchers, and the resurgence of interest in black historiography in the 1960s led to two more studies—George Salvador's *Paul Cuffe, The Black Yankee, 1759–1817* (1969), and Sheldon Harris's *Paul Cuffe, Black America and the African Return* (1972). Like Sherwood's work, these biographies almost totally depended on the limited Cuffe collection at the New Bedford Library; neither man believed that adequate material could be found elsewhere. Thus, although Salvador's brief portrayal of a frugal black Yankee still has considerable validity, it fails to treat the later, crucial stage of Cuffe's life. And Harris's narrow interpretation of Cuffe as a Christian missionary to Africa is grossly misrepresentative due to an overdependence on zealous American missionary propaganda.

The previously unexamined, substantive material I have pulled together breathes new life into an only partially understood and inadequately researched historical figure, and also offers new perspectives on the activities of free blacks on both sides of the Atlantic. Countless newspapers and periodicals of Cuffe's day enable us to trace more accurately his astute and unrivaled business expansion, first as the founder of a most successful Afro-Indian enterprise in the late eighteenth century, and later as architect of the prestigious, thriving black partnership of Cuffe & Howards, in New Bedford. The United States' printed media suggest that he was the most widely publicized black American in the early 1800s. British media portrayed him as an "African Captain," the first to reach Europe with an all-black crew. Still, volumes of American Colonization Society documents reveal how desperately that white organization craved his endorsement for racist purposes—the deportation of blacks to Africa. A newly discovered 1807 British publication of a Delaware biography links Cuffe's African activities to the Anglo-American anti-slave-trade movement. Friend William Allen's 225-page letter-copy book, a pivotal source entitled "African Correspondence," located in a remote pharmaceutical warehouse on London's East End, closely ties the Pan-African to an advocacy role for disenchanted black settlers fighting Sierra Leone's white economic monopoly. And Quaker records in England and the United States show his innovative role as a black Friend. In short, Paul Cuffe may be the most historically accessible black American until the mid-nineteenth century.

Readers have been spared the tedium of proof of this historical accessibility in the form of lengthy documentation within the text, but are encouraged to peruse, and I hope in many cases to probe, the sources listed in the notes and the extended bibliography. Periodically, explanations in the notes expand on material in the text; I consider the notes section indispensable for the serious scholar.

My deepest gratitude goes to the countless people who have so generously assisted and unfailingly encouraged me in this undertaking, especially Glenn Weaver, Letitia Brown, and Christopher Fyfe, each having entered at a crucial point in the work. I also am grateful for Friend Henry Cadbury's humble suggestions, Friend Frederick B. Tolles's early assistance, John Hope Franklin's repeated encouragement, and the guidance of Nantucket historian Edouard Stackpole. Additional sources were suggested by David B. Davis of Yale, Philip Curtin of the University of Wisconsin, Norman Bennett of Boston University, Roger Anstey of the University of Canterbury, and Kenneth Charlton of the University of Birmingham. I would like to thank as well Llewellyn Howland of Boston, Westport residents Mrs. Louis H. Tripp, Margaret D. Quilin, and Julius T. Smith, Esther M. Douty of Washington, D.C., and Emil F. Guba of Nantucket. If suggestions by any of these individuals, and others I have failed to name, have not been followed, the fault is mine.

The staffs of the following libraries have been of great help: New Bedford Free Public Library; Library of Congress; National Archives; Federal Records Center, Waltham, Mass.; Boston Public Library; Baker Library of Harvard University; Nantucket Historical Association and Peter Folger Museum, Nantucket, Mass.; Old Dartmouth Historical Society, New Bedford, Mass.; Marine Historical Association, Mystic, Conn.; and Massachusetts Historical Society. Special thanks to Leo Flaherty, curator of the Massachusetts Archives for the Secretary of the Commonwealth.

Thanks are extended also for assistance from the Historical Society of Pennsylvania; Haverford College Archives; Friends Historical Library of Swarthmore College; New York Public Library; New-York Historical Society; Olin Library of Cornell University; Howard University Archives; Maryland Historical Society; Chicago Historical Society; William R. Perkins Library of Duke University; Rhode Island Historical Society, and the Society of Friends Collection in that library; John Carter Brown Library of Brown University; Delaware Historical Society, and Eleutherian Mills Historical Library of Wilmington; Georgia Historical Society; and Trevor Arnett Library of Atlanta University.

The staffs of British repositories helped to authenticate Cuffe's activities in Europe and Africa. A special thanks is due for the kindly assistance of Edward Milligan at the Friends House Library in London. I am grateful to the firm of Allen and Hanbury, Ltd., and especially its president, John Hanbury; the Church Missionary Society Library; Methodist Missionary Society Library; British Public Record Office; Liverpool University Library; and Liverpool Record Office of the Liverpool Public Library.

My indebtedness extends to the educational institutions that have so generously permitted this teacher-writer a flexibility in scheduling of classes and the use of their library facilities. I particularly must thank Philip Anderson and Rhoda Neuman, formerly of Montclair Academy, Montclair, N.J.; John Stander and Jim Heryer of Sunset Hill School, Kansas City, Mo.; and Joan Neuwith and the supportive staff and students of Bolton (Conn.) High School.

Early drafts of this book were diligently typed in Kansas City by Claire Hildebrand and Saundra Master. In Connecticut, Janet Carson dedicated countless hours and loving care to type the final draft. Ann Orlov of Cambridge, Mass., painstakingly edited portions of earlier drafts, as did Sue Brander of Tolland, Conn. Theresa Sears, of the University of Illinois Press, labored to delicately refashion the manuscript for publication, and Susie Warren keyboarded it. I also thank August Meier, series editor, for his insistence that I persist in my efforts to produce something of historical value.

I express a special gratitude to my late grandmother, Clara Moulton Thomas, and to my parents, James Moulton and Antoinette Dominick Thomas, for their generosity, perseverance, and love.

Lamont D. Thomas
Tolland, Connecticut

RISE TO BE A PEOPLE

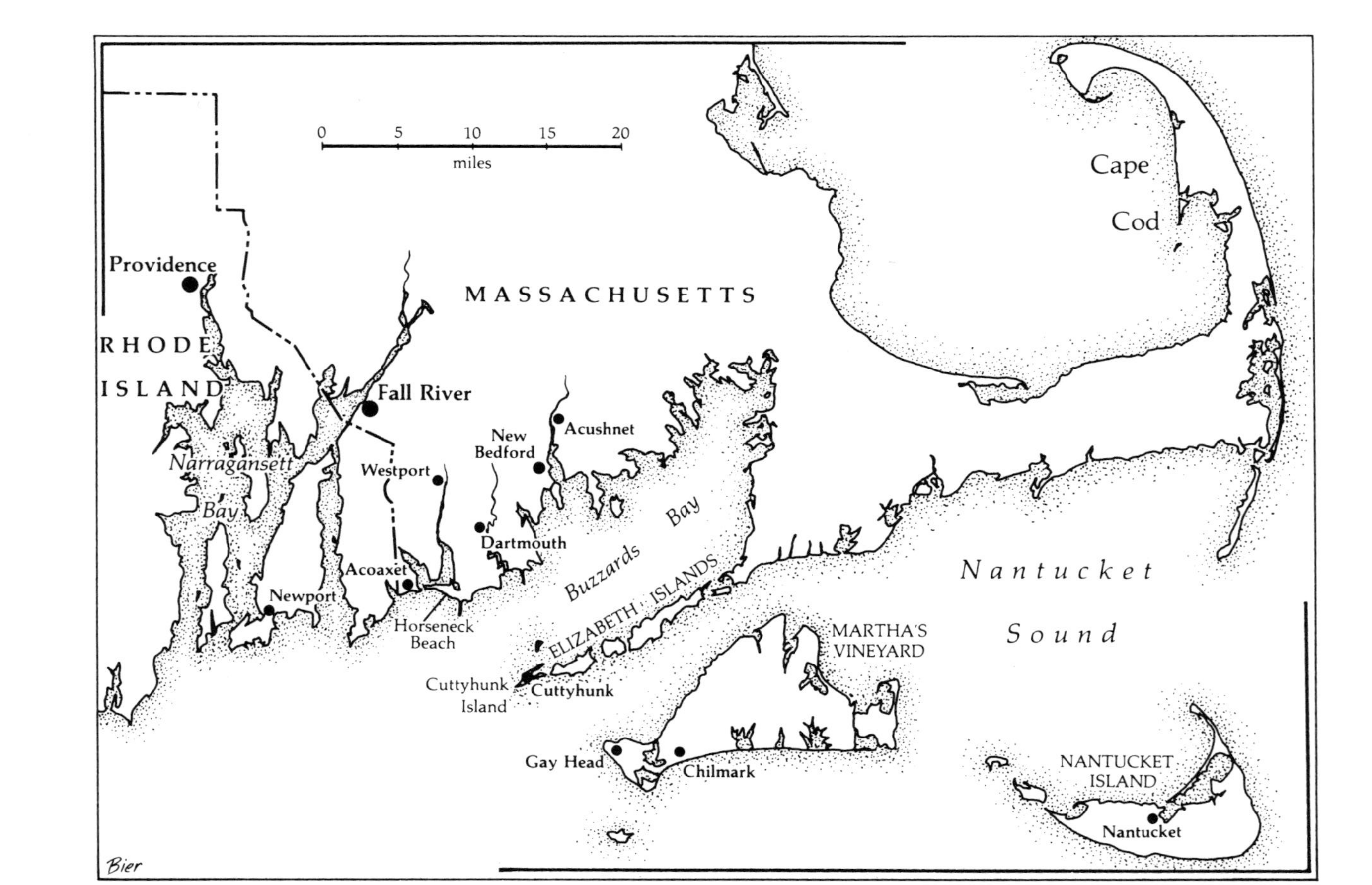
0
5
10
15
20
miles
Providence
RHODE
ISLAND
MASSACHUSETTS
Cape
Cod
Fall River
Narragansett
Bay
Westport
New
Bedford
Acushnet
Dartmouth
Acoaxet
Newport
Horseneck
Beach
Buzzards
Bay
ELIZABETH ISLANDS
Cuttyhunk
Island
Cuttyhunk
Nantucket
Sound
MARTHA'S
VINEYARD
Gay Head
Chilmark
NANTUCKET
ISLAND
Nantucket
Bier

1

COFFE SLOCUM MISTER

"VIRTUE outlives the grave" was Peleg Slocum's family motto. A virtuous Quaker by contemporary standards, Peleg lived in Dartmouth, in the Massachusetts Bay Colony, at the close of the seventeenth century and bore all the outward signs of the elect. A prosperous farmer, merchant, and preacher, he almost single-handedly financed the building of Dartmouth's first Friends Meeting House. Peleg Slocum also owned slaves.[1]

Slocum descendants aspired to Peleg's status. Sometime during the late 1720s Ebenezer Slocum acquired a young Ashanti slave of Akan ancestry. The youth's name was Kofi, which in his native tongue meant "born on Friday."[2] Kofi had also been a slave in West Africa, but slavery was very different there. Ashanti slaves could marry and own property, even their own slaves; they could swear to an oath, bear witness, and inherit their master's lands. When Kofi was about ten years old he was seized by or sold to Fanti middlemen, who delivered him to the Royal African Company slavetraders on the Guinea coast.[3] The slavetraders, in turn, bound Kofi and other Africans for the dreaded middle passage to the lucrative slave markets of colonial America.[4]

Kofi reached Newport, Rhode Island, by 1728, the same year that Ebenezer Slocum married Bathsheba Hull at the Newport Friends Meeting.[5] Either as part of Bathsheba's dowry or by Ebenezer's purchase, Kofi became the property of the Slocum family. Few records remain to tell us how Kofi perceived his youth in this strange land or what tasks he performed in the Slocum household. We may assume, from later developments, that the African received mild treatment and a basic education in Quaker values. He was fortunate to avoid the harsher upbringing of slaves on nearby Narragansett Bay plantations. Eventually, however, Ebenezer sold Kofi to his nephew John

Slocum, also of Dartmouth. This bill of sale, the earliest record documenting the existence of Paul Cuffe's family in North America, is dated February 16, 1742:[6] "Know all men by these Presents that I Ebenezer Slocum of Dartmouth in the County of Bristol and Province of Massachusetts Bay in New England yeoman for in Consideration of the Sum of one hundred and fifty Pounds Current Money . . . deliver to the Said John Slocum acertain Negro Man of about twenty five years of age Named Cuffe. . . ."

Quaker philosophies were shaping a new destiny for the Ashanti-born slave. Thirty years before, when a Dartmouth woman had ordered her slave stripped and hung for alleged sexual advances, local Friends had queried at their next Quarterly Meeting whether slavery "be agreeable to Truth." Dartmouth Friends maintained a thriving commercial relationship with Quakers on nearby Nantucket Island, where the whaling industry was beginning to flourish, and in 1733 Nantucket Friends became the first in America to collectively denounce slavery at their Meeting. Five years later Philadelphia's outspoken Friend Benjamin Lay vehemently attacked the "Hellish Practice," saying it represented "the very worst part of the old Whores Merchandize, nasty filthy Whore of Whores, *Babilon's Bastards*."[7]

Such news flowed on the tides between the colonial port cities. Friends in Dartmouth knew of ideas taking shape in Nantucket, Philadelphia, and elsewhere. The virtuous Slocum motto still ran deep in the family's Quaker conscience, and so it was that sometime during the mid-1740s John Slocum freed Kofi. Other Dartmouth slaves would not be so fortunate for another thirty years. The appointed liberation day caught Kofi completely by surprise. The African wept when hearing the news, then worked an additional period to earn two suits of clothes and some cash.[8]

In 1745 the man "born on Friday" announced his intention to marry Ruth Moses, a local Indian woman. Her Wampanoag forebears had welcomed the first settlers, assisted them, and joined them at the Thanksgiving feast of 1620. When Nantucketers had wanted to learn how to catch whales, a Wampanoag named Ichabod Paddock had taught them. Dartmouth originally belonged to the Wampanoags, and its seafaring commerce owed its beginnings to Ruth Moses's people. She owed her biblical name to the Christian missionaries who took the land. Kofi Slocum, who had taken his master's surname, and Ruth Moses married in 1746.[9]

The couple lived first in Dartmouth, the only town they both knew well. Later they moved to Cuttyhunk, one of the bleak, windswept

Elizabeth Islands nine miles to the southeast, near Martha's Vineyard. The island had once belonged to Peleg Slocum, then to Captain Holder Slocum. Although the rocky terrain offered but a harsh subsistence even for the industrious farming couple, it afforded the advantage of isolation from the negative aspects of encroaching civilization. Ruth bore ten children, most of whom received good biblical names, as their mother had: David, Jonathan, Sarah, Mary, Phebe, John, Paul, Lydia, Ruth, and Freelove.[10] Theirs was a closeknit family.

Ruth and Kofi Slocum "followed the Quaker Meeting." Although they were not accepted as Friends they espoused Quaker principles and raised their children to labor "in the Light." They believed that acceptance by both God and man depended on hard labor, honesty, frugality, prudence, and order. Yankee practicality had to be tempered by humility, particularly when dealing with European society. No task was considered too great an undertaking.[11]

During the years at Cuttyhunk the family maintained its ties with the outside world. At first venturing out into Buzzards Bay in crudely constructed dories, and later in more sturdy craft, the family traveled north to Dartmouth and southeast to the large Indian settlement at Chilmark near Gay Head on Martha's Vineyard. The children thrived on their contacts with others, and their aging father learned to write. Aided by a literate benefactor, Kofi laboriously copied neatly rounded letters into a faded notebook. Business entries attest to his extraordinary progress. In 1763 Kofi paid, or promised to pay, £100 in the town of Dartmouth. A year later he and a son received carpenter's fees for erecting a new residence on Cuttyhunk. Kofi Slocum, once a slave, now kept a business ledger.

During the early 1760s the white Slocums sailed to Cuttyhunk fairly frequently. Kofi moved his family to Chilmark, a move that in effect drew them away from the white Slocums and into the Indian community on Martha's Vineyard. The following journal entry records their progress: "Chilmark, 1764, March, Argus Allen for promis me wife to pay for your bord, your and your mans for three day bord, three pounds old tenor." Income was derived from carting sails, rigging, hawsers, and anchors. Vessels carried workers "to the main," and Kofi hired people to help him. He had become a small, independent merchant in the Buzzards Bay community.[12]

In 1766 "Coffe," as he now spelled his name, bought a 116-acre farm in Dartmouth, "with appurtenances, buildings, and fences," from David and Grace Brownell for 650 Spanish-milled dollars. Two thousand pine and oak boards were to be delivered by Brownell by March

25, the accession date.[13] That same year Dartmouth residents hotly debated something far more threatening to them than this black freeholder's purchase: how would they respond to the oppressive terms of Britain's Stamp Act? Colonists should not be taxed without representation, they argued.

All four sons and six daughters, ranging in age from two to nineteen years, moved to the mainland with their parents. Paul, at eight years of age, joined the others in enlarging buildings and farming the land. The older children worked neighboring property, and at least one son continued caretaking duties on Cuttyhunk. However, the short runs into Buzzards Bay became increasingly dangerous as political tempers flared. In June 1772 Rhode Islanders from nearby Warwick attacked and burned the *Gaspee,* a British customs schooner, amid public demands for freedom from Britain's "slavery" of America.

Coffe Slocum died in the spring of 1772 at the age of about fifty-four years, a man who recognized the meaning of freedom more than most. He left his Indian widow and their ten children to preserve the best of the Yankee and Quaker values he had come to live by. He also left a journal that is extraordinary for its painstaking entries. The core of Coffe Slocum's life and ambition, and his legacy, emerges in one poignant entry: "Daarmouth Chechiemark Cullhonk Nossnour and Romykes and Care Dare Ere Fear Give We Heare Are . . . good Do good all Do good to All . . . Give Give Give . . . Good Do Good at all times I lern read AbcdABBBDDJAATM Coffe Slocum Mister."[14]

2

THE STRUGGLE FOR INDEPENDENCE

THE political climate became more tense with each passing day. Dartmouth resident Joseph Rotch, owner of the ship *Dartmouth*, learned firsthand the price of political unrest when his ship's cargo was pitched overboard during the Boston Tea Party. The people of Dartmouth voted at their town meeting in July 1774 to reject further trade with England, so as to save themselves "from Bondage and Slavery."[1] The town's Afro-Indian community, all of whom were disfranchised, heartily concurred but undoubtedly wondered why the same logic did not apply to those brethren still enslaved in Dartmouth.

Coffe Slocum's family, now without its African father, struggled to stay together, despite Jonathan's withdrawal to Chilmark on Martha's Vineyard, David's return to Cuttyhunk, and Paul's adventures at sea.[2] Since his father's death, Paul later boasted, he had shifted for himself. Whaling merchants like Joseph Rotch and Joseph Russell welcomed crewmen without regard to color, so the teenager shipped aboard. Whalers sailed for the Bay of Mexico, hunted near the West Indies, or searched off western Africa. By 1773, when fourteen Nantucket whalers crossed paths with slavers off the Guinea coast, Paul already was sailing aboard vessels bound for the West Indies.[3]

Although for a short time whaling was quite profitable, with some 360 vessels employing 4,700 men, prosperity abruptly ended with the rise in British captures along the eastern seaboard. Seizures included New Bedford vessels with black and Indian crew members. Paul's third voyage ended in a British prison in New York.[4]

Three months later Paul was back in Dartmouth, freed from the rapidly overcrowding British jails and wanting nothing so much as security and an identity. At the time that meant going by his father's African name but his mother's Indian identity. "Musta is my Nature," he wrote, meaning he was a *mustee*, or of part-Indian descent. His brother John, the only one who had remained at home with his mother and sisters, vacillated, first referring to himself as "John Slocum of Dartmouth . . . *mustee* man"; the next year his signature read "John Cuff."[5] Mary's Indian husband, Michael Wainer, became a likely role model on the family farm, as it seemed safe to be Indian.[6]

Or was it? In the winter of 1778 no place was safe from British landing parties. Even more unnerving was word from Boston, where the state legislature had concluded a controversial constitutional draft. According to the proposed Article 5, every male, "being free, and twenty-one years of age, excepting Negroes, Indians, and molattoes," would be entitled to vote. Even a war for independence would not bring representation for people of color. In May, to the relief of Dartmouth's nonwhites, the town meeting rejected the state constitution, including Article 5. The exclusion, whites had argued, "deprives them [Negroes, Indians, and mulattoes] of the natural right all men have to make their own laws, and dispose of their own property."[7]

On September 5, 1778, Tory sympathizers signaled for a timely attack on Dartmouth: Bristol County's Second Regiment was out of town. The Elihu and James Akin shipyard, just one of the local firms supplying the patriot cause, was planning to launch several new vessels, which the British hoped to destroy, along with supplies from the oil factories, rope walks, and a rum distillery. Two frigates, eighteen gun brigs, and thirty-six troop-transport vessels descended on Dartmouth, with the invaders outnumbering the defenders ten to one. Massive destruction resulted. The palatial homes of propertied aristocrats such as the Rotches, Russells, and Howlands were leveled.[8] The resulting hardships for the colonists intensified their struggle, which in turn molded character and identity.

Taxes had risen in 1777, two increases were required in 1778, and three more were ordered the following year. Although Indian lands were tax-exempt, Negro lands were not. Thus, town fathers levied heavy taxes on the Coffe Slocum family farm as though it were Paul's and John's, and even though Paul was not twenty-one years old. Paul continued to use his father's African name: his African identity grew as well as his opposition to taxation. His desire to be independent of the community exceeded that of his brothers.[9]

Paul Cuffe became a maritime trader and blockade runner, for he relished the challenges of the sea; profits also promised to be far more substantial than those from farming, despite the danger of being seized. Seaside communities such as Martha's Vineyard, Nantucket, and Warren, Rhode Island, had been plundered by British marauders, who roamed along the coast. Blockade runners thus had to sail on the darkest nights and through the stormiest seas to avoid capture.[10]

Nantucket lay over the horizon, a passage of eight soaking hours at best. Yet the island's lack of perishable goods and timber made it an ideal market for Paul's venture. His brother David, back from Cuttyhunk, helped him build a small boat and joined Paul on trading expeditions. David withdrew as a member of the crew, however, when Paul suggested running blockades—crossings to Cuttyhunk were enough danger for him. Cuffe's earliest biography recounts the mariner's solo outings: "He launched into the ocean and was steering for the island . . . when Refugee Pirates discovered, chased, and seized himself and treasures. Robbed of everything, he returned home pennyless but not discouraged." Several more attempts to cross to Nantucket resulted in his reaching the beaches, only to be attacked by "Refugees . . . acquainted with his arrival."[11] He tried yet again and finally succeeded in making Nantucket his first maritime market.

The "Hard Winter" of 1780 kept the intrepid mariner on the farm. John noted "a Very Long Snow Aboute knee deep upon the Level." It so froze Buzzards Bay that horses were able to cross to the islands. Paul's landfall, Nantucket, was reduced to a "state of penury," wrote another contemporary. Islanders dug up peat moss to fuel their stoves.[12]

Lawmakers in Boston, after trudging through the snow to draw up a new state constitution to be submitted to voters, frantically approved three more tax levies in 1780; and Dartmouth selectmen added a fourth for local residents. Town petitions against taxation, as from Cape Cod's Yarmouth, Barnstable, and Truro, reached the Massachusetts General Court. A massive tax revolt was under way.[13]

On February 10, 1780, John and Paul Cuffe were joined by recently liberated Dartmouth blacks Adventure Child, Samual Gray, Pero Howland, Pero Russell, and Pero Coggeshall in presenting their plea to the state. "We apprehend ourselves to be aggrieved in that while we are not allowed the Privileges of freemen of the State, having No vote or Influence in the Election with those that tax us, [the state has acted] . . . against a familiar Exception of Power . . . too well known to need a Recital at this place."[14] The petitioners noted that they could not inherit "as our Neighbors, the white people do"—both Cuffes had thus far been deprived of their father's estate. Most signators had suffered in hard slavery without due reward, some for as long as thirty and forty years. They had neither livestock nor land, and a few survived as "Distressed mongrels," living no better than the legislators' dogs. Collectively, the Dartmouth petitioners were

"Chiefly of the African Extraction," which meant that as "Poor Despised black People" they experienced equality "Neither by Sea nor by Land." "Oh God, be merciful unto the poor," they humbly prayed, " . . . grant us Relief."[15]

"Interesting Petition or Memorial from Negroes of Dartmouth for exemption from taxation," read the entry to the state's record of this petition for May 14, 1780.[16] Two days later a committee of three was formed to study the petition. Representatives William Stickney, Benjamin Thomas, and Captain Seth Sumner realized the sensitive nature of their task, since over the past several years the issue of black rights had been an embarrassment to the legislature.[17] Earlier, Massachusetts blacks had sought an end to slavery "within the bowels of a free Country" and had harped on "the inconsistency of acting, themselves, the part which they [legislators] condemn & oppose in others [the British]."[18]

Finally the lawmakers responded, prompting John Cuffe's terse appraisal: "But We Received None." The petition had failed in the House of Representatives. Harrassed legislators had chosen to believe that the state's new constitution, now devoid of language that would withhold voting rights solely on the basis of race, would guarantee Negroes and Indians the rights they sought.[19] Property value, not color, would determine the franchise; by implication, blacks who qualified by reason of property would be allowed to vote.

The Cuffes dropped their role as public defenders in October 1780 when the town meeting levied yet another tax. They allegedly owed in excess of £154 in back taxes for three years. John decided to try once again to escape taxation based on his Indian heritage, and he was probably responsible for persuading Paul to join him in litigation. The brothers drew up a petition for the Bristol County Court of Common Pleas, claiming to be "Indian men and by law not the subject of Taxation for any Estate Real or personal." The petition further argued that they had been unjustly assessed a double poll tax because Paul, who had turned twenty-one on January 17, 1780, was a minor at the time of the initial levy.[20]

This attempt to avoid taxes only exasperated authorities. Assessors Benjamin Russell, Richard Kirby, Christopher Gifford, and John Smith ordered Constable Collins to seize the delinquents and "commit [them] to the common gaol of the said County of Bristol." Four days later the brothers were incarcerated. However, the court did respond to a writ of habeas corpus for "the bodies of John and Paul Cuffe said to be Indian men," signed by the powerful Walter Spooner, Dartmouth's council member to the General Court, delegate to the Constitutional Convention, and personal advisor to Massachusetts Governor John Hancock. The writ specified that the Cuffe brothers were to be released until the tax assessors showed just cause. Spooner's display of justice emboldened the tax protesters.[21]

When a February 18, 1781, resolution from Governor Hancock called for new taxes, John Cuffe recopied the petition sent to Boston the previous winter, although he carefully omitted all references to "Despised" blacks and "Distressed mongrels" living in huts. Instead, he exercised tact and restraint, referring to the petitioners only as "Chiefly of the African Extract." But the memorial never reached the legislature. Instead, on March 8 the board of selectmen appointed Walter Spooner to respond to the Cuffes' claim to be Indian. Edward Pope, Dartmouth's representative to the House, was also alerted.[22]

According to Spooner, the issue at hand was the Cuffes' right to vote, not their identity. Although the state constitution inferred enfranchisement for Negroes and Indians, townships were responsible for implementing that right. Forthwith, the Cuffes appealed to their white neighbors of Dartmouth. Would the town approve of de facto exclusion, in spite of recently declared constitutional rights? The challenge to selectmen was clear: "Put a stroke on your next Warrant for calling a town meeting so that it may legally be Laid Before said town By way of vote to know the mind of said town whether all free Negroes and molattoes shall have the same Privileges in this said town of Dartmouth as the white People have Respecting Places of profit, choosing of officers, and the Like . . . or, that we have Relief granted us Jointly from Taxation . . . under our depressed circumstances."[23] The wording offered a hard choice to financially strapped selectmen: either the town would accept tax payments from blacks, which implied equal status and voting privileges, or it would reject sorely needed revenue.

The selectmen chose silence, and nothing in the existing records indicates that residents ever voted on the question at a town meeting. Freedom from Britain was a more compelling issue than the rights of a few disgruntled, disfranchised blacks who were lucky enough to be out of bondage. Yet on June 9, 1781, Constable Richard Collins accepted £8, 12*s* "in full for all" the brothers' taxes and court costs, a substantial reduction in the £154 originally owed. Three days later the charges against John and Paul Cuffe were dropped. With concessions on both sides, an out-of-court settlement peacefully resolved the protracted legal encounter.[24]

Hard times persisted, and the fate of the new nation hung in the balance. Dartmouth selectmen had to petition the state legislature because of their own distress. The Cuffe brothers also struggled on a private level: beset by personal frustrations, Paul turned to liquor, and John, the vigilant moral guardian of the family, lashed out at his seafaring brother. In a journal note he wrote of Paul's character, "Excess of Drinking Burns up Beauty, hastens age, makes a man a Beast, a strong man weak, and a Wise man a fool." On February 25, 1783, Paul Cuffe and Alice Pequit, a local Indian woman who may have lived among the Pequots on Martha's Vineyard, were married by Justice of the Peace Benjamin Russell. As one of Dartmouth's tax assessors and selectmen, Russell needed no introduction to the groom. Two weeks later the couple's first child was born, and within days the United States of America celebrated its independence from Britain.[25]

The nation's celebration coincided with Cuffe's decision to intensify his own struggle for independence. Now over twenty-one, he was assuming family responsibilities of his own. He had emerged from the Revolution as a veteran of political, economic, and social conflict. He fully identified himself as a black American, both in words and action. Dartmouth officials tacitly had acknowledged that the ideals of democracy could serve minorities as well as whites. But just how much freedom could Paul Cuffe expect in the new nation?

3

RISING PROSPERITY AND AFRICAN AWARENESS

EARLY in life Paul Cuffe had discovered that prominent and powerful whites would tolerate useful people of color. Now Dartmouth needed enterprising citizens to rebuild the town. Antislavery Quakers such as the Rotch family dominated political and economic life in the community, and these Friends knew the grim legacy of ostracism, which had driven them from England. For a black man seeking opportunity, Dartmouth was a more favorable locale than most in Massachusetts—or in the nation, for that matter.

At the age of twenty-four, with his family begun and an array of working skills on which to draw, Cuffe sought economic independence in the evolving American civilization.[1] He knew he needed wealth to achieve social status in the fledgling republic. And though he had already developed basic seafaring skills and proved his willingness to take risks, he still had to learn the subtleties of entrepreneurial success. In the expansive postwar years an astute observer could learn by example from those who already knew how to amass wealth.

Cuffe learned just that by observing the burgeoning family enterprises of local Quakers such as the Rotches. He did so from the precarious vantage point of a black freeholder. After renting a shoemaker's shop with profits from his maritime ventures, he later was able to purchase the property on the Acoaxet River from Isaac Sowle for forty pounds on June 2, 1789.[2] The value of the property qualified him to vote, but apparently he did not do so. Laws enacted at that time made it clear that black people were tolerated at the pleasure of the white community. In 1786 Negroes, Indians, and mulattoes were forbidden by law to marry whites. Two years later the state lashed out at runaway slaves with a law to punish "Rogues, Vagabonds, common Beggers, and other idle disorderly and lewd Persons." Criminality was defined by race. No person "being an African or Negro" could reside in Massachusetts for more than two months without a certificate from the secretary of state; a mere complaint to any justice of the peace could lead to their removal.[3] Whether a runaway or a resident, blacks faced potential legal exclusion.

Inasmuch as the Rotches were, in effect, the only business mentors a man like Cuffe could hope to have, the building of their empire bears recounting. The rebuilding of Dartmouth began with the return of Friend Joseph Rotch, who had spent the war years on Nantucket. It was Rotch who named Dartmouth's eastern portion New Bedford, and it was his family more than any other that brought prosperity to the town. Settling atop Johnny Cake Hill, Joseph and his son, Joseph, Jr., rebuilt the family business. By 1788 William Rotch, Jr., had joined them, and William Rotch, Sr., "by far the richest man on Nantucket," soon followed. William, Sr., married off his children with a good eye toward preserving the family fortune: Elizabeth, Thomas, and William, Jr., all married into a single Newport mercantile family. The firm of William Rotch & Sons came to include William, Jr., Thomas, and Elizabeth's husband, Samuel Rodman.[4]

The Rotch family fortunes increased dramatically, and their power soon extended from the Rhode Island line to the east bank of the Acushnet River. By the 1790s they owned factories producing spermaceti, iron, and cordage, as well as a ropewalk, a warehouse, a sawmill, a sail loft, a coalhouse, and a blacksmith shop. Several of William Rotch, Jr.'s, mills prospered only a few miles from the Cuffe home at the head of the Acoaxet River, in the western third of Dartmouth, which had been incorporated as a separate township called Westport. The Rotch whalers continued to be "fortunate" in the Bay of Mexico. A 1791 letter from William, Jr., to his uncle Francis reports that "the convenience for conducting" business in New Bedford was "very great."[5]

In short, the Rotches epitomized the "minor virtues" of the Quaker elect: honesty, truthfulness, fulfillment of promises, thrift, and hard work. Whenever possible they did business with other Quakers, both at home and abroad, and they maintained a lively correspondence with English Friends both during the War for Independence and afterward. They possessed the innovative spirit in manufacturing, trade, and banking that made British Quakers such valuable commercial partners. They were a power to be reckoned with.[6]

Paul Cuffe, born in 1759, as was William Rotch, Jr., began his quest for success within sight of Johnny Cake Hill and the Rotches' New

Bedford residential compound. He may even have been whaling from the Rotch island refuge of Nantucket soon after the war. In a diary entry dated August 24, 1783, a local Tory may have been referring to Cuffe: "Paul Negro came in from whaling last Friday with G. Clark brought 140 bbls was gone 12 or 13 weeks."[7] He certainly knew Nantucket waters and the people, as he continued to make trading runs to the island and also did business with Samuel Rodman of William Rotch & Sons. From the countinghouses at the foot of Nantucket's Main Street to the New Bedford waterfront, Cuffe had ample opportunity to observe—and strive to duplicate—the Rotch family business.[8]

The Westporter selected his brother-in-law Michael Wainer as his business partner. A talented seaman and trusted friend, Wainer also had fathered a potential crew of six boys. Cuffe hired someone, presumably his brother-in-law, and began sailing the Connecticut shoreline in a twelve-ton schooner built of "cold box iron," purchased with profits from his other business ventures. His next vessel, a sixteen-to-eighteen-ton schooner, permitted him to sail for several seasons. Cuffe and Wainer headed the schooner toward the Grand Banks off Newfoundland on several codding runs, where they joined other barrel-bottomed Yankee codders called "heel-tappers," known for their low waists and high quarterdecks. Later, Paul shipped out as mate aboard a trader bound for North Carolina, returning as the ship's captain. By 1790 Michael and Mary Wainer's family was ready for sea duty: Thomas, Gardner, Paul, Jeremiah, David, and John ranged in age from seventeen to eight years. Paul and Alice Cuffe's four daughters would eventually lure their own captains of industry.[9]

Between 1787 and 1795 Westport shipbuilders registered three vessels, presumed to be those belonging to Cuffe and Wainer.[10] The first of the trio was a twenty-five-ton schooner, *Sunfish,* so named for her first catch. During the years she sailed Paul enhanced his reputation for daring at sea. At one point whaling masters on four other vessels insisted that the black captain was unprepared for whaling and thus refused to join with him, as was customary. Cuffe insisted on being lowered over the side in his one small whaling boat, whereupon the other masters ceased their opposition.[11] During that season the *Sunfish*'s crew brought six of seven whales to shipside, two of them harpooned by Cuffe himself.

Their second schooner, the forty-two-ton *Mary,* slid into the water in the fall of 1792.[12] Wainer commanded the *Sunfish* to Newport, Rhode Island; Cuffe followed in the *Mary.* On March 20, 1793, the

Mary, named after Cuffe's sister and Wainer's wife, was entered at Newport's collector of customs for a fee of $2.52, in the very port Cuffe's father had entered as a slave some sixty-five years earlier. The brig *Hannah* would soon depart from those same docks for a slaving run to Africa's Guinea coast and then to Havana, Cuba.[13] Cuffe's growing presence as a reputable and prosperous black merchant would silently refute the very essence of the Atlantic slave trade.

Although William Rotch, Jr., advertised Philadelphia and Russian bar iron, the black captain sailed off to the Quaker City for his own iron to build a third vessel. His Westport shipyard, built at the homestead on the east branch of the Acoaxet River, hummed with activity, and the double spars of a sixty-two-foot square-sterned schooner—the *Ranger,* perhaps the family's most cherished vessel of all he constructed—towered above the farm. To pay for the *Ranger* Cuffe sold both the *Sunfish* and the *Mary,* thus displaying in finance the same daring that had earned him respect at sea, for one disaster would have wiped out his maritime investment. He bristled on the subject of diversifying ownership for the *Ranger.* This sacred cow would never be owned outside the family; her masters would be from the family, as would her crew, whenever possible.[14]

After launching the *Ranger* in about 1796, the black captain had more to worry about, as he navigated her past Horseneck Beach for a southern voyage, than just foundering on the rocks. While gathering supplies in New Bedford, Cuffe had learned of continuing strains in Anglo-American relations which threatened ships along the eastern seaboard. His own government's Fugitive Slave Act, which legalized seizures of any blacks suspected of escape, clearly endangered an all-black ship's company. And though every state except Georgia had ostensibly ended its Atlantic slave trade, free blacks at sea were always vulnerable to capture.[15] Yet his crew continued to trim canvas as the *Ranger* headed for Virginia, the heart of the most dangerous territory into which a free black could go.

In Norfolk Cuffe heard reports about a large shipment of Indian corn available at Vienna, the official port-of-entry to Maryland's Eastern Shore. He welcomed the challenge and sailed up the Nanticoke River, passing slaves tilling the fields. A few miles south of Vienna the *Ranger* came into view of Lewis Wharf and of Weston, the prosperous plantation home of U.S. Senator John Henry. The somber captain's words to his crew could be heard above and below deck: practice exemplary conduct, avoid intemperate behavior, abuse no man. A shocked crowd gathered as the *Ranger*'s crew came into view, recounts Cuffe's first biographical sketch: "On arrival the people were filled with astonishment and alarm. A vessel owned and commanded by a person of color, and manned with a crew of the same complexion, was unprecedented and surprising. The white inhabitants were struck with apprehension of the injurious effects which such circumstances would have on the minds of their slaves, but perhaps they were still more fearful that, under the veil of commerce, he had arrived among them with hostile intentions."[16] Confrontation appeared certain.

By their reasoning residents of Vienna had good cause for alarm. These crewmen were not Indians like the nearby Nanticokes but of African ancestry. The townspeople still complained bitterly about slaves who had deserted their owners for British vessels during the Revolution; in fact, slave masters called them "stolen" property. Moreover, Maryland's large free Negro population reputedly held goods stolen by slaves. As a result of these experiences, in 1796 a law was passed that bound suspicious free blacks to six months' servitude. The people who crowded the docks that morning also had fresh recollections of the frightening news of the successful slave rebellions in Haiti. So terrified were Marylanders of possible rebellion among their own slaves that they had put a stop to the African slave trade.[17] Clearly, they now feared that the *Ranger*'s crew might try to incite their slaves to rebel.

Paul Cuffe confidently stepped ashore as a man in command of his own business. He had impeccable mercantile credentials: proof of registry at New Bedford—one of New England's most illustrious ports—and receipts from such reliable merchant houses as William Rotch & Sons. The crowd's attention shifted to the federal collector of customs, James Frazier, as they demanded that he seize the black captain and prohibit his return to the ship. Frazier's decision appalled the crowd: the captain's credentials were flawless; he would be permitted to unload the *Ranger*'s cargo.

Cuffe had more sense than to flaunt his victory. Instead, he conducted himself "with candour, modesty and firmness, and all his crew behaved not only inoffensively, but with a conciliating propriety."[18] After several days suspicion subsided and residents extended respect, "even kindness." Prominent citizens toured the vessel in awe that a black crew could manage such a craft and a black man could own it. One citizen even invited Cuffe and his family to dine in town. When the *Ranger* set sail a full cargo of Indian corn—which would bring a thousand dollars on the New Bedford market—lay in the ship's hold. His voyage had netted an equally profitable cargo of experience.

By displaying exemplary conduct the crew had made social gains that yielded economic rewards. Cuffe proved that his black crew, armed with conciliating propriety, might profit almost anywhere. The *Ranger* would soon return south.

Due to the easing of Anglo-American hostilities vessels once again could trade freely with a British cargo. At Passamaquoddy, Maine, directly across from St. Andrews, New Brunswick, Cuffe met Friend James Brian, an Irish-born merchant from Wilmington, Delaware. Brian needed a vessel to transport Nova Scotian plaster of paris to Wilmington's farming community, and the liberal terms he offered appealed to Cuffe. Soon the black captain sailed up the Brandywine River to Wilmington, twenty-eight miles south of Philadelphia. Brian and Cuffe trusted and respected each other as frugal men of principle, and as a result of this voyage they struck up future terms.[19] On August 18, 1798, Cuffe closed out the *Ranger*'s foreign registry; domestic routes would serve quite well, including those to Nantucket.[20] His partnership with Michael Wainer remained firm, but the merger with James Brian opened a potentially lucrative market. *Claypoole's American Daily Advertiser,* a Philadelphia publication, carried the following entry for April 10, 1799: "Schooner Ranger, Puffer [*sic*], New Bedford, 10 days." Wilmington's *Delaware and Eastern-Shore Advertiser* for July 22, 1799, recorded another Cuffe visit. "Schooner *Rambler* [*sic*], Capt. Cuffee, from Passamaquoddy." The black captain's name and vessel were yet unfamiliar to the maritime press, but such inaccuracies would not persist.

Profitmaking led to further expansion of the family enterprise. In February 1799 Cuffe paid $3,500 for a 140-acre waterfront homestead farm owned by Ebenezer and Rachel Eddy. This land may have adjoined his original shoemaker's shop. On March 16, 1800, Lemuel and Mary Sowle, friends of the family, transferred a few rods of land to "yeoman" Cuffe's farm, and within another twenty-four hours three-quarters' interest in the farm quietly shifted to his brother-in-law and longtime business partner, Michael Wainer. On the death of his mother Cuffe had acquired an additional 50 acres, bringing his total landholdings to an astonishing 200 acres.[21]

Such diversification required a reassignment of responsibilities. Michael Wainer began to devote all of his time to managing the farm, and his son Thomas was given command of the *Ranger,* sailing the now-familiar north-south route to Wilmington, Delaware. After the completion of a third coastal run by the end of August 1800, Thomas's uncle took a new and significant step. To process more of their own cargoes locally, Cuffe bought a gristmill from Philip and Humphrey Macomber. And their windmill, which stood on the west bank of the Acoaxet, also brought in new partners: two local black entrepreneurs, Washington Davis and Samuel Hicks. Paul Cuffe now controlled an increasingly black-oriented enterprise within Westport's shipping, farming, and milling operations. His total assets amounted to $10,000, and this in little more than fifteen years since the American Revolution.[22] For a man whose formal education lasted only two weeks, and that in navigational training, he had learned well from watching others.

By the turn of the century Cuffe's extraordinary accomplishments marked him as a black Yankee entrepreneur without peer in white America. But was this his only goal, to rise financially within the evolving American civilization? Cuffe's historical contributions typically are linked to black colonization in Sierra Leone, not to the founding of a modest financial empire in the United States. Thus, we must pause briefly to examine what channels of communication with Africa were available to him and to note his response to African affairs at the time.

First knowledge about the area of Sierra Leone, where Paul Cuffe would eventually sail, came from Friends in and around Westport. As it happened, William Rotch, Sr., traveled to Europe in 1786 to promote an international whaling industry, abolition of the Atlantic slave trade, and the Society of Friends. At the time of Rotch's return to Nantucket, in January 1787, British philanthropist Granville Sharp sent three shiploads of former American slaves (since residing in London) to West Africa. Sharp intended to establish a Province of Freedom for the unwanted blacks, known as the Black Poor of London. Rotch discussed the Province of Freedom with Friend William Dillwyn, formerly of New Jersey, before sailing for home.[23]

News of this African refuge spread quickly among New England Friends, thanks in part to Rotch, who, soon after his return, left Nantucket for Newport to bring the information to Friends at the Rhode Island Yearly Meeting. Among them was William Thornton, a former medical student from the University of Edinburgh who desperately sought an African haven for his own inherited slaves, now living on the island of Tortola in the West Indies. He spoke with Rotch at length, then carried the news to Newport blacks, some of whom decided to go to Africa.[24] New Bedford, Dartmouth, and Westport Friends, including Rotch's family, returned to Cuffe's neighborhood with the news of Africa.[25] Word of the settlement along the Sierra Leone River, and proposals for black emigration, also came to Cuffe from Boston, where seventy-three free blacks had petitioned in December 1787 for return passage to Africa. Prince Hall, who ten years earlier had pointed to the contradiction of freedom from England while maintaining American slaves, now led these blacks to cite "very disagreeable and disadvantageous circumstances, most of which attend us so long as we and our children live in America."[26] William Thornton soon was boasting enthusiastically that hundreds of blacks had decided to leave Boston for Africa.[27]

Emigration from America to the African Province of Freedom was clearly not Cuffe's choice. He remained resolute in his belief that the United States, and particularly Massachusetts—which had ratified the federal constitution in February 1788—was his own province of freedom. Further, he felt that the powerful social forces of alienation were not so overt in Westport. Only nine Negro householders appeared on the tax lists there, two of them being Cuffe and his brother John, and the fifty-six blacks in the town comprised less than 2.5 percent of the local population.[28] Life ashore meant relentless exposure to white society; yet survival—and independence—for free blacks required assimilation with the white majority.

Cuffe's commercial ties to Newport, New England's slave-trading center, brought him further African news, and the enticements to sail to Sierra Leone may have been considerable. By March 1793, when his ship *Mary* sailed regularly to Newport, residents and the press smuggly boasted of the continuing role of their community in the Atlantic slave trade. Samuel Hopkins, Newport's Congregational minister and a champion of the cause of African resettlement, was searching, with the town's African Union Society, for a Sierra Leone–bound vessel and predominantly black crew. Newport blacks complained of their "calamitous state . . . being strangers and outcasts in a strange land." They had asked free Philadelphia blacks to join them in "their return to their own country." Hopkins pleaded: "A vessel must be procured, and proper sailors provided, to go to Africa. . . ."[29] Meanwhile Newport's legitimate traders predicted that handsome profits were to be made in African trade.[30] Yet Cuffe continued to resist the idea of emigration.

During this period of time Philadelphia reigned as the center of commercially successful Friends, abolitionist societies, and free African unity in the United States.[31] The mutual respect which helped to solidify white abolitionists and the city's black elite pleased Cuffe when he arrived there in the mid-1790s for trading purposes. The city's thousand or more free blacks formed their own African societies and African churches in response to the white trend toward exclusion. Yet they, like Cuffe, fervently seemed to cling to the goal of assimilation within American society.[32] James Forten, a Philadelphia black maritime entrepreneur, epitomized that goal yet carefully followed Granville Sharp's accomplishments in the Province of Freedom. In town, African peddlers along the wharves spread subculture gossip among incoming shipmasters and the black community.[33]

Just to the south, in Wilmington, Delaware's abolitionist stronghold, Cuffe received more news of Africa. His commercial liaison, Friend James Brian, spoke for the town's antislavery leaders.[34] After 1797 either Cuffe or one of his shipmasters would appear at Brian's docks, where antislavery supporters and the press continually tracked Sierra Leone's progress, or lack of it.

In addition to the news of Africa, and particularly Sierra Leone, which he heard in various ports-of-call, Cuffe also confronted pro-African abolitionist views which frequently appeared in the papers he perused for essential commercial news. For example, on December 29, 1792, the *New Bedford Medley* published Delaware Friend Warner Mifflin's petition to the president and Congress: "If anti-slave trade measures are not taken to redress the wrongs and alleviate the sufferings and oppressions of the African race in these States, the Almighty will manifest his displeasure in a more conspicuous manner than has yet appeared. . . ."[35] On October 24, 1794, the *Medley* attacked chattel slavery.

While others were speaking out for resettlement in Africa and against the Atlantic slave trade and chattel slavery, Paul Cuffe was quietly establishing a Westport-supported, racially integrated school. Fifteen children in his extended family living in the Westport area needed formal education, and he allowed that others could attend if they so chose. The idea at first aroused his neighbors' suspicions; education to most of them was an exclusively religious matter. Their opposition notwithstanding, a schoolhouse was constructed on Cuffe's land, financed entirely by him. Neighbors called it "Cuff's School," yet some of them sent their children to it.[36]

Clearly, no one, least of all Paul Cuffe, could foresee the reputation he would acquire as a humanitarian, philanthropist, and selfless African benefactor. Too many unfulfilled goals remained in his rise within the evolving American civilization to allow him to be distracted now.

4

FEDERALIST SHIPPING MERCHANT

By the early years of the nineteenth century Paul Cuffe was most likely the wealthiest black in America. He certainly enjoyed the most favorable maritime conditions the country had ever known. When Republican Thomas Jefferson won the presidency, the golden days of Federalist maritime policies appeared to be at an end. Yet maritime successes associated with Federalist protectionism continued, and national import-export profits more than doubled over the next four years.[1] In this economic climate the frugal black Yankee Federalist merchant thrived.

If Cuffe flinched at sober reminders of slavery in the press, such reports only confirmed how fortunate he was. New Bedford's *Columbia Courier* reported that the British frigate *Chesapeake* had seized a United States schooner importing forty-two slaves from Africa. New York letters, reprinted in other newspapers, recounted an uprising in North Carolina among "TROUBLESOME" slaves. Reports from Sierra Leone were equally distressing: eighteen settlers had been wounded and fifty-six killed by the "treachery" of Timmany natives. Disgruntled Nova Scotians and West Indian Maroons had so disrupted conditions in the colony that some members of the Sierra Leone Company had proposed abandoning the experiment altogether. The British Parliament, moreover, had failed to muster the necessary support to pass its anti-slave-trade bill.[2]

Cuffe opted to stay at home instead of going to sea. Ostensibly, he shared parenting duties with his wife, Alice.[3] Caring for his attractive daughters, some of whom were approaching marriageable age, mainly meant keeping a judicious eye on prospective suitors; and his spacious home and burgeoning business made his daughters all the more attractive. While staying ashore involved Cuffe more in family life, it did nothing to slow the pace of his entrepreneurial affairs. Years had now passed since the building of the *Ranger,* and it was time for a new ship, one that would involve the entire family. Although Cuff's School trained the children in letters and arithmetic, the essential practical education began at dockside. Working with Thomas Wainer he began to accumulate shipbuilding supplies. Thomas's brother Jeremiah now commanded the *Ranger,* with a cargo of Nova Scotian gypsum, on the blue-chip run from St. Augustine, Maine, to Philadelphia, then made two more runs carrying plaster of paris from New Brunswick to James Brian's Wilmington docks. Westporters Nicholas Davis and Bevian Howland followed Cuffe's lead, sailing their ship, the *Hope,* with the same profitable cargo. Indeed, such trade was considered so lucrative that Nova Scotian legislators attempted to block Yankee merchants from participation.[4]

Although a reticent man by nature, Cuffe's social relationships within the community broadened during his time ashore. Two constant visitors, who may also have been shipbuilders, were Friends Isaac Cory and his son Isaac, Jr. They knew the black merchant's reputation of pursuing a cautious policy of Afro-Indian partnerships and crewmen. The successes of his enterprise awed them and countless other white residents. Yet Cuffe realized that his restrictive policy would eventually impede expansion. It is not surprising, then, that he reached a major turning point in his evolving assimilation into white society and offered the Corys one-quarter ownership in the 162-ton brig *Hero,* now being built in his shipyard.[5] Certain early investments would remain safely within the family, but his prominence, and his prosperity, produced a noticeable shift toward greater confidence in the white business community. Together Cuffe and his newest partners launched the *Hero* in late January 1802, under the command of Isaac Cory.[6]

With the coming of the spring thaw, Captain Jeremiah Wainer weighed anchor aboard the *Ranger.* Meanwhile, the *Hero* dodged past Gooseberry Neck and up the Acoaxet to pick up Cuffe, then headed for New Brunswick to join the *Ranger.* The two ships departed for southern waters, and like a proud mercantile family the captains orchestrated a tandem entry up the Brandywine River that fall: "Arrived. Brig *Hero,* Cuffee, St. Andrews; Schooner *Ranger,* Wainer, St. Andrews."[7] Local Delaware abolitionists, who within weeks were discussing the release of a slave child named Cuffe,[8] cheered Paul Cuffe's impressive accomplishment.

Opportunities for profits in Europe caused the black merchant to pursue that market as well. He ordered the *Hero* prepared for transatlantic trade with a suitable local crew. Twenty-nine-year-old Thomas

Wainer assummed command of the brig and set sail for Le Havre, France. Her forty-three-day run back to Philadelphia in the spring of 1803 met with Cuffe's instructions for an immediate return to Europe, this time to Oporto, Portugal, north of Lisbon. Cuffe read of the *Hero*'s progress in New Bedford's *Columbian Courier:* "Oper to [*sic*]—Aug. 1 no American vessel in port—sailed this day the brig *Hero,* of Westport, for Philadelphia." In September Captain Wainer eased her up the Acoaxet, and then she was off again, this time to St. Andero, Spain, from where she returned the following summer. Jeremiah Wainer pushed the *Ranger* to her limits, racing from New Brunswick to Wilmington four times in five months to outstrip his competitors. In a year and a half the *Ranger* posted seventeen ports-of-entry, a record which may have netted the Westport merchant as much as $5,000.[9]

In the fall of 1804 reports of whaling profits from southeast African voyages caused the black merchant to dream of his own whaling fleet. Although such routes would mean entering African waters where slavers lurked, Cuffe decided to take the risk. The *Hero* received a new registry, sailed once under Wainer for St. Andrews, and then underwent a major overhaul. The newly re-registered *Ranger* may have gone to Philadelphia on a related mission.[10] Then sometime in December 1804 the family bid farewell to the *Hero*'s crew and to Captain Samuel Tobey, a white Nantucketer, as the *Hero* set sail for the Cape of Good Hope to hunt for spermaceti. In June 1805 Captain Tobey went ashore for supplies at Delagoa Bay, Portugal's permanent African outpost south of the Limpopo River. There he signed a financial statement connecting Paul Cuffe with William Rotch, Jr., Tristram Folger, and Obed Coffin, America's most prestigious whalers. Later, though merchant James Brian eagerly awaited the arrival of the brig's oil shipment, Cuffe sent much of the cargo on to Philadelphia.[11] His first venture into African waters had been a profitable one and would certainly not be his last.

Preparations for the second voyage required fitting a third mast on the *Hero* to improve her maneuverability for whaling. On June 9, 1806, she was re-registered as a bark, but under the same ownership, and was prepared for sea. Cuffe's nephew Paul Wainer signed aboard as mate and keeper of the log. On June 16, 1806, his entry read: "Left Westport at 9 A.M. all Well on board the Ship *Hero* Bound on a Whaling Voyage to the Cape of Good Hope." The *Hero* encountered merchant ships from Salem, Philadelphia, and London in the East India trade. The varied names of the vessels rekindled Wainer's memories of home: the *Essex* of Nantucket, David Harris in command; the *Acushnet* of New Bedford, Lewis Tobey in command; and the *Triton* of New Bedford, under Eban Clark. Captain Clark, an old friend of Cuffe's, sailed as the *Hero*'s consort for more than two months. He then departed for home with news that the bark carried 270 barrels of oil.[12] Again a profitable cargo arrived from Africa, a reminder to the frugal black merchant to look more favorably on continental African business.

Expanding on his basic trade routes of coastal and European traffic, Cuffe decided to embark on a trade run to the West Indies. Enticements came from the French Guadaloupe colonial administration, which guaranteed a three-dollar bounty on imported cattle and comparable incentives for other livestock brought for slaughter. In contrast to other Cuffe departures, this one seemed doomed from the start. The *Ranger*'s space was hastily partitioned to accommodate 250 turkeys, 500 chickens, plus some hogs and cattle. Trouble began on the second day at sea when strong winds began shredding the sails. Gale-force winds set the deck awash, and much of the livestock had to be cast overboard. Finally, a quieter Gulf Stream carried the schooner to the Leeward Islands. Tragically, Captain Jeremiah Wainer had died and two other crewmen were lost at sea. Word was sent to Westport, a makeshift crew was assembled, and the *Ranger* limped home.

The solemn occasion prompted by the loss of three mariners from a single community dependent on the sea demonstrates the pivotal role played by Cuffe in both his family and the community. A worshipful gathering at the Friends Meeting House, called by Elder Peckham at Cuffe's request, shows that his financial, personal, and spiritual affairs had become intricately entwined within the economic and social fabric of the Westport Quaker community. His letters to scattered brothers and sisters confirmed his role as family patriarch: "Therefore We thought and felt Willing to have you to come together if agreeable & convenient," he humbly pleaded on behalf of Michael Wainer. "I Remain your Loving Brother."[13]

Cuffe also was bound to black brethren in other communities, and particularly to acquaintances in New York's African Methodist Episcopal Zion church, chartered on February 5, 1801. "Give my love to all well-wishing friends, to our Zion," he wrote to his youngest sister, Freelove, who was living in New York, "wishing that we may stand fast in the Lord and walk in his Statutes." To this he added the fruits of his own black Yankee experience: "and let us Endeavor to Establish the Corrector of Colour that it may shine brighter and brighter."[14]

Westport Friends maintained a white facade in their meeting, bolstering Cuffe's opposition to all but selective participation in business opportunities with whites. His social encounters throughout the New Bedford, Dartmouth, and Westport regions also reflected such racial exclusion. One anecdote recalls his experience at a local inn. When appearing for dinner with payment in hand he was told that his meal had been set in the kitchen. Cuffe mortified listeners by pointing out that William Rotch, Sr., had served him in his parlor.[15] His own insistence on racial and family unity persisted. Masters of the family schooner *Ranger,* like prospective sons-in-law, had to be black. Alvin Phelps, a free person of color from nearby Rochester, assumed the post of *Ranger* captain in the fall of 1805, and a year later married one of Cuffe's daughters.

Early in 1806 the *Hero* returned from Africa and was outfitted for a July departure. The *Ranger*'s participation in domestic trade ended on April 11, and Samuel Tobey resumed command of the *Hero.* White Dartmouth residents George Sanford and Isaac Howland invited Cuffe to invest in their schooner *Hope;* she had been constructed in 1795 by Bevian Howland and Nicholas Davis, at the time Cuffe had built the *Ranger.* He accepted for reasons that are not clear, the only case in which he held less than half ownership of a vessel. Master Shubel Baker immediately entered the *Hope* into the New Bedford–Philadelphia traffic.[16]

Cuffe's most consuming work during this time involved the construction of the largest hull ever produced in his Acoaxet shipyard. Family and neighborhood builders swarmed over a double-decked, three-masted ship. Scrutinizing details with him was Friend Lemuel Milk, a white Dartmouth surveyor who was a partner in the ship's construction.[17] Cuffe's daughters Naomi and Ruth paid special interest as well, enraptured as they were by two handsome New Bedford carpenters working on the new ship. By August 18, 1806, the ship *Alpha* stood ready, a 268-ton vessel measuring ninety-one feet overall. A family crew was assembled and Cuffe took immediate command.

Neighbors and friends who had dropped by or watched the *Alpha*'s construction from Hix Bridge were aware that, by the summer of 1806, Paul Cuffe was to Westport what the wealthy Rotches were to New Bedford. A guest to the Rotch parlors gave this portrait of the black Westport celebrity: "In the next township lives Paul Cuff, the owner and master of a fine ship. He is a man whom I suppose to be worth 20,000 dollars, of more extensive credit & reputation than any other in the township—and has his family settled about him who are also much respected." He added that two Cuffe daughters had married former slaves, now New Bedford carpenters, who were "finishing for themselves in this town, a most commodious & comfortable house."[18]

According to this guest of the Rotches, Cuffe was "averse to all mixtures," although his mother had been Indian, as was his wife. When he entertained white friends they were given separate tables and beds, and the Cuffes "reluctantly partook of vituals with persons of other colors." The captain appeared to be a man of "diffident manner" who felt "himself as one of a degraded class," even though he was more respected than whites in similar circumstances. The correspondent concluded, Cuffe "has observed he would willingly consent to be skinned if his black could be replaced by white."[19] The latter remark struck at the heart of Cuffe's quest for equal status in a whitening American civilization. As a black man he wrestled with "the system" as he climbed the ladder of white respectability. Such an admission, even if made only once, sums up his acute awareness of social forces then in command. The closer he came to the pinnacle of respectability, the more his own aspirations pressured him to conform.

Prior to the *Alpha*'s departure Cuffe and some local Quaker merchants joined forces. With William Rotch, Jr., Cuffe negotiated for a certain cargo to be traded on the best of terms in Savannah, Georgia, in Liverpool, England, and then in St. Petersburg, Russia.[20] With Lemuel Milk, Cuffe planned yet another hull to be constructed at his Westport shipyard, a brig of approximately one hundred tons with a high, square stern. In the rush of activity to complete the *Alpha*, however, Cuffe missed a traveling Nantucketer, Mary Barker, "Speaker in the Friends Meeting." He humbly regretted his absence, blaming it on the Lord's will rather than his own. "I am much pleased to see that thee has been so favored as to be suffered to make me a visit," he added. "I cannot write enough to express the goodness of the Lord. . . . I remain thy ever well-wishing friend till death."[21] His sentiments and terminology read like those of an aspiring Friend.

The *Alpha*'s departure commenced Cuffe's sixth and most optimistic shipping season of the nineteenth century. Relieved to be at the helm once more, the Westporter headed first for Passamaquoddy, Maine, and the usual cargo of Nova Scotian gypsum. By mid-September the *Alpha*'s bow pointed toward James Brian's docks in Delaware. Cuffe's most trusted nephew, Thomas Wainer, with two European voyages behind him, sailed as the ship's first mate. Fourteen-year-old Paul

Cuffe, Jr., was on his maiden voyage as one of the six remaining family crew members.

The appearance of the *Alpha* on the Brandywine River caused the usual stir, thanks to Cuffe's trademark of an all-black crew. The layover in Wilmington was extended as members of the Delaware Abolition Society wished to speak at length with this remarkable black captain, a man who nobly embodied the arguments for abolishing the slave trade and, perhaps, domestic slavery as well. He met with Rev. William Price, president, and John Jones, then acting-secretary, of the Society and with other delegates who had returned from that year's American Convention of Abolition Societies: Joseph Bringhurst, Cyrus Newlin, Allen Lane, William Poole, and Daniel Lowber. While Cuffe leisurely conversed with abolitionists, Thomas Wainer impatiently tended to dockside business. The crew emptied the ship then stowed flour, apples, and Windsor chairs into the hold. No one could have imagined the future significance of those talks with Delaware abolitionists: a biographical tract to appear a few years later in England.[22]

The *Alpha* headed past the Carolina coast, where slaves were still legally imported, and on to Savannah, arriving by December 13, 1806. The aristocratic city stretched out before the black merchant's eyes, first reminding him of the opulent New England shipping centers he knew so well. Cuffe entered the *Alpha* at customs and advertised for the next leg of her voyage, to Liverpool. Dockside duties for the black crew continued through Christmas, as slave-auction notices appeared in the press: "20 New NEGROES of the Angola Country" had arrived; all sales would be under $300. The crew was surprised to learn that under current Georgia law free people of color were subject to the same restrictions as slaves within the city.[23]

Captain Cuffe confidently strode ashore, despite the restrictions. Yankee traders like himself were welcome at Jacob Idler's counting-house, where the most successful American and European shipmasters conducted business. As the days passed Cuffe began to hear grumblings about the ominous Little Emperor, Napoleon Bonaparte, who had blockaded England in retaliation for Britain's Orders in Council. The Westporter, like others, faced a dilemma: he could not set sail for Liverpool, where imprisonment by the French fleet seemed a foregone conclusion; neither could he have his ship lay idle in slave-ridden Savannah without incurring heavy personal as well as financial losses.

The unhappy turn of events perplexed another New Englander in Savannah—William Ladd, a New Hampshire-born trader whose advertisement for Liverpool had adjoined Cuffe's the first day in town. This Harvard-educated Yankee earlier had commanded his father's fleet out of Portsmouth, married a British wife, and traded along the southern seaboard. He also had attempted to introduce Dutch redemptioners into Spanish Florida to reduce the black slavery he had once fostered there. Only recently Ladd had returned from his father's funeral in New Hampshire.[24] The Napoleonic blockade now drew the two Federalist merchants together, as both halted publicity for Liverpool.

Nearly three uneasy months passed. The black shipmaster gained white allies by his serious, unobtrusive, and gentle manner. The crew, like their captain, conducted themselves with the same conciliating propriety that had won over residents in Vienna, Maryland, ten years earlier.[25] Cuffe's ship stood ready for sea by early March 1807, late enough for the captain to know that President Jefferson had signed legislation prohibiting America's continuation in the African slave trade.[26] Canvas went aloft, lines came aboard, and the *Alpha* slipped into the channel, bound for Russia. Beside the black captain on the quarterdeck stood William Ladd, "the only white person on board." Below was a securely stowed cargo of 251 bales of Georgia cotton, a product of slave labor preferred by prosperous merchants out of Savannah. Cuffe's cargo, consigned to the Rotches, had originally been intended for Liverpool contacts William and Richard Rathbone, who welcomed Georgia cotton.[27]

At Göteborg, Sweden, the *Alpha* made the normal stopover for Massachusetts bottoms en route to St. Petersburg.[28] Again Napoleon threatened the Yankee's progress. With only the Russian tsar Alexander standing in the way of the advancing Frenchman, Cuffe risked sailing further into the Baltic. However, in Elsinore, Denmark, at the four-mile stream opposite Cronberg Castle, he conceded the eastward race, a fortuitous decision. On June 14 the Russians lost to the French at Friedland in Prussia, thus closing the eastern Baltic to American shipping. Frightened Philadelphia-bound passengers rushed aboard and the *Alpha* sailed for Göteborg, where Cuffe ordered Swedish glass and iron stowed in the ship's hold. There, onlookers goggled at the unprecedented sight of a black captain commanding an all-black crew, the decorous William Ladd and bustling Philadelphia passengers adding to the extraordinary American mosaic. Out of the crowd stepped a young Swede, about the same age as Paul Cuffe, Jr., who begged for passage to America.

On June 22 Abraham Rodin signed papers to sail aboard the *Alpha* as an indentured maritime apprentice to the black captain. The Yankee's terms for Rodin's six-year apprenticeship were predictably stern: Rodin must always obey his master, protect his goods, and indicate his own whereabouts at all times; he must avoid fornication, marriage, cards, dice, haunted houses, taverns, and "playhouses."[29] In return the apprentice was guaranteed food, lodging, clothes, health care, and instruction in reading, writing, "seamanship & other industry." A Bible and new clothes would be his when his apprenticeship had been served. Three weeks later the *Alpha*'s multiracial complement headed for the United States. Narrowly escaping Britain's bombardment of Copenhagen, she safely reached the Baltic sleeve. Other dangers lay ahead, however. Tremendous gale-force winds off Greenland pummeled the ship for eighteen hours. Her quarterboards, caboose, and coops washed away, along with part of her foremast and a longboat. Crashing seas dangerously weakened the hull, requiring the crew to cast fifty tons of valuable iron overboard to save the ship from foundering.

With the storm scarcely behind them the *Alpha*'s company learned of new hazards. The crew from the passing schooner *Hannah,* out of Lynn, Massachusetts, shouted news that the HMS *Leopard* had seized the USS *Chesapeake* and impressed various crew members. The incident, which had occurred off the coast of Virginia, had provoked renewed anti-British protests throughout the United States. Even home waters would now be more dangerous. Cautiously the *Alpha* continued southward past Nantucket and turned up the Delaware River toward Philadelphia. On September 21, 1807, her battered hull, weary passengers, and exhausted crew gratefully rested in the Quaker City.[30]

Grim political news assailed the black captain as he headed back to his Federalist stronghold. Republican Thomas Jefferson had summoned Congress to deal with the *Chesapeake-Leopold* affair. Earlier the *Chesapeake* had been associated with illegal slavers from Africa; now the same name symbolized a new form of tyranny, this time to Yankee shipmasters. Cuffe could only hope for the best. At home he registered his newest brig, *Traveller,* under Captain Asa Bly and sent her to New York. He negotiated the sale of the *Hero*'s imported oil from Africa, signed additional papers for the *Alpha,* and inspected the *Ranger* for future service.[31] His fleet stood ready when disaster struck: first came Jefferson's Embargo Act in January 1808, then the Enforcement Act. Edged in black, the *New Bedford Mercury* shrieked for Federalist New Englanders: "Our Constitution Is Dead!" Legislation forbade international maritime trade, and all departing coasters or whalers had to post double bonds. The booming Federalist shipping era was over.

So ended, for a time, Cuffe's maritime plans, and with them the means to fully attain his American dream. Present ownership included controlling interest in a schooner, a brig, a bark, and a ship, all four constructed at his Acoaxet shipyard, and he still held part-interest in a second schooner. Farming, milling, whaling, and trading interests from British Canada to the Caribbean and from Portuguese East Africa to Sweden brought continued profits to the Westport merchant. Racial frustrations notwithstanding, the black entrepreneur maintained great faith in the United States, his home. But Cuffe was about to discover that to many others his accomplishments aroused enormous sympathy for Africa. An established Anglo-American communications network was searching for a civilizing African agent, a search that would eventually lead them to Paul Cuffe.

5

INTERNATIONAL FRIENDS OF AFRICAN CIVILIZATION

"MEMOIRS OF AN AFRICAN CAPTAIN," read the headlines of the British *Monthly Repository of Theology and General Literature* in April 1807 as the *Alpha* bypassed Liverpool and headed for the North Atlantic.[1] Paul Cuffe, the celebrated captain, did not get to read about himself, and he also lost the opportunity to meet British supporters of civilization in Africa who were subtly recruiting new philanthropists for their cause.

In March 1807 British abolitionists had celebrated a notable Parliamentary victory: they had passed legislation designed to ban Britain's participation in the Atlantic slave trade. These "friends of humanity" convened at London's Freemason Hall to praise one another. Prayers and speeches showered tribute on legislative strategist William Wilberforce, rising propagandist Thomas Clarkson, and Granville Sharp, who had watched his Province of Freedom become the colony of Sierra Leone. The Duke of Gloucester, nephew of King George III, sat as president of the newly founded African Institution.[2]

Directors claimed to be "anxious" to "adopt such measures as are best calculated to promote . . . [the native African's] civilization and happiness." Too often, the portrait of the Negro had been drawn "by the pencil of the oppressor, and [had] sat for it in the distorted attitude of slavery." Native Africans had suffered enormously due to the fatal Atlantic trade perpetuated by Europeans, but now British, Danish, and United States anti-slave-trade legislation would serve to end their suffering. The directors swore not to undertake religious missions or commercial speculations in Africa themselves, "to prevent misconceptions"; they did not want the African Institution to be confused with the trouble-ridden—and now defunct—Sierra Leone Company, which many of them had backed.

The African Institution's directors promised to accurately inform the British public of African political and agricultural developments. The Institution would promote literacy, "useful" arts, "impliments of husbandry," and modern medical techniques; moreover, it would "employ suitable agents" to encourage individual enterprise and advisable correspondence. The directors felt that by doing so the Institution would spread "the blessings of civilized society among a people sunk in ignorance and barbarism."[3] Friend William Allen, a British industrialist who would figure prominently in Cuffe's future recruitment as a civilizing agent, perceived the African Institution in appropriate Quaker terms: these were the "Friends of Civilization of Africa."[4]

The biographical tract written as a result of Cuffe's visit to Wilmington, Delaware, set the stage for his recruitment. It first appeared in the *Monthly Repository* in April 1807, with the following preface:

> The subject of the following narrative is a FREE NEGRO. He is a Captain of an American vessel, now on her passage from Savannah to Liverpool, and the whole of the crew are also FREE NEGROES. The Delaware Society for promoting the Abolishing of Slavery have authenticated this narrative, for the purpose of shewing that, with suitable culture and a fair opening for the exertion of talents, the NEGRO possesses a portion of intellect and energy by which he is enabled to form great designs, to adopt means to the end in the prosecution of them, to combat danger, to surmount difficulties; and thus to evince that, with equal advantages of education and circumstances, the Negro-race might fairly be compared with their white brethren on any part of the globe.[5]

The story of Cuffe's ancestry and commercial successes clearly spoke for the cause of the African Institution.

Cuffe's admirers published installments of the Delaware Abolition Society's tract through June 1807. Divine observations and lofty achievements were chronicled, interspersed with the narrative of one born to an African father and an Indian mother. It said that Cuffe willingly gave "the right hand of fellowship to that people who walk nigh to God, called the children of Light." Unlike others who "would have abandoned in despair the trackless ocean for the furrowed field, or [would have] sunk victims of misfortune," he courageously overcame all barriers. In short, this virtuous African descendant, endorsed by the "unimpeachable character" of William Rotch, Jr., qualified "for any station of life to which he may be introduced."

The account also described briefly another exemplary African descendant: "As a tribute due to merit it may be stated, that there is now resident at Philadelphia, James Torten [*sic*], a man of colour." He had been educated at a school founded by the Society of Friends, and he carried on a sail-making business "more extensively than any other person at Philadelphia." Later, at the African Institution's July meeting, William Sancho,[6] born in England to African parents, would be the center of attention.

Directors of the African Institution sought support from an American civilizing mission directed by the Society of Friends. Three days after Cuffe's homeward voyage began from Sweden, the directors praised a report entitled *Accounts of Two Attempts Toward the Civilization of Some Indian Nations in North America.*[7] It recounted civilizing achievements by the Philadelphia and Baltimore Yearly Friends Meetings. The publication vindicated Quaker nonconformist beliefs that Indians worshiped the Great Spirit, long "the Indian appelation of the Almighty." This proved to Friends that Christ's Inner Light was universal. Schemes of civilization did not have to "immediately attempt to plant Christianity." The Quakers were "brothers" because they "never wished any part of our land," an Indian chief was quoted as saying. The report stated that members of the Oneida, Stockbridge, and Tuscarora tribes knew how to work sawmills and gristmills. Onondagas and Cayugas possessed improved farm implements and had acquired skills such as knitting, sewing, and blacksmithing. Members of the Society of Friends stressed techniques of industry and changes in social values; they were teaching "a way of life rather than a religion."[8]

In associating themselves with the selfless American Friend's mission, the directors of the African Institution observed that in North America were "a people, to whom might have been speciously ascribed, even at a very recent period, invincible sloth, and irreclaimable vagrancy of manners." But Quakers had vindicated the Indians, finding that the native American's "barbarism" was chargeable less to their own indolence and prejudice than to "those of their civilized neighbors." The British report judiciously avoided mention of the destruction brought about by "civilized" European slave traders in Africa. It concluded that plenty, sobriety, and order had come to native Americans touched by the Quakers. Could there be more striking proof that private philanthropic bodies such as their own could spread benevolence?[9]

The pivotal figure in postwar transatlantic Quaker communications was William Dillwyn, the "great medium" between English and American abolitionists. By 1780 he had moved from Burlington, New Jersey, to England. Once the secretary for Philadelphia Friend Anthony Benezet and a frequent petitioner against American slavery, Dillwyn had joined five others in 1783 to form Britain's earliest anti-slave-trade society. Thereafter, American Friends such as William Rotch, Sr., visited him to learn of British philanthropy. Dillwyn's principal American correspondent was Friend James Pemberton, president of the Pennsylvania Abolition Society. On August 13, 1807, Dillwyn wrote to Pemberton about a "new association for civilizing Africa," though he failed to name the African Institution. He hoped the Society's benevolent object would be "perused with Prudence and Spirit."[10] His letter reached Pemberton a few days before Cuffe arrived in the Quaker City from the Baltic.

On disembarking from the battered *Alpha,* Cuffe found that Philadelphians were unusually receptive to African developments. Rev. Absalom Jones's African Episcopal Church advertised a lottery to raise money for a new African church in the city; the enticement was to spin a lottery wheel with the city's most respectable black and white citizens. Philadelphia papers summarized the American Friends' account published earlier in London, which promoted "the improvement and gradual civilization of the Indian natives." Thomas Clarkson's *The History of the Rise, Progress and Accomplishment of the Abolition of the African Slave Trade* went on sale. Elsewhere, New York's black churchman Peter Williams, Jr., and Boston's white evangelist Jedediah Morse showed similar enthusiasm for African improvement.[11]

Cuffe remained in Philadelphia for several weeks, meeting with Absalom Jones, Richard Allen, and James Forten, among others.[12] Friends Alexander Wilson, Samuel R. Fisher, Jr., and John James became acquainted with the black captain, as did Dr. Benjamin Rush, soon to succeed James Pemberton as head of the Pennsylvania Abolition Society. Rush's correspondents included William Thornton, the quixotic emigrationist-turned-architect, and President Thomas Jefferson. Pemberton, another Jefferson admirer, also made a point of meeting with Cuffe. His commodious South Street home was the focal point for antislavery activity among whites. Visits by his niece Ann Emlen Mifflin, who probably had heard about Cuffe in New Bedford some years earlier, helped to keep Pemberton appraised of the antislavery thinking of Friends in other areas.[13] And together they kept William Dillwyn informed of current views.

At this time both Pemberton and Mifflin were vaguely aware of the Royal African Institution but not the publication of the Delaware memoir about Cuffe. So, in their initial conversations with him they only theorized about the plight of African inhabitants abroad.[14] Ann Mifflin did ask Cuffe if he would assist in the emancipation of blacks by transporting to Sierra Leone free persons who chose to settle there. Cuffe indicated that he had thought about sailing there for trade purposes, as inhabitants of the African continent surely were in a dreadful state. Pemberton praised Cuffe; more importantly, Mifflin recorded her impressions of the black captain and sent them to William Dillwyn, casting Cuffe within her proposition for eliminating slavery. Pemberton wrote to Dillwyn on related matters.[15]

That correspondence reached Dillwyn on December 11, 1807, and he immediately responded. He enclosed African Institution reports to better inform the American philanthropists and in the hope that news about the group might encourage others to so organize. Pemberton read the abolitionist news from England and then informed President Jefferson. He also wrote to the black captain, quoting Dillwyn: "I have had a conversation with Zach Macaulay . . . in which he said that if Captn Cuffey should incline to make a voyage to Sierra Leone altho no longer under the Company's Government he will take care that he shall there receive every encouragement which the Governor can afford."[16]

Although denying that he was doing so, Pemberton subtly tried to lure the Westporter into service. "Diverse persons of eminent Stations and Character" wished to prohibit the slave trade and promote civilization, he told Cuffe. The new association (African Institution) had "raised a Considerable Sum of money to engage persons of Sobriety" able to teach farming in Africa. The plan obviously offered respectable contacts plus remuneration and was to change the Africans' "former course of Living," just as Friends had been successful among native Americans.[17]

Dillwyn's correspondence during the summer of 1808 stressed Cuffe's dazzling attributes. Sierra Leone Governor T. P. Thompson had been instructed by Zachary Macaulay to offer Cuffe "every assistance in his power."[18] The African Institution's principal difficulty, Dillwyn wrote, would be in finding "suitable agents in Africa" familiar with plans adopted by "Friends for the Civilization of the Indians." Influenced by the Institution's eagerness, Dillwyn conjectured that Cuffe "must be well qualified to be essentially useful in prosecuting their views." Late in August he forthrightly pleaded for "a few *colored* volunteers from America" of the caliber of Paul Cuffe and Absalom

Jones. The Institution's recruitment campaign had swung into high gear.

Cuffe applied for admission to the Westport Friends Meeting in February 1808. Nonmembers of the Quaker Meeting, like his father and mother, always had been told that revelation of the Divine Principle could enlighten "the soul of every man." And many Friends were convinced that native Americans knew the Almighty by another name, thus revealing the universal Inner Light. But the scarcity of black Friends militated against Cuffe's request, although his respectability implied a certain spiritual compatability. A committee was appointed "to visit him and take a Solid opertunity with him in order to Discover the Motive and Sincerity of his Request." Moreover, the Friends needed to examine his "fittnness to become a member of our Society." Did he characterize the "minor virtues" of honesty, truthfulness, fulfillment of promises, thrift, and hard work, so admirably reflected by lucrative and prestigious Friends?

In March 1808 Jeremiah Austen, Abner Potter, and Prince Wing asked the women's meeting to concur with the men in accepting Cuffe, which they did. Six days later the men withheld approval and the case was continued for another month. Finally, on April 16 the committee reported "several opportunities with him, [who] appeared to them to be Sincere in what he has requested." They resolved to "Receive the Said Paul Cuffe," and Elder Wing carried word to the Acoaxet farm that Cuffe now belonged to the Westport Meeting.[19]

The newly enacted maritime embargo made the next several months difficult for Cuffe and his fellow Federalist merchants. This undoubtedly led to his delay in responding to a very flattering letter from James Pemberton. A deepening spiritual awareness brought the subject of African civilization into full focus, and Cuffe wrote to Pemberton, "I desire ever to humble myself before my maker." He continued: "As to Poor me i feel very feeble and almost Worn out in hard Service and incapable of doing much for my Brethren, the African Race, but blessed be god i am What I am and all that I can conceive that god please to Lay upon me, to make an instrument of me for that Service. I Desire Ever to be Submissive that his will may be done." Cuffe asked the Philadelphian to send along further information when it became available. The African Institution's request for a civilizing agent needed far more consideration.[20]

Pemberton had every intention of securing Cuffe's services. God had brought an end to the slave trade, he promptly reminded the black Friend, and the African Institution, divinely inspired to promote "the civilization of the Blacks in their own country," sought to "draw them off from the wild habits of life" and teach the arts of agriculture, mechanical labor, and domestic industry. Religious information could follow, if educated minds were prepared sufficiently. England's "friends of humanity" sought to teach Africans a way of life, as they had done with native Americans. He advised Cuffe to counsel with Friends for strength and encouragement.[21]

Nearby Newport was an appropriate place to do so while hearing the latest news of Sierra Leone. A free black school had been started there under the new African Benevolent Society, and Newport Gardner, the town's most educated person of color, taught the young scholars. Cuffe, as founder of a school in Westport, had every reason to meet with Gardner and other brethren. They also updated him on emigration efforts to the British colony. At the Yearly Meeting of Friends, on the afternoon of November 13, Cuffe took tea with Stephen Gould, and four days later they worshiped together. "Paul Cuff was at meeting," Gould glowingly related, "& I believe was the first black man that ever set in a preparative or any other meeting of business in Newport."[22]

Cuffe continued to watch and pray as he pondered his future. Why not attempt to break the slave trade at its roots, in Africa? Sierra Leone seemed secure, and the profitability of African whaling grounds had been proven. Could transatlantic trade become the basis for philanthropy in Africa?

6

ECONOMIC AND PHILANTHROPIC PARTNERSHIPS

ON June 9, 1809, the *New Bedford Mercury* proclaimed "the commencement of commercial intercourse between this country and Great Britain." Yankee merchants dutifully praised the Almighty and schoolchildren danced for joy. Amid the celebration Cuffe surely recalled the difficult times since the embargo had gone into effect. Congress had "authorized the absolute detention of all vessels bound coastwise, with cargoes *exciting suspicion* of an intention to evade [embargo] laws." That summer Cuffe and his Dartmouth co-owners had allowed their schooner *Hope* to transport flour between New Bedford and Alexandria, Virginia. In August the schooner had reentered New Bedford, not as a free vessel, but as a pawn of the federal government: guilty of "suspicion."[1]

Jingles such as the following, which appeared in Newburyport, Massachusetts, had spoken for Yankee Federalists: "Our ships all in motion once whitened the ocean, / They sailed and returned with a cargo; / Now doomed to decay, they have fallen a prey / To Jefferson—worms—and embargo."[2] Inflated insurance rates and double customs bonds for coastal and whaling vessels had threatened the maritime industry. Massive unemployment also had seriously affected mechanics and laborers. Then in March 1809 President Jefferson had insisted on a Non-Intercourse Act against English and French trade as soon as the embargo was lifted. Massachusetts voters retaliated by wrenching political power from short-lived Republican officeholders, and Federalist mercantile priorities again dominated state politics.[3]

On May 15 "Paul Cuffe of Westport in the County of Bristol and State of Massachusetts, merchant," had taken a bold step, swearing for the first time to be the sole owner of a registered vessel, the 109-ton brig *Traveller*.[4] The stage was set for his next move when he read in the *New Bedford Mercury* that native chiefs in Sierra Leone had halted trading slaves from the interior to European slavers on the coast, in return for profits from selling cattle and agricultural goods to legitimate European and American merchants.[5] Moreover, Mungo Park, Britain's explorer of the African interior, had opened West Africa for civilizers. The question now was whether humane merchants could sufficiently satisfy African commercial demands by legitimate civilized trade.

The fifty-year-old black merchant wrote to Philadelphia Friends John James and Alexander Wilson—James Pemberton having died a few months earlier—that "I have for some years had it impressed on my mind to make a voyage to Sierra Leone" to inspect the situation of the colony.[6] He stressed commerce and racial identity over direct religious conversion, and wished for the African inhabitants "to become an enlightened people." He wanted, however, "to give general satisfaction" to all those seeking to establish Christianity there. "I am of the African race," he continued, and "I feel myself interested for them." Masterfully understating his own commercial accomplishments, Cuffe spoke of having "some concern in navigation," which, if he were convinced to emigrate, he would transfer to West Africa. Furthermore, since whaling was an integral part of that business, he wished legal concessions such as bounty for oil imported into Sierra Leone or duty-free status in England. He would sail by the fall of 1810, if given proper encouragement; and, he added, he already knew of several creditable families that might possibly settle there.

The idea of his own emigration was the outgrowth of many months of consideration while deprived of Anglo-American commercial options. Certainly, an African whale fishery offered practical advantages for emigration. William Rotch, Sr., had tried to launch a foreign whaling industry in Europe for some years after the War for Independence, first along southern England and then at Dunkirk under the French government. Neither scheme had succeeded, but the bold initiative was worth repeating.[7] African whalers under Cuffe's management made sense; faultless credentials as a respected Yankee whaling merchant surely qualified him for the venture.

The bark *Hero*, owned with the Corys, was already thousands of miles to the southeast in African waters. Captain Latham Paddock had just put to sea from Portugal's Delagoa Bay northeast of Cape Town in company with several other vessels.[8] Perhaps, thought Cuffe, the *Hero* would be the first of many ships to sail under Sierra Leone registry. Why not let his commercial enterprises, coupled with agricultural potential, prosper for the benefit of indigenous inhabitants of Africa, as they had in North America?

Friends James and Wilson, accepting the last wishes of Pemberton, leaped at the opportunity to forward Cuffe's plan to the African Institution.[9] They promptly informed England's William Dillwyn that the black merchant was ready to act "on account of his brethren in Africa." The venture could not be approved fully unless Cuffe and others had reasonable prospects of a "comfortable support for themselves and families, and something more." In the process, they said, Cuffe sought to promote civilization so as to "gradually" prepare native minds for the principle of Truth. Ground rules for Cuffe's civilizing mission thus were established.

The reopening of international commerce also led to a bold and racially significant business venture for Cuffe. Proof of his genius as an entrepreneur materialized in the heart of New Bedford's prestigious maritime district in the form of a partnership with Peter and Alexander Howard, selling West Indies goods and groceries from a shop on Water Street.[10] Black capitalism, rooted in family cohesiveness and black crews, thus entered a more overt phase. This son of an African slave, in partnership with his sons-in-law, themselves former slaves, would persist in seeking ever-higher status within the American civilization while simultaneously preparing for an active civilizing role in Africa.

The current climate of maritime relations favored both objectives. Cuffe and John James ordered their ship *Alpha* to Europe after restrictions were lifted. Captain Alvin Phelps hurried the *Ranger* into service to Bath and Passamaquoddy, Maine, and then to the Wilmington market. The *Ranger* and the *Traveller* supplied Cuffe & Howards from James Brian's West Indies supplies; Naomi and Ruth Howard aided their husbands in the store's opening. The Cuffe family's financial power in the Westport, Dartmouth, and New Bedford areas increased, and the patriarch's membership on various committees and representation at the Preparative Meeting assured patronage by Friends. West Indies goods were in great demand and business thrived.[11]

Suddenly, in late July 1809, commercial prospects declined with the publication of England's Orders in Council: Ambassador Erskine had misinformed Thomas Jefferson that England would withdraw her embargo against the United States on June 10. Immediately, the new president, James Madison, reenacted the embargo on trade with England. Once more Federalist merchants suffered, as did Cuffe's pros-

sider, whether a State Bank can be established in this Commonwealth, which will be more equal and useful in its operation than the present Banking System; and to make report at the next session.

The Commitee consists of the Hon. Messrs. Brooks, King, Bridge and Welles, of the Senate; and Messrs Head, Story, Page, Bates, and Davis of the House.

Narrow Escape.—As Mr. *Mordecai Lewis*, and wife, were riding in a chair, near *Philadelphia*, the horse was struck instantly dead, by lightning; while they escaped without suffering any material injury.

Farm for Sale.

FOR Sale, a FARM pleasantly situated in the town of *Little Compton*, county of *Newport* (*R. I.*) lying 2 1-2 miles from the Four Corners, in *Tiverton*—three miles from the Common, and six miles from *Seconet Point*, on the West Road, or Great Highway, next the sea shore—containing about 140 acres of good Land, for grain or grazing, and has produced from twenty to thirty tons of Hay per season; well watered for Cattle, summer and winter. On said Farm there is a convenient House for a large family, Stable and Crib, with an excellent Orchard, and two good Wells of Water. Any person wishing to purchase, with or without the Crops, may know the terms, (which will be reasonable) by applying to the Subscriber, on the premises.

ROBERT WOODMAN.

Little-Compton, July 4, 1809. (tf.)

Entertainment.

THE Subscriber takes this opportunity to express his gratitude for the encouragement which he has received, and to request a continuance of the favours of the public. He is constantly provided with the best Liquors, Meats and Vegetables, which can be procured, and assures his customers, that no exertions on his part shall be wanting to render their Parties pleasant and agreeable; and hopes that his unremitted endeavors to please will not be unavailing.

☞ Parties may be served with Tea and Coffee, at the shortest notice.

NATHAN WINSLOW.

Dartmouth, June 1. (6w)

Blank Manifests,

For Sale, at the MERCURY-OFFICE.

sortment of Women's and Children's SHOES, direct from the manufacturer, which are for sale at her Shop, in the Main-Street. *N. Bedford, 7 mo.* 6.

Henry Clapp,

BOOK-BINDER,

RESPECTFULLY informs the inhabitants of *Nantucket*, that he has taken the North end of SAMUEL MACY's Shop, near the Brick Insurance-Office, where he intends carrying on his business.—Also intends keeping for sale, all kinds of School Books generally used, with a variety of other Books—a general assortment of Stationary, Blanks, &c.

Account Books ruled and bound to pattern, at short notice. Old Books neatly rebound.

Nantucket, July 3, 1809.

☞ Cash or Books paid for Rags and old Canvass. (6w.)

Copartnership Formed.

THE Subscribers would inform their friends and the public, that they have lately commenced business under the firm of CUFF & HOWARDS—and have taken the Store lately occupied by RECORDS HEATH & SON, in *Water-street*, where they intend keeping a general assortment of

W. I. GOODS & GROCERIES;

and respectfully solicit a share of their custom.

PAUL CUFF.
PETER HOWARD.
ALEX. HOWARD.

They have now on hand—Fresh superfine Alexandria Flour, Rice, Philad. Pilot Bread and Biscuit; loaf, Havana and brown Sugars; Hyson, Souchong, and Bohea Teas, Coffee, Chocolate, Pearlash, Ginger, Allspice, Pepper, Cinnamon, Cloves, Nutmegs, Honey, Vinegar, Allum, Sulphur and roll Brimstone, Copperas, Logwood, Redwood, Spanish Flotant Indigo, Flax, Soal and upper Leather, Calf-Skins and Boot-Legs, an assortment of Philadelphia Earthen Ware, and a variety of other articles.

New-Bedford, 7th mo. 6, 1809.

FOR SALE,

THE DWELLING-HOUSE and LOT, next north of *Wm. Kempton's* Store, in the north part of the village of *Bedford*. Apply to

JONATHAN PARKER, *on the Premises.*

Who has also for sale—A new birch CANOE; a new Iron VICE.—*Also*, An East-India Directory, containing *sixty-four* Charts, with a large quarto Book of Directions. *June* 23.

smooth.

☞ The above Medicines may be had at the Shop of CALEB GREENE, *Water-street, New-Bedford*, wholesale or retail. (3m.) *5th mo.* 5, 1809.

New-Bedford, June 2.

Manufactured Tobacco,

SNUFF, and CIGARS.

TO be sold, for cash, on the most reasonable terms, at the *New-Bedford Tobacco Manufactory*, head of Taber's wharf,

Maccoboy, of a superior quality.
Rappee, scented and plain, suitable for the West-India market.
Negro's Head and Cut Tobacco.
Spanish and East-India Cigars.
American do. scented and not scented
Also, Cephalick Snuff, a well known and approved remedy for the head-ache.

☞ If the purchasers of the above articles do not approve of them, they will have their money repaid them; provided they return the goods uninjured in the course of a month after the purchase.

N. B. Snuff or Tobacco given in payment for empty Snuff-Bottles.

RAN AWAY

FROM the Subscriber, on the 8th inst. an indented Apprentice, named *Perry Cornell*, aged 16 years, small of his age. Whoever will return said Boy to the Subscriber, shall receive *one cent* reward.—And I hereby forbid all persons harboring said Boy, or taking him to sea, on penalty of the law.

JOSHUA BARKER.

New-Bedford, July 13, 1809.

Horse Strayed.

STRAYED from the pasture of the Subscriber, on the 5th instant, a whitish-grey HORSE, about 13 1-2 hands high, 7 years old, has a bunch on his nigh gambrel. Whoever will give information of said Horse, so that the Subscriber may obtain him again, shall be handsomely rewarded.

THOMAS SAVORY.

Rochester, July 12, 1809.

To be sold at Public Vendue, by order of Court, on TUESDAY, the first day of August next, at 2 of the clock in the afternoon,

ONE half of the DWELLING-HOUSE, and a small lot of Land, of John Hull, late of *Dartmouth*, in the county of *Bristol*, deceased;—the same lying conveniently situated in said Dartmouth, at a place called *Russell's Mills*, in said town.

ABIGAIL HULL, } *Administratrix to said Estate.*

Dartmouth, June 27, 1809.

Cuffe & Howards, the pioneering local black business advertised here, was founded by Paul Cuffe, with his former slave sons-in-law, in the heart of the New Bedford merchant community. The establishment was formed at the peak of Cuffe's business prosperity. All subsequent ads corrected the misspelling of Cuffe's name. From the *New Bedford Mercury*, July 7, 1809. Courtesy of the American Antiquarian Society.

pects for sailing to Sierra Leone. Cuffe & Howards placed their last advertisements for three months, just prior to the August 9 trade curtailment: herbs, vegetables, cotton, and pins were on hand; ladies Moroccan shoes were available for the discriminating wearer.[12]

The family-owned *Ranger* and *Traveller* now were pressed into Nova Scotian trade with Wilmington. On September 23 the two captains, Thomas Wainer and Alvin Phelps, managed a dual entry into Wilmington harbor, duplicating the feat by Cuffe and Jeremiah Wainer seven years earlier. It was an unmistakable display of economic achievement when most blacks remained in slavery. At Christmastime the *Traveller* supplied Cuffe & Howards with Spanish cigars and Cuban brown sugar, and the firm also advertised powder and shot—unusual items for a Quaker merchant to offer for sale.[13] The *Alpha* made unscheduled runs between Portugal, London, and parts of Spain, which left Cuffe and James perplexed; yet she was safer in Europe than at home, even if unproductive. The *Hero* was reported around the Cape of Good Hope, presumably homeward bound. But the *Ranger* ran into trouble when a gale between Cape Ann and New Bedford blew her off course, producing a frightening adventure for Thomas Wainer and his crew, which ended three weeks later at Perth Amboy, New Jersey.[14]

Meanwhile, Cuffe & Howards' competition increased. Pardon Tillinghast assumed sole ownership of a West Indies and grocery goods shop, and Uriah Brownell sold identical items in town. The Cuffe family store was not to be outdone, however. Potash, demanded by local farmers, headed the list in Cuffe & Howards' advertisement on the *Ranger*'s return. African riches again reached Cuffe's Acoaxet docks with the return of the fully laden *Hero* on March 2 after eighteen months at sea. Captain Latham Paddock presented 480 barrels of sperm and right oil to the bark's owners and related tales of fellow Nantucket and New Bedford whalers off the Dark Continent. He also offered details about Delagoa Bay and Saldanha Bay on the continent's southern tip. The crew of thirteen, including seasoned cabin boy Abraham Rodin, had their own stories to tell. The bark netted $5,000 before lays to officers and crew, leaving some $1,700 in profits for Cuffe.[15]

If the first trade embargo had afforded Cuffe time to consider sailing for Sierra Leone, this second curtailment eliminated the slightest doubt that eventually he would go. A packet of letters about the African voyage lay on his desk. By rereading them he was able to roughly reconstruct events on the British scene, developments that strengthened his decision to sail for West Africa when trade permitted.

Zachary Macaulay, the African Institution's director and secretary and the former Sierra Leone governor, had written to William Dillwyn that "a person like Paul Cuffe would most unquestionably be a desirable accession to the population of Sierra Leone." Directors would grant him "every encouragement." The prospective civilizing agent could hardly have asked for better news, except guaranteed trading terms.[16] Unknown to Cuffe, Macaulay's influence also extended within the Church of England's evangelical Clapham Sect, which almost single-handedly had controlled the Sierra Leone Company. Macaulay represented the most formidable voice for the colony's trading community, since he was a partner in Macaulay & Babington, Freetown's leading commercial firm.

Avoiding sentimentality, Macaulay got right to the point, appealing to the Yankee's incontrovertible practicality. Cuffe should "minutely" inspect the state of things before "shifting his domicile from America to Sierra Leone." His own extensive experience in the colony prompted a call for critical examination of "all those local advantages and disadvantages which ought to enter into the decision." Cargo instructions were enclosed as well. Cuffe could profit from flour, tar, molasses, masts, oars, Virginia tobacco, spermaceti candles, rum, and gin. Further data included a personal recommendation to Macaulay's friend, Governor Thomas Ludlam. The secretary's introduction, for use on Cuffe's arrival, spoke of this "person of great worth"; he wished to advance Cuffe's countrymen's civilization and make his "commercial objects" important. This delighted Cuffe.

In another letter, one of the African Institution's directors, William Roscoe, unabashedly urged the president, the Duke of Gloucester, to advance mercantile interests to Cuffe and others: "One of the *first objects* of the institution should be, to encourage, as much as possible, a fair and peaceable traffic with the natives of Africa."[17] Britishers should "keep up an intercourse equal to, and if possible, greater than that which existed during the continuance of the Slave Trade." William Wilberforce, also a director, convinced that civilizing values should be implanted by means of legitimate commerce, sent this and earlier reports to John Jay, president of the New York Abolition Society, and Macaulay mailed the same packet to Benjamin Rush, president of the Pennsylvania Abolition Society. Directors also called for America's "friends of humanity" to step up their efforts and match England's stricter enforcement of anti-slave-trade laws.

Friend William Allen, a well-known British chemist, knew of Cuffe through William Dillwyn, among others. One of many directors of the African Institution, Allen was deeply involved in Quaker science and philanthropy in British society. He belonged to the Slave Trade Committee of the London Meeting for Sufferings, the London Committee for the Abolition of the Slave Trade, the Physical Society at Guy's Hospital, the Royal Jennerian Society, and he served as a Fellow of England's most prestigious scientific body, the Royal Society. He had established the Spitalfield's Soup Society and belonged to the Committee of the Society for Bettering the Condition of the Poor. Although secular by traditional standards, his philanthropy "was a 'spiritual' outlet that balanced worldly success in business and science."[18] Allen was impressed by Cuffe's financial expertise and his ownership of a "vessel only with black seamen," and he was pleased to learn that the Westporter belonged to the Society of Friends. Cuffe's concept of philanthropy also met with Allen's approval: he, too, "felt a religious concern" to assist the African Institution. Allen noted that Cuffe would investigate prospects for sober blacks moving to Sierra Leone and proceeded to relay his optimism to William Rotch, Jr.[19]

Meetings among the elite Westport and New Bedford merchants ensued, with frequent updates of the fragmentary news from England. William Rotch, Sr., returned visits to the Cuffe home, at least once taking along some traveling English Friends. On that occasion Paul and Alice Cuffe waited on them but refused to sit—conciliating propriety apparently merged with "diffident" behavior until they were assured they would not offend their guests. Ideas from Macaulay and Dillwyn were discussed, as was Thomas Clarkson's masterpiece on abolition, available in New Bedford bookstores. That work "baptised my mind," the black Westporter wrote later.[20] Advertisements for Cuffe & Howards reappeared as its founder reluctantly prepared the *Traveller* for Lisbon, not Freetown. Sierra Leone, a British colony, continued to be off-limits due to trade restrictions.

Paul Cuffe was determined to see what could be done for his African brethren in a partnership with British philanthropists. His experiences in black capitalism would prove as useful now as they had for Cuffe & Howards. He wholeheartedly endorsed—in fact embodied—the principles of an existing civilizing mission as broadly outlined by the directors of the African Institution. Cuffe was sure that the Divine Hand moved toward the day when his African brethren would cease to be taken from their homes and enslaved, and he was committed to do his part, as soon as commerce permitted.

7

EMBARKING ON A CIVILIZING MISSION

"OUR Bable at Washington . . . [has] dispersed without being able to agree on any anti-commercial plan," read the triumphant announcement on May 11, 1810, in the *New Bedford Mercury.* Almost immediately vessels departed for London. One of them carried news, via Philadelphia, of Paul Cuffe's plans: he intended to take "a voyage, or visit" to Sierra Leone that fall if God and Friends concurred. Cuffe wrote to Friends James and Wilson to ask if "some solid Friend" would accompany him, as if still unconvinced of the safety of sailing in slave-trading waters. The Quaker City Friends delightedly relayed Cuffe's decision to British Friends, reminding the Londoners of the necessity for commercial incentives.[1]

Essential support for the civilizing mission clearly would depend on directors of the African Institution, among whom were Anglican bishops, earls, viscounts, members of both the houses of Parliament, and leading bankers and industrialists. Their aristocratic and social breeding allowed for potentially fruitful opportunities to rectify the injustices that had been forced on African descendants, but they were prone to zealous, disjointed action.[2] American Friends sought out this select company in England. Benjamin White, carefully briefed in Delaware on Cuffe's achievements, set off on a religious journey. He spent many months meeting key abolitionists in Britain, including William Allen; Pennsylvania Friend George Logan, President James Madison's trouble-shooting emissary, did so as well.[3]

Englishmen who took notice of Cuffe disagreed among themselves as to what action to take on his behalf. Liverpool's William Roscoe argued that African chiefs could best be dissuaded from selling their brethren by trading native goods for English goods. George Harrison cautioned against inhumane commercialism by drawing an example from North America: American traders had first made the Indians drunk, then bought furs and skins; their hands had offered "a *pound weight*" but their feet struck with "two pounds." In the charitable atmosphere of William Allen's Plough Court apothecary firm, Harrison, Thomas Clarkson, and others compiled the *Philanthropist*. Unlike publications of the established Anglican Church's Claphamite Sect, the *Philanthropist* stated that the plow and mechanic should humanely precede the Bible and priest in Africa.[4]

Differences notwithstanding, various factions attempted a united front to advance Cuffe's mission. Allen met with William Wilberforce, England's antislavery parliamentarian, in sessions that included Henry Brougham, of the House of Lords, and James Stephen, both members of the Clapham Sect.[5] Stephen proposed that a memorial be introduced to the Lords of the Privy Council, which sat as the Board of Trade, to assure profit for Cuffe in Sierra Leone. Wilberforce wished to tie Cuffe's proposed whale fishery to a scheme for a British whaling industry.

Eventually, the directors of the African Institution decided to ask Cuffe to meet with their board in late November of that year, at which time he could talk with powerful ministers in the British government and then take an English vessel to inspect Sierra Leone. Cuffe's own ship could return to the United States with a cargo. Allen invited the black Friend to stay at Plough Court when in London and assured him that everyone wanted to come "more clearly in possession of [his] views." This latest information was sent to Cuffe via his ship, the *Alpha*, which had sailed to London and was returning on the outgoing tide.

Selected as representative to the upcoming New England Yearly Meeting in Newport, Cuffe modestly increased his efforts to make new acquaintances and influence them. Quakers saw more than a stout, grey-clad shipmaster milling among the assembled worshipers. Stephen Gould, who was very much taken by his eastern neighbor, recorded the historical significance of Cuffe's presence for Friends: "This is the first time that ever a man of colour delivered his opinion in our Yearly Meeting & I guess in any in the World." Matthew Franklin sent word to New York that he had seen Cuffe in the gallery of the New Bedford Meeting with the venerable William Rotch; he had even closed the worship.[6] It is hard to imagine how Cuffe could have further improved his standing within the Society of Friends. Not surprisingly, he easily obtained the needed endorsements for his voyage to Africa.

In September 1810 the black Friend announced to the Westport

Meeting that he wished to make "a voige or visit to Africa if his friends had unity with his Prospect." John Mosher, Abner Potter, Benjamin Davol, Philip Dunham, Joseph Tripp, and Resolve Howland were chosen to study the matter. A month later they presented their recommendation, over Clerk Ebenezer Baker's signature. Cuffe was "a man whose orderly Life and Careful conduct has recommended him to the esteem of his friends———Desiring that he may experience Divine preservation in his present undertaking, we recommend him to the friendly attention and assistance of all well Disposed people where his Lot may be cast."[7] Friend William Rotch, Jr., sent a draft for £250 to Liverpool Friends for Cuffe's use in Sierra Leone.

Meanwhile, the Westporter continued to build his own financial reserves. West Indies goods sold steadily at the firm of Cuffe & Howards: one could buy molasses, Havana sugar, Sea Island cotton, kegs of mustard, Madeira nuts, and Charleston biscuits; discreet buyers were offered Lorrilard's Snuff by the bladder in elegant snuff boxes; and ladies could purchase the latest white kid gloves. Cuffe and the two Corys hired Nantucket officers and a diverse crew for the *Hero*'s fourth whaling voyage, this time heading around South America to the Pacific whaling grounds. Commercial prospects in Sierra Leone would have to be extremely good to entice Cuffe to shift his enterprises to Africa.

When the *Alpha* finally reached home from London she carried the request that Cuffe travel to England within the month. But the Britishers' plan was clearly not feasible. Instead, the *Traveller,* which had returned from Lisbon in September, would be outfitted to sail directly for Freetown. Cuffe's involvement in business and family affairs would be suspended during an expected absence of one to two years. John Cuffe accepted appointment as guardian over Paul's "lonely family" and personal interests. Four days before weighing anchor, Peter and Alexander Howard reluctantly accepted the fact that Cuffe & Howards had to close.[8]

A crowd flocked to the Acoaxet farm after the Friends Meeting on November 25. The Cuffes, Wainers, Howards, families of the nine crew members, and neighbors assembled on shore or waited aboard bobbing craft at the river's edge. Abraham Rodin, the Swedish apprentice, originally scheduled to sail with Cuffe, was omitted from the brig's roster. Captain Thomas Wainer and crew were "all people of color," boasted Cuffe, who listed himself as "owner of the Brig & supercargo." John Wainer came aboard as first mate, followed by his brother Michael and brother-in-law John Master; other crew members were Samuel Hicks, Zachariah White, Joseph Hemnaway, Charles Freeberg, Thomas Paton, and Prince Edwards. On shore Cuffe affectionately bid family and friends farewell; he was followed into Buzzards Bay by brother John, sons Paul and William, Abraham Rodin, and Paul Wainer. They "left us at 2 o'clock," the family patriarch wistfully noted as he headed south. "All well. Wind at North, pleasant weather and smooth sea."[9]

Their first stop was Philadelphia, where John James urged Cuffe to be more practical and at least carry old corn to Spain or Portugal before sailing to Africa. He demanded half of the profits when he heard about good trading conditions at Sierra Leone, and then complained when Cuffe included Alexander Wilson in the venture. The black Friend indignantly observed how "prospect of gain did catch his eyes."[10] Cuffe and James did agree to turn over the *Alpha* to Nantucket's Thaddeus Coffin, whereupon she departed for New Orleans.

The sturdy sixty-nine-ton *Traveller,* dwarfed by freighters bound worldwide, had her cargo of 1,100 pounds of barley exchanged for African-bound goods from James's countinghouse. News of Cuffe's intended voyage swept quickly from the customs house through the merchant quarters, the Quaker Meeting houses, the free black community, and the antislavery strongholds. Friends appointed a time to offer a recommendation from the Arch Street Meeting House, site of many yearly meetings. "After a feeling conference," Cuffe recalled, "they expressed satisfaction and left me at liberty." His preaching at that Meeting moved William Savery to offer his seat to the black Friend, but Cuffe "made a gesture of dissent and walked back down the aisle, to his place among his own people."[11]

The pragmatic captain knew the necessity of impeccable credentials when entering slave-trading waters. "I have had the pleasure of a personal knowledge of Capt. Paul Cuffee for several years," began one of his most cherished testimonials, prepared by Benjamin Rush.[12] Rush vouched for the Westporter's "integrity and other moral virtues," stating that Cuffe's mission was to aid the benevolent views of England's prestigious African Institution "toward the African nations." Thus, Rush summoned "the friends of Liberty, humanity, and religions in every part of the world" to protect this extraordinary company. With this and other endorsements stowed safely in the owner's quarters, the *Traveller* cleared Philadelphia for Freetown, Sierra Leone, on December 27, 1810. The wealthy black American was embarking on an extraordinary African adventure.

The *Traveller's* eastward passage tested the company's skill and resolve. The brig plowed through thundering squalls that splintered yardarms and washed crew members overboard, including Captain Wainer's brother-in-law, John Master, who seized some loose rigging and was able to pull himself to safety. By early February 1811 the *Traveller* cruised in North African shipping lanes. Cuffe's log noted passing vessels of Portuguese and British registry. The encounters conjured up haunting tales of the slave trade, first learned from his father. He meditated on Thomas Clarkson's "Records on Abolishing Slavery, which often baptised my mind in the sense of his proceedings." It brought "consolation and comfort" from the Lord. Finally, near month's end, the "dust of Africa lodged on our rigging."[13] A week later the Cape of Sierra Leone lay three leagues away.

The black company passed the Cape at dawn on March 1, and "at half past 8 o'clock we came to in Sierra Leone Road," wrote Cuffe. First impressions confirmed what he had heard in America: vessels condemned for transporting slaves rimmed the shoreline. His Majesty's Frigate *Crocodile* dominated the harbor, symbolizing Britain's attempt to halt these traders of human flesh. Symmetrical rows of small earthen houses lined the streets leading to the beach. Above the town loomed the walls of Fort Thornton, which in turn were dwarfed by verdant, towering mountains that seemed to jut through the clouds.[14]

Initial efforts to contact Governor E. H. Columbine proved fruitless. When he finally appeared he invited the Friend to church and then to a private conference. The encounter stacked a distraught colonial administrator against Zachary Macaulay's approved black emissary. The two dined at the governor's house, where Columbine felt at ease discussing controversial issues: the continuing slave trade and "the unsuccessfulness of the Colony." He spoke of his personal tragedy: during thirteen months in the West African climate he had suffered repeated malaria attacks, his wife had died, and his children had been sent home, where one had died. Administrative headaches abounded as well, caused in large part by the former governor, T. P. Thompson. Just before Cuffe's arrival Columbine had felt compelled to defend British abolitionists against Thompson's charge that they had enslaved natives in order to civilize them. No doubt Cuffe heard a flood of derogatory comments about influential black Nova Scotian settlers who formed the backbone of the settlement. Cuffe later listened to an informed governor tell his council that he was "about to quit the

Colony."[15] The Westporter shuddered at such a skeptical introduction to Africa.

Notwithstanding pleas on Cuffe's behalf from London, government and commercial restrictions added to his initial disappointment. On March 2 "his Excellency permitted all of our Cargo to Be Landed but the 6 Bales of India goods," Cuffe noted in the brig's log. His tone changed four days later: "17 $ is the highest price I can get for my flour. and No Permit to Land the Merchandize in the colony." The personal initiative by Zachary Macaulay had not effectively safeguarded Cuffe's losses. Macaulay's own firm, which monopolized much of Freetown's commerce, aggravated the situation. Duties and wharfage and craneage fees were increased. Local officials treated Cuffe little better than any other American merchant. In turn, he avoided the powerful English traders whenever possible: on one occasion he bartered goods for 316 elephant "teeth"; another time he made £130 by directly selling to His Majesty's Brig *Protector,* about to depart for Goree. The black Yankee discovered that his ideas for trade ran directly counter to the colony's commercial establishment.[16]

Cuffe's interests quickly shifted to the former American slaves and freemen, the Nova Scotians, whom Columbine had found to be the most troublesome.[17] There were 982 of them, as opposed to 28 Europeans who controlled three-fifths of all the property. Others in the Freetown vicinity included a few families from Granville Sharp's original settlement, 807 Maroons from the British West Indies, 100 local Africans, 601 Kru tribesmen, and over 1,000 Africans recaptured from slave ships.[18] But the most educated, republican-minded, and prosperous of the inhabitants were the Nova Scotians. Some of these black entrepreneurs, who acted as agents for Europeans dealing in up-country produce, owned coastal trading vessels. They also comprised the bulk of the colony's church-going population, aside from the established white Anglican congregation. Many flocked together with their own preachers to Methodist, Baptist, and Countess of Huntingdon's Connection meeting houses. Although they also were recognized for their liquor consumption, they were Cuffe's kind of people, and likely agents to further promote civilization.

These settlers provided Cuffe a contact with indigenous people. Soon after his arrival a "King Thomas" and his retinue of thirteen came aboard the *Traveller.* They were welcomed "with civility," Cuffe pointedly observed, adding that he gave his guest a Bible, a Quaker history, and an essay on avoiding war. He also presented the visiting monarch with appropriate advice for a head of state, intended for "the use and encouragement of the Nations of Africa."[19] He expressed ethical principles without once mentioning Christian conversion, thus upholding his Quaker principles of advocating a civilized way of life. Africans should be sober "by doing justly, loving mercy, and walking humbly." Youth should be shielded from "corruptions of the world" like swearing, bad company, and spiritous liquor. And servants should be faithful and industrious "so that we may become a people," thereby thanking those "who have borne the heat and burden of the day, in liberating us from a state of slavery." Cuffe noted in his log that the Africans departed without receiving any rum.

Other encounters with local Africans followed. King George from Bulom Shore honored the black American with three chickens and an invitation to visit his village. Cuffe did so, traveling six miles in a long canoe with settlers David Edmonds, John Morgan, and Henry Warren. They were cordially received, and gift giving of Christian material again marked the event. On another occasion the civilizer mistakenly challenged the Mandingo people for "doing wrong"; he called them "Professors of Mahamet" who memorized the Old Testament and read backwards. Unlike earlier acquaintances, the Mandingo gave Cuffe a lesson in indigenous African pride: "They are no white men and their fathers taught them thus," he quoted them as saying. Kru people, he noted, worshiped "the new moon"; they, like most Africans, lacked a recognizable religion, although there was evidence of some sort of deity. Others who had the Bible lacked the "Living Substance."[20] Cuffe's civilized Judeo-Christian perspective prevented much comprehension of indigenous values.

He did appreciate humane, Western values, however. One morning Cuffe visited a school with thirty female "Scholars, Which Was a Pleasing prospect in Sierra Leone." He welcomed Britain's efforts to stop slave traders who, a short distance to the south, demanded a larger quantity of Vai slaves and ravaged the Sherbro area. Sadly, he reported an incoming British man-of-war had seen but was unauthorized to capture Portuguese slavers along the Leeward Coast. Another time Cuffe gratefully observed a Vice-Admiralty Court trial in which Acting Judge Alexander Smith condemned a Portuguese schooner captain for trading "Contrary to the Law of Nations."[21] Based on all that he saw, he pondered whether the colony represented the best chance for saving his enslaved brethren in America.

Methodist preacher Henry Warren, whom Cuffe proudly noted was originally "a black man from Philadelphia" but was now "Henry Warren of Sierra Leone in Africa," may have been the first person to convince Cuffe of Sierra Leone's advantages for black Americans. On March 11 the two men had a particularly lengthy conversation. The next day Thomas Wainer rented a house from Nova Scotian carpenter Peter Francis; Cuffe followed suit, bettering Wainer's rent by one pound per month. The Westporter clearly intended to rent from and live among the settlers, despite Columbine's warnings to the contrary.[22] They held out the most hope for the colony and African brethren in the interior.

Toward the end of March, as both Cuffe and Columbine were preparing to leave the colony, they spoke on the "Subject of the Country & Settling in it to good Satisfaction."[23] The ailing Columbine offered assurances that industrious and Christian persons would be welcomed. He told Cuffe that the directors of the African Institution wanted to know the financial burdens he bore; the next day accounts were forwarded to London. By early April the *Traveller* stood ready for sea. Her cargo had come from black merchants rather than English trading houses. Cuffe particularly liked trading with boatbuilder David Edmonds and local entrepreneur Sarah Holiday, who provided lumber. Kru woodcutters brought camwood and furwood from the interior. James Reid, one of Cuffe's admirers from among the early settlers, offered him a copy of an original bill of "sale" from the late 1780s, which asserted that Africans had granted land rights for the beginning of Sierra Leone.

The essential matter of a petition to further black emigration from America was delayed until the arrival of John Kizell, the most respected black merchant doing business out of Freetown. Kizell came from Sherbro Island, his birthplace and now his residence after many years as a slave in Charleston, South Carolina, an immigrant to Nova Scotia, and then a petitioner to England on behalf of those who wished to settle in Sierra Leone. On Sunday, April 7, 1811, the Sherbro merchant knelt in prayer with merchant-preacher Warwick Francis and Paul Cuffe at the Baptist Meeting House.

That day marked the rebirth of local black incentive. After worshiping together, Cuffe, Kizell, Edmonds, Francis, Reid, Thomas Wainer, and others withdrew to the privacy of the *Traveller,* where they "Stated a sketch of a Petition to Lay before the People for their approbation."[24] Cuffe recorded the final draft intended for the British Parliament:

> His Excellency Governor Columbine Esqr Governor of His Majesty's Colony Sierra Leone

We the undersigned do Wish to Lay before your Lordship the following circumstances as under viz

---

1st That Encouragement may be given unto all our Brethren who may Come from the English Colonies or America and become farmers in order to help us to Cultivate the Land
2nd our foreign Brethren who may have Vessels that Encouragement may be given to them to Establish Commerce in S. Leone
3d Would Encouragement be given unto all those Who May Establish the whale fishery in the Colony of Sierra Leone.

Twelve of Sierra Leone's most respected citizens backed Cuffe's prescription for reviving black industry in the British colony. They knew full well that the wrath of the English merchant community, which had thwarted local trade since the settlement's inception, had to be avoided.

Just before sailing for the United States Cuffe received essential news from William Allen in London: directors of the African Institution wished to meet with him. Britain's Privy Council had voted him extraordinary commercial privileges, allowing the American a six-month trading license between Sierra Leone and England. Immediately, crew members exchanged the brig's cargo for items to suit the Liverpool market.

Cuffe's excitement grew as he envisioned the possibility of triangular trade between Africa, Europe, and America. Henceforth, "Paul Cuffe and his concern" could promote commerce and emigrants from the United States and Britain for Sierra Leone. "I have thought if commerce could be introduced in the colony," he wrote to Allen, "it might have this good tendency" of training seamen to enter business for themselves as well as prepare native minds "for the reception of better things." Financial expansion would lead to national self-determination. Sierra Leone would "be numbered among the historians' nations of the world." The settlers' three-point petition for black farmers, traders, and whalers would be an important beginning.[25] Cuffe's goal remained "the civilization of Africa."

The settler population of Sierra Leone began to share Cuffe's enthusiasm. They followed his and John Kizell's lead in forming the Friendly Society, a mutual aid society that would concentrate on commercial concerns.[26] Its first action came less than two weeks after the meeting on the *Traveller*. On April 20, 1811, sixteen people, half of them petitioners for Cuffe's commercial proposals, drew up an antislavery petition. Their proclamation was given the impressive title

"Epistle from the Society of Sierra Leone, in Africa, to the Saints and Faithful Brethren in Christ." The epistle queried in typical Quaker form whether it was agreeable to "Jesus Christ for one professor to make merchandise of another." Cuffe would carry that message to London.

Such proclamations fit perfectly into the local scene. Sierra Leone governors like Columbine ruled by proclamation. Before Cuffe's arrival Columbine had proclaimed that malicious women addicted to defaming neighbors, the courts, and the police would be publicly doused in the harbor, "such dunking to consist of three complete dips." Cuffe had heard the governor threaten idle young men and women "in the habit of disturbing and insulting the Religious Worship" with a twenty-pound fine. The Westporter recorded another government proclamation: slaves freed by their African masters could reside in the colony.[27]

Freetown's waterfront bustled while efforts to further subvert the power of black merchants increased. Robert Bones now headed the Governor's Council, Kenneth Macaulay became secretary to Bones, and George Macaulay received an appointment as writer for the secretary. The firm of Macaulay & Babington would gain considerable power in the governor's absence. On May 6 members of the European and settler communities united in a rare display of cooperation at "A General Meeting of the Society for the Relief of the Poor of this Colony." The ailing Columbine, probably already aboard the *Crocodile,* was listed as having donated thirty pounds. None of the several Macaulays made donations, unlike Cuffe's associates Joseph Brown, David Edmonds, Peter Francis, Warwick Francis, John Gordon, and James Wise, who gave their share.[28]

Would Cuffe's challenge to the economic status quo in the colony end with his departure for England? Alexander Smith, perhaps acting for the English merchants who monopolized trade there, feared not; moreover, Cuffe might reveal the settlers' side of the story to the British. Smith wrote a scathing denunciation of Cuffe to Zachary Macaulay in London, saying that he had never known a more unprincipled, mercenary individual, that Cuffe was no better than a slave trader. Unfortunately, Cuffe's journal entries for those volatile days, otherwise meticulously kept, have disappeared.[29]

On the morning of May 10 the frigate HMS *Crocodile* headed for open water with the dying Columbine on board. The brig *Traveller* followed in her wake, commanded by Cuffe rather than his nephew, who had remained in Freetown. He ordered one crew member about with particular care: Aaron Richards, the son of cooper Thomas Richards, a black settler, had come aboard as Cuffe's apprentice, to learn navigation. It was hoped that he might eventually command a trading vessel between England and Africa for the black settlers.[30] Future voyages to England for the purpose of increasing black commercial trade would depend on the success of Cuffe's present undertaking.

8

TAKING HIS MISSION TO ENGLAND

As the *Traveller* pierced through a thick fog off Wallesby in July 1811, her crew discovered that the Liverpool wharves were "lined with people who had assembled to gaze at them as they approached the shore." The *Edinburgh Review* guessed it "must have been a strange and animating spectacle to see this free and enlightened African entering, as an independent trader, with his black crew, into that port which was so lately the *nidus* of the Slave Trade." The *Times* (London) commented on the entry: "The Brig *Traveller* . . . is perhaps the first vessel that ever reached Europe, entirely owned and navigated by Negroes."[1] A visiting American Friend, Stephen Grellet, later expressed hope that the vessel's cleanliness and excellent order would open "the minds of many in tender feelings towards the poor suffering Africans."[2] Ironically, the Liverpool docks onto which Cuffe stepped were those from which the last British slaver, *Kitty Amelia,* had sailed just four years earlier. And only nine years prior to that, 149 slave ships had departed from Liverpool for Africa, the trade on which "the greatness of 'the old town' was suckled."[3]

The day after the *Traveller*'s entry with her cargo of elephant "teeth," camwood, palm oil, and copal gum—products of free African labor—Cuffe's ship *Alpha,* commanded by Thaddeus Coffin of Nantucket, reached Liverpool from New Orleans. She carried a lucrative cargo produced by slave labor: 532 bales of plantation cotton. Both cargoes were entrusted to William and Richard Rathbone, members of Liverpool's American Chamber of Commerce.[4] No one, including Cuffe, thought it unusual that prominent Britishers could benefit financially from slave labor while espousing a policy of humanitarianism toward Africans. What did confound the black American was that members of Liverpool's African Company of Merchants simply sat by as his young Sierra Leone apprentice and two fellow crew members were taken captive by a press gang. Authorities later insisted on detaining Aaron Richards despite Cuffe's proof that he was legally indentured for the voyage to and from England. They also knew that Cuffe had a Privy Council trading license for that voyage, but such papers apparently meant little in view of worsening Anglo-American trade relations.

Aaron Richard's captivity both infuriated and worried Cuffe. Such was his frame of mind as he boarded a stagecoach for London. Wearing a wide-flapped hat, and dressed in a drab grey suit, Cuffe journeyed through the well-cultivated countryside for thirty-two hours, providing a welcome opportunity to relax and sightsee. By dawn of the second morning he reached the throbbing British metropolis, and after resting and dining at a local inn he hailed a "pilot" for Lombard Street. At last he stood in the small confines of Plough Court, the site of William Allen's home and apothecary shop.[5]

The two Friends greeted each other as spiritual brothers on a joint African rescue mission. They discussed the detainment of Aaron Richards and the damage to Cuffe's reputation by Alexander Smith's poisonous letter. Allen had already talked to Zachary Macaulay and Lord Henry Brougham about the impressment; and Macaulay, in turn, had contacted James Stephen in the Colonial Office. It seemed clear that the two issues were related. As Allen later confided to Thomas Clarkson, "It appears . . . remarkable that Smith showed every kindness and attention to Cuffe *till he* found him determined to come to England."[6] Ironically, Smith's complaint had initiated disclosure of the very issue—the white commercial monopoly—that most bothered Cuffe and black settlers in Sierra Leone.

Restoring Cuffe's reputation would be easier to do than freeing his apprentice. Bureaucratic red tape slowed progress on the latter for weeks. Allen set out with his black Friend for the office of William Smith, in Parliament, and then for the Board of Trade. Finally William Wilberforce summoned the two Friends to his office at the Palace Yard, where they received word that Richards had been removed from Liverpool to the prison ship *Salvatori Mundi* in Plymouth. Allen later noted that "Wilberforce immediately called for pen, ink, and paper, and wrote to the Board of Admiralty." Five days later Thomas Clarkson arrived at Allen's Plough Court home; he had come to London "entirely to see Paul Cuffe." The black Friend gratefully watched Clarkson "set to for Aaron's liberation."[7]

Orthodox Claphamites competed with the Plough Court mavericks to resolve the Richards affair. Wilberforce lavished praise on this

"Black man [Cuffe] of singular Talents Qualifications & Merits" to Admiralty Secretary Croker. The African Institution needed him as a permanent settler, hence the necessity for immediate action on Richards's release. "I need not point out to you what an acquisition this could be to a new colony of which ye worst circumstance has been the bad character of the population." Clarkson and Allen called at the Admiralty Office and then wrote to Mayor Henry Woollcombe and Friend Francis Fox of Plymouth and Thomas Thompson of Liverpool to say that Richards must be kept safe.[8] Finally Allen noted that "we have got off Aaron Richards, the impressed man," after "an explanation" with Macaulay. Richards remained close to the *Traveller* after that ordeal.

Now free to travel to the comfortable Walthamstow estate of William Dillwyn, Cuffe and Allen conversed with Dillwyn on recent activity among Philadelphia blacks, on Friends' work among American Indians, and, Cuffe noted dryly, "on the subject of importance." The black American did not advocate Ann Mifflin's theory on "Returning Societies";[9] he had not sailed to empty the United States of unwanted blacks. Perhaps another meeting would be necessary between the Friends to clarify that point. Later Dillwyn skeptically called Cuffe "an innocent well intentioned man . . . more useful in other lines." Cuffe skirted any direct criticism but found Dillwyn "very unwell," one whose "glass is almost run."[10] John Clarkson obviously was more to Cuffe's liking. The black Friend dubbed him a "goodlooking man and well-wisher of the cause."[11] Clarkson had led black settlers from Halifax, Nova Scotia, to the Sierra Leone River in 1792; and in 1811 the displaced Nova Scotians still considered him their favorite governor.

Philanthropist Allen set aside long periods of time to learn of Cuffe's African ideas. Cuffe probably showed Allen and others the settlers' petition to increase black trade and entice new immigrants. By the end of July the two men had grown in "nearness of spirit" thanks to Friends Meetings and conversations late into the evening. Cuffe's economic plan gradually took the form of a Pan-African triangular trade, or what he referred to as the "African traffic," which would mean keeping "a constant road open from England to America and to SL & from thence to England." The *Times* (London) suggested that all-black crews in European waters would be the mark of the future. Cuffe utilized such publicity where it would be most productive: he sent copies to New York, Boston, and New Bedford. He also mailed recopied Sierra Leone and English documents to Philadelphia churchmen and to his brother John in Westport, whom he instructed to search for "some of our folks who might visit the colony."[12] He told John that labor in the colony was so cheap that one only had to oversee the work of others.

Social engagements in Liverpool also bolstered the cause. On August 7 Cuffe dined with William and Richard Rathbone, Lord John Russell, and William Roscoe. Roscoe, a prosperous merchant and one of the directors of the African Institution, was the first Liverpool member of Parliament to oppose the slave trade. Cuffe must have been relieved to hear someone adamantly favor unilateral seizure of slave traders on the high seas, regardless of national registry. The practice complied with "the law of nations," a term Cuffe had heard in the Admiralty Court in Freetown. Roscoe also campaigned against the Portuguese slavers off the Calabar coast, and, like Cuffe, believed that commerce was the best means of spreading civilization in Africa.[13]

Personal affairs needed Cuffe's attention as well. The captain saw to repairs for the *Traveller* and a cargo for the *Alpha*. At one point he decided to switch vessels with Thaddeus Coffin and sail for home, so as to make a "full settlement" with the *Alpha*'s co-owner, John James, and recruit a few select persons to examine Sierra Leone. Coffin would take the *Traveller* to Freetown under the British license, pay its debts, and sail for Westport.[14] But good news about a King's Council decision and a meeting of the African Institution's directors, scheduled for August 27, sent him scurrying back to London.

Cuffe and Allen, his Quaker host, once more communed together, and the two faithfully attended Grace Street Meetings twice weekly. Each reinforced the other's ethic of responsibility toward the mistreated Africans. They yearned to civilize Africa from Christian impulses, to teach humane values with technical know-how. Both were secular social reformers by traditional standards.[15] Nevertheless, evangelical publicity conveyed the opposite view. The *Monthly Repository*'s August 1811 installment rejoiced that Cuffe "looked up with reverence and gratitude to a crucified Saviour, and sought these [British] shores for a better acquaintance with his name. . . ." Christ's "Name would shortly be made known in all the regions of Africa!" The ever-increasing publicity also attracted flocks of male and female admirers to Plough Court, including an old New Bedford Friend and shipmaster, Eban Clark.[16]

Claphamites William Wilberforce and Zachary Macaulay continued to work, often unsuccessfully, on Cuffe's behalf. The Board of Trade had issued the American a special trading license, although it had failed to grant a protective license for the *Traveller* should a British ship seize her en route from Sierra Leone to America. Nor was the license valid for the continuation of a Sierra Leone–English trade route. Wilberforce offered to begin "another Effort" if Cuffe considered the refusals to be "of great Importance." Wilberforce regretted that various rules prevented the African Institution from providing housing allotments to new immigrants whom Cuffe might transport to the colony, but he offered to raise funds separately to stimulate land allotments. There was also the matter of certain embarrassing political realities: agricultural produce raised by Cuffe's clients, the free black settlers, must not "give occasion for jealousy to the West Indies."[17] In other words, cotton raised by slaves in the British West Indies was preferred on the English market. It is unlikely that the latter topic came up on the evening Cuffe was graciously dined by Macaulay. Primarily, the Institution's secretary wished to ease the tensions created by Alexander Smith's vitriolic letter.

On August 27, 1811, a large number of the directors of the African Institution, chaired by King George III's nephew, the Duke of Gloucester, convened to meet Paul Cuffe. William Allen gave a short introduction, and then the featured speaker turned to the Duke of Gloucester and presented him with native African crafts, to prove, as he said, "that the African was capable of mental endowments." Cuffe told the gathered dignitaries that he could not guarantee the good character of all new settlers, but persons "of steady habits" were likely to go "if the channel could be kept open." A successful African traffic required trading privileges from the United States to the colony and to England. No, he did not intend "at present" to settle in Sierra Leone. Yes, Nova Scotians needed economic stimulus; as an incentive, he felt the establishment of a whale fishery would contribute toward that end. The directors graciously thanked Cuffe for the presentation and then appointed a committee to study his proposals, including reimbursement for his expenses while in England. Surely he represented "an instance of the practicability of African improvement."[18]

The generous reception and lofty praise notwithstanding, promises for future action were open to question.[19] Cuffe candidly hoped that "the subject may not fall beneath the level where we found it." Allen went a good deal further. Sierra Leone had been at "so low an ebb" in 1807, he later wrote in the *Philanthropist,* that the government had had to take over the colony from the Sierra Leone Company. Cuffe had arrived to find it "in this state"; it continued to be mismanaged and lacking in influence. The American's information had emphasized the necessity for "sufficient stimulus" to settlers. In contrast to Cuffe's and Allen's reactions, the official directors' publication maintained that Cuffe had given an "encouraging account of what he had seen in Africa" and that Sierra Leone was "in a state of visible improvement."

Allen, as but one director of the African Institution, now looked at the problems in Sierra Leone from a black perspective. Two days after the special meeting he formally established a compatible position with Cuffe. He addressed a lengthy diplomatic and inquiring letter to Sherbro merchant John Kizell, which, if passed into the wrong hands, would not seriously offend the English merchants: "From the representations made to me by my Friend Capt. Paul Cuffee, of thy zeal to promote the great and good cause of the Civilization of Africa, I am inclined to wish to open a correspondence with thee . . . [to be] kept informed of the exact state of things among them (the people of colour) . . . and what in thy opinion would tend to excite a spirit of industry among the settlers."[20] Henceforth the black settler population of Sierra Leone would have at least one staunch sympathizer in England, perhaps the first since John Clarkson had defended black interests there.

A gratified Cuffe left London by stagecoach for Manchester, England's showcase of the burgeoning Industrial Revolution. The progress he witnessed in the factories there staggered his imagination. The thirty-six-mile ride to the coast from Manchester to Liverpool gave him time to reflect on all he had seen and heard. At the docks he was met by the Rathbones, the Thompsons, William Faner, and George Briggs, among others. Methodist Bishop Thomas Coke paid the captain for four passengers to Sierra Leone—finally, the settlers would get their long-overdue Methodist missionary and teachers.

Once more the black American spoke of a Pan-African trading scheme. He called on England, the United States, and France to protect cohesive African commerce as though visualizing a "Holy Alliance" on Africa's behalf. Twice he insisted that the triangular traffic should maintain "communication between America, Africa, and England." "Building a vessel in Africa" would also help. Many people gathered to talk with Cuffe on "the most expedient method of civilization." Navigation, cultivation, and communication were needed "whereby Africa might be advantaged."[21]

High media visibility and low financial returns characterized the final phase of Cuffe's journey to England. The *Liverpool Mercury* reprinted the black settlers' epistle while the paper's drama editor ad-

Liverpool 9th mo 9th 1811

Esteemd friend

William Allen

after my best wishes to thee & family

these may inform thee that I Expect to be

in Readiness to Sail after first day next Ensuing

if thou has any further communication to me

it will be kindly Excepted

Will thee be so kind as to Send me the copy of

the minites of african institution so fare as it

Consernes Africa

I have too Long neglected forwarding the payment

for the goods but I have Recived the goods and

to morrow the orders will be Sent forward to

London to meet the payment for the Amount

I hope the board of trade will further consider

the Necessetty of a further Exstention of a Lisene

to Enabel a communication between Africa England

and America

my Love to thee and family and to thy Dear moth

and am thy Assured friend Paul Cuffe

PS francis tompson holds out yet

This letter, sent to William Allen just prior to Cuffe's embarkation from Liverpool for Sierra Leone, mentions several factors important to the success of his plan for a triangular Atlantic trade. Both men were determined to foster a black enterprise among harrassed merchants in the British colony. Paul Cuffe to William Allen, Sept. 9, 1811, Loose Letters, William Allen Papers, Allen and Hanbury, Ltd., London.

vertised a contrasting image of Africa: Liverpool's Academy of Arts was presenting a play entitled "AFRICAN: or War, Love, and Duty," which stacked Ferulho the Priest, Terribal, and Henry Augustus Mug against virtuous, responsible European merchants.[22] The black captain sat in his cabin, not in the theater, recording expenses of at least $1,200, which he hoped the African Institution would pay. Medgley flannels, Herculaneum pottery, flour, sugar, and shoes were on board, as well as numerous English and Arabic Bibles for the missionaries and used books gathered from about town.

At ten o'clock on Friday morning, September 20, 1811, the brig *Traveller* departed St. George's docks for West Africa. Sundry papers from the British customs house and the United States consul were stored below with the usual collection of authenticating documents. "A great many attended our departure," wrote the celebrity. Several more sailed aboard for a few hours to witness the black crew at work. Bishop Coke tearfully watched the brig recede into the mist with his Methodist missionaries on board. "The vessel sailed amidst the prayers of the pious," he glowingly reported, "and the admiration of all who saw her leave the British Coast."[23] British publications rushed to reprint the 1806 Delaware-originated memoir of Cuffe. It was carried in provincial newspapers, William Allen's *Philanthropist,* Zachary Macaulay's *Christian Observer,* and the *Universal Magazine.*[24] Publishing houses reproduced the biography in Liverpool and in York, and a copy eventually reached Sierra Leone and the United States.

Paul Cuffe had made a deep impression on three levels of British society. The printed media had alerted the general public to his wide range of African accomplishments. Further, Cuffe personally had reached the most instrumental policy-making segment of British society—the royalty sympathetic to Sierra Leone and the abolition movement, elected and appointed government officials, and the leading philanthropists for the African cause. Interdepartmental communications, conferences, and a special meeting of the African Institution had netted him a one-way trading license to Sierra Leone, with possible benefits to come. But his most important success came at the individual level. Henceforth, William Allen, a director of the African Institution and England's Quaker editor of the *Philanthropist,* would go on record as the advocate for Africans under British rule. With Allen in London and Cuffe in Westport, a developing African traffic might funnel trade, settlers with maritime and agricultural expertise, and encouragement to Sierra Leone.

9

THE FRIENDLY SOCIETY OF SIERRA LEONE

THE civilizing mission nearly ended for Paul Cuffe in early October 1811. Missionary George Warren, on board the *Traveller,* wrote that "The [French] Schooner continues to gain on us," presumably to take the black Westporter and his crew captive. Two hours later Cuffe noted the pursuer was "nearly in our wake, 1 league off." Within minutes a great squall providentially brought driving rain, high winds, and heavy seas. In the commotion the captain ordered extra sails aloft and the *Traveller* escaped certain seizure. Earlier, Warren recalled, "we had taken an opportunity, the Captain with us in the cabin, to . . . commend ourselves by solomn prayer to the Divine protection."[1] Now the brig with a British trading license had escaped England's continental enemy. It appeared that only with such Divine assistance could the black Friend expect to continue to assist his brethren.

"It is Calm & Warm," wrote Cuffe on November 12, 1811, "Sierra Leone Looks Natural." Word of his return spread through Freetown. Kru fishermen were the first to board, followed by the captain of the brig HMS *Protector.* Other craft came alongside, and a welcoming committee that included merchants David Edmonds and nephew Thomas Wainer arrived. The black captain ordered a boat prepared for shore, where he led the four Methodist missionaries to the governor's house to meet its new resident, Charles William Maxwell. Governor Maxwell warmly welcomed the new arrivals, including their reputable captain. On the way they encountered the colony's chaplain, Rev. Reinhold Nylander, a German-born Lutheran missionary from London's Church Missionary Society. Up Charlotte Street they proceeded, to the refined abode of European carpenter George Nicol and his Nova Scotian wife, Sophia. Along came Methodist preachers

John Gordon and Joseph Brown, signators of the settlers' epistle published in England; Brown had been the first to ask Bishop Coke to send Warren and the three schoolteachers. Cuffe led the entourage to the home of Alexander Smith, "who showed every mark of friendship."[2] After briefly chatting with Baptist preacher Warwick Francis, the new Methodist missionaries returned to the Nicols' home for a rest.

Governor Maxwell had taken command of the colony on July 1, after which he ordered that all foreign vessels could import only lumber, candles, soap, and food provisions. Naval officers were to check immediately the papers and health of persons aboard, ship's documents were to be held in the secretary's office until departure, and duties on foreign vessels were to be three times the fees for British bottoms.[3] Thus, although Cuffe's British license had to be honored, it was subject to strict interpretation by the governor. The normally calm Friend first complained that Maxwell gave him conflicting orders regarding the cargo. Then he was piqued to learn that his was the first bottom ever to have a customs official ordered aboard to see that all goods were landed at Freetown. He quickly recorded small orders from the brig's hold for the governor and "Esqr. Smith," without further comment, probably relieved that at least his British license exempted him from Maxwell's elaborate prohibition against American vessels. This second trip must show some profit, both for his benefit and for the proposed African traffic.

The British license, Cuffe's diplomacy, and Maxwell's generally amenable conduct protected the American from exploitation, and sales ensued for weeks. Crates, boxes, and chests were carted ashore; some were opened for display, others delivered directly to storerooms or homes. Cuffe's policy was one of "Selling to those Who Would buy & pay," giving first choice to black settlers. Goods included linens, hats, candles, tea, pork, and bread. Forty bushels of salt went to Nova Scotian Charlotte Simpson; eighty bushels were loaded aboard John Kizell's schooner *Adventure* after payment of local charges. "I Sold Very Smart of the tin & hardware So that there Was Constant Employ," Cuffe wrote on November 18, the same day 385 Herculaneum iron pots reached shore. Meanwhile, palm oil and several tons of camwood were shipped off to London aboard HMS *Umbro.* Settlers "were closely advised to make good use of the *Traveller*'s books, ec." Cantankerous Alexander Smith disliked Cuffe's tobacco, told Charlotte Simpson to complain about hers, evaded Cuffe's offers to replace the goods, and disputed the price. "This appears to me to have been too much the mode of his way of Dealing," noted Cuffe in disgust. Yet letters to England never mentioned any problems.[4]

The black civilizer again embraced Christianity as an extension of his mission. He and David Edmonds unsuccessfully tried to stop former Philadelphian Henry Warren from dividing the Wesleyan community. Cuffe asked George Warren and Methodist teachers John Healey, Thomas Hirst, and Joseph Rayner if they would like "an interview" with King George of Bulom, who had welcomed Cuffe on his first trip to the colony. Warren and Rayner met the affable ninety-two-year-old monarch, who wore his most civilized attire: an old satin coat, an unfashionable silk waistcoat, a pair of coarse blue trousers, and "a middling pair of shoes, but no stockings."[5] Warren pressed for a mission school and the king welcomed the idea, promising that all of his children would attend. The next day Cuffe introduced the Methodists to a Christian "mulatto" from the Guinea coast.

Sometime during his stay the Westport Friend presented a pointedly Christian address to his "scattered brethren and fellow countrymen of Sierra Leone."[6] He prayed for "Ethiopia [to] stretch out her hand unto God. Come, my African brethren and fellow countrymen," he appealed, "let us walk together in the light of the Lord." Later, England's Bishop Coke would note Cuffe's contribution to the Methodist mission.[7] The Christian approach had its limits, however. Although subject to the influence of evangelicals in London and Freetown, the Quaker civilizer still believed in the power of the Inner Voice rather than imposed conversion. Early in December 1811 he circulated a letter from the Oneida Indians in America to prove the success of a mission that primarily emphasized a way of life rather than a religion.

Missionaries themselves were not immune from Cuffe's advice on good conduct and industry. Shortly before Christmas, Zachary Macaulay's brother Alexander brought missionaries John Wilhelm and Jonathan Klein into port.[8] Reinhold Nylander, the ailing colony chaplain, dutifully took them to the governor's house, as Cuffe had for the Methodists. But the anxious Lutheran was incapable of much more than spurring on the newcomers to excede Methodist conversions. Cuffe welcomed them to Freetown but felt compelled to offer some sage Quaker advice: "I then Endeavored to hold out the Necessity that good may be done Even in goods and industry ec ec ec." Moreover, he felt uncomfortable talking of "converts."

Settler and commercial affairs consumed most of Cuffe's time and energy. He found the weakened Friendly Society caught in the crossfire of discontent. On November 20 the Governor's Council passed the Militia Act, which required all inhabitants to sign an oath of allegiance to King George of Britain; two weeks later the government threatened settlers to sign or leave. This was a painful reminder to Nova Scotian and Maroon settlers of alleged earlier deception by colonial officials, who had imposed unexpected quit-rents (taxes) on new land. Many misinterpreted the preamble of the Militia Act to mean that males between the ages of thirteen and sixty who signed would be deported for military duty.[9] In addition, the government already had unsatisfied land claims against four-fifths of the disgruntled Nova Scotians.

As animosity increased Cuffe attempted to calm the settlers. He circulated among his neighbors with seeds and plants from William Allen, speaking of Allen's eagerness to help with the population's agriculture and trade. James Reid, at first a governor and now the colony's jailer, took the next step, calling on Cuffe to meet with prominent settlers at his own home. At a Friendly Society meeting to be attended by most of the elite black citizens, the discussion would center on how they could improve their economic and social status without antagonizing the governor.

They met on December 11, Cuffe proudly noted, "with the inhabitants of the colony." Policies were formally established: a monthly meeting, a written record, and an official title, the Friendly Society of Sierra Leone. The black Friend initially stressed that every matter be "for the beneficial good of the universe and glory of God," thereby removing distinctions between temporal and spiritual welfare. The pious settler-merchants endorsed Cuffe's religious practicality: God blessed a humble servant in the marketplace. The Friendly Society intended to "excite industry," give "such advice as may be serviceable," and open communication with "distant Countries." The meeting was an important step in the evolution of the organization begun on Cuffe's first visit to the colony. In the most practical terms the Friendly Society of Sierra Leone was a cooperative black trading society,[10] modeled after the Society of Friends, the Anglo-American chain of correspondence, Allen's initiative, and Cuffe's black experience.

Unfortunately, Cuffe had to face current realities of drunkenness, disease, and challenge from European merchants. Some of his own crew drank excessively; when Prince Edwards, for one, begged release from the crew, Cuffe ordered him ashore without hesitation. Charles Durror became ill, then Thomas Wainer, Samuel Hicks, Charles Freeberg, and Zachariah White. Wainer narrowly escaped death thanks to plaster of flies, blood suckers, and fervent prayers to his Maker. Then, on Christmas Day the ailing Freeberg and White were discovered "in a rum drinking noisey house." Cuffe soberly concluded that doctors were not needed for "men that was well enough to stand houses of mirth." Along the waterfront John Kizell's camwood lay unattended in the absence of healthy shiphands to load it onto the *Traveller*. "The government men" criticized Cuffe for irresponsibility, and Alexander Macaulay ignored his promise to collect three tons of wood for the *Minerva*.

Cuffe anxiously watched as settlers, who felt they had legitimate complaints against the governor, drowned their sorrows in rum. Maxwell again summoned them to sign the oath: their choice, noted Cuffe, was "to obey the King's Decree in all Cases or . . . forfeit their Houses and Lots of Land." The black civilizer candidly recorded "pretty general objections" but refrained from urging compliance. As a Quaker pacifist he could not imagine being "subject to the commanding officer's directions whatever." Repeated musters at year's end only persuaded some to sign. The Governor's Council lashed out at the settlers' "dangerous and seditious practices," which arose because of "false and wicked constructions to the aforesaid Act."[11]

Cautiously the Americans sidestepped the furor. After signing papers to lease his East Street residence,[12] Cuffe headed up-country, umbrella in hand, with Englishman James Carr to investigate farming possibilities. The two plodded on for several miles among cattle, sheep, Indian corn, and buckwheat. The following morning, on horseback, Cuffe rode with Lazarus Jones to former governor Thomas Ludlam's old plantation, where lush fields of coffee, cassava, and yams grew. Jones also showed a plantation he owned with George Nicol and Warwick Francis, and they visited one of the several villages established for recaptured Africans who had been freed on the high seas and carried to Sierra Leone.

Sherbro's proponent of African commerce, John Kizell, finally appeared in town on January 6, 1812. Officers Henry Warren, David Edmonds, and James Wise mobilized leading citizens for a pivotal Friendly Society meeting that evening. Opening ceremonies concluded, Kizell stepped forward to read from William Allen's initial letter to the black settler population, the most sincere offer of concrete assistance that those merchants had heard for years. Written in late August, with Cuffe present, the epistle from England appealed for a new beginning, suggesting that, with Cuffe's help, economic change could indeed adjust in favor of the black majority. Kizell's enthusiasm showed as Cuffe's additional remarks fueled the spirit of optimism.

The next morning several would-be shiphands called at Cuffe's home. Now his dream of a black ship's company engaged in the Sierra Leone–British trade seemed more probable. Thomas Richards wanted to be sure that his son Aaron, who had been detained for a time in England, could continue as Cuffe's maritime apprentice. Anthony Davis and his wife asked for their son George's passage to America, and Moses Jenkins, a native Kru inhabitant, applied in order "to see what sort of a place America was."[13] Meanwhile, the civilizer explored business sites for future Friendly Society and new settler investments. He tried to purchase additional land, examined conditions for cotton production, and surveyed for a sawmill, a gristmill, a saltworks, and a rice-processing factory. A healthy, prosperous African nation required productive employment opportunities.

As a succession of Friendly Society meetings took place, Cuffe and the officers cautioned against offending the governor, yet everyone sought a scapegoat for the unrest. After one heated meeting, Warren, Edmonds, and Wise decided to compile a suitable diplomatic reply to Friend Allen. Yes, they united "in sentiment with our respected Friend Capt. Cuffe," enthusiastically calling for commercial intercourse under the British flag. Yes, too often settlers neglected industry, and "Spiritous Liquors" were disruptive. Yes, they conceded, it was necessary to satisfy those "who hath borne the heat and burden of the day." Preliminary remarks aside, they got down to specifics. The solution to local lethargy was "*this*: if . . . you will have the goodness to give directions to the master of some vessel" to load their African produce at Freetown for sale in England to the settlers' advantage, "we would most assuredly turn our attention to our farms." Then they outlined an elaborate hierarchy for handling the business of their cooperative trading society, without a word of criticism against the English merchants' monopoly.[14]

Kizell and Cuffe were pleased with the progress being made. Black merchants heartily supported the Friendly Society of Sierra Leone, their new commercial outlet in the colony. Undoubtedly, this was the solution to "whatever may tend to excite industry among" the settlers, noted Kizell. Moreover, Kizell and Cuffe knew that natives repeatedly asked for legitimate commerce as a means to halt the slave trade. Before leaving for Sherbro Island, Kizell wrote to Allen, "If we had Factories on the coast to purchase the African produce," the African participation in the slave trade would cease. Cuffe wrote that he intended to return in a year with settlers, machinery, and an incentive for profits.[15] The message came through loud and clear from Britain's West African colonial possession: civilization required economic self-determination.

Arguments with Alexander Smith continued as Cuffe prepared to depart for the United States. Governor Maxwell offered a well-intentioned assurance that "every protection and encouragement" would be given to industrious emigrants from America.[16] As a final insult, however, the governor retracted and then burned documents naming Cuffe's maritime apprentices: apparently one had failed to sign the oath of allegiance. When two officers boarded the *Traveller* to learn her intended course, Cuffe worried, "I cannot feel much liking to their conversation." Log entries record that Captain Tillard of HMS *Sabrina* forced the *Traveller* back to Freetown on the grounds that a ship with a black captain, a black crew, and Sierra Leone youth on board must be a slaver. Later, the overzealous Captain Tillard apologetically released the ship and Governor Maxwell reissued apprenticeship papers. The brig finally headed down the Sierra Leone River for open water on February 19, 1812.

When Paul Cuffe left Africa he surely carried a part of that land with him. On the shores of his father's birthplace he conceived of "a nation to be numbered among the historians' nations of the world." Disappointments notwithstanding, he seized on a new and lasting pride as an early-nineteenth-century proponent of Pan-Africanism.[17] One century later, W. E. B. Du Bois would define such Pan-Africanism as "the tendency of some Africans and New World Negroes to unite their efforts in a common struggle to destroy the derogatory image of Africans and Negroes." As a legacy of the slave trade, Du Bois continued, Pan-Africans united in "the struggle against racial discrimination everywhere and for African self-determinism."[18]

10

A PAN-AFRICAN RETURNS

ON April 14, 1812, *Poulson's American Daily Advertiser* complained of deteriorating relations with England. It also announced that the "brig *Traveller*, Cuffy from Africa" was nearing Philadelphia. That very day in London, William Allen told the Duke of Gloucester: "The colonists of Sierra Leone want only a stimulus to their industry, . . . they are looking to us for it. . . . The present opportunity, through the medium of Paul Cuffe, seems providentially afforded."[1] A stimulus to industry became the central task for the Pan-African supporters on three continents.

Cuffe took a well-deserved rest on this voyage, aware of the enormous extent to which American cooperation would be required in the year ahead. Glimpses of humor and verse in his journal reflected the mood on board: "Plenty of flying fish . . . fly on board. They met with kind reception." Thomas Wainer again captained the brig, with the three African apprentices following his orders but looking to Cuffe for navigational instruction. His own learning experiences had taught him the importance of simplicity, and Cuffe, in teaching them the three "L's" in navigation—"latitude, lead, and lookout"—used rhymes: "If the Wind Come before the Rain / Lower the topsails & hoist them again / If the Rain Comes before the Wind / Lower the topsails and take them in."[2] The all-black company sailed peacefully for North America.

Once past Bermuda, Cuffe scuttled plans to enter Philadelphia and instead continued northward. He hired a passing craft off Block Island, Rhode Island, to carry him ashore, where he wished to acquire a special permit to unload imported merchandise from a British territory. That evening, April 19, Alice Cuffe answered a knock on the farmhouse door to find her drenched husband. The family rejoiced and gave thanks, but Cuffe soon disappeared into the night to awaken the New Bedford customs collector. Meanwhile, unknown to him, the *Traveller* was seized and taken to Newport by a customs cutter. Deteriorating Anglo-American relations not only threatened peace but also the continuation of Cuffe's scheme for an African traffic.[3]

The fate of the brig's entire cargo was at stake, not just the $1,570 worth of English woolens that Cuffe had been unable to exchange at Freetown for African wares. Customs also seized 36 tons of camwood, 582 pounds of elephant "teeth," 800 cattle hides, 603 goat skins, 477 gallons of palm oil, plus small amounts of rice, peanuts, and mats. Newport customs collector William Ellery, signator of the Declaration of Independence and former owner of two slave ships, claimed to be following the letter of the law, which only could be waived by U.S. Secretary of the Treasury Albert Gallatin. Cuffe responded that, having received a British trading license from King George's Privy Council, he would take his case to President James Madison. Stephen Gould, a close companion in Newport, opened his home and clocksmith shop for three days to assist Cuffe.[4]

Many people of high rank rushed to defend the black Yankee Federalist. Newport's U.S. District Attorney Asher Robbins assisted with Cuffe's legal documents and wrote several letters on his behalf. Recommendations came from the city's past customs collector and presidential elector, Constant Tabor. Rhode Island Governor Simeon Martin, Senator C. G. Champlin, and Dr. Walter Channing, son of the state's attorney general and brother of Rev. William E. Channing, joined the crusade. In Providence, at Obediah Brown's, Cuffe gathered up letters from William Rotch, Jr., and former U.S. House Speaker Joseph B. Varnum, introductions from wealthy merchant Thomas Arnold, and a note from the state's leading antislavery spokesman, Friend Moses Brown.[5] Dinner engagements and Friends Meetings concluded his stay in Newport. The stout Westporter, dressed in his best grey flannels, awaited the stagecoach to New York.

The Washington-bound petitioner reaped the benefits of earlier publicity. "In travelling through the country," wrote Cuffe, "I perceived that the people seemed to have great knowledge of me ec." He passed through Norwich and New Haven, Connecticut, boarded a different stagecoach at dawn in New York, spent a trying time discussing financial matters with John James in Philadelphia, then nearly lured James Brian to accompany him from Wilmington. Four days after leaving Providence, Cuffe reached Friend Samuel Hutchinson's home in Washington City. One incident marred the trip: when instructed by a servant to dine apart from other clientel, the black traveler noted firmly, "I told him as I rode with the company, I could eat with them. So we all sat down and ate at one table." A "southward man there, not of the best character," was sorely tried but did nothing.[6]

Cuffe's deepest penetration by land into the South was a sobering reminder of the situation in which many of his black brethren found themselves. Two-thirds of the 8,000 blacks in Washington City were in bondage; the remainder, although free, were excluded from white society. Hutchinson's companionship seemed advisable at all times. On Monday, April 27, the U.S. Senate considered a bill to establish a Department of War; this hardly illustrated a democratic effort to maintain peace with England. The nation's capital looked more like a struggling country town in comparison to venerable London, where Cuffe had been less than a year earlier. Yet the urbane traveler admired the "magnificent" construction of Congress's "representatives House," designed by Friend William Thornton, formerly of Tortola in the West Indies, a one-time proponent of black emigration, and now head of the U.S. Patent Office.

On Saturday, May 2, 1812, at 11:00 A.M., Cuffe and Hutchinson "waited on the President."[7] James Madison, who like Thomas Jefferson preferred a plan to remove blacks to Africa as a means of ending slavery in America,[8] listened attentively to his callers. "James," Cuffe firmly began in the manner of Friends who traditionally shun titles, "I have been put to much trouble, and have been abused. . . . I have come here for thy protection" to request Newport customs "to clear me for New Bedford, Mass." Cuffe's visit to "aid his unhappy brethren" should not be rewarded by confiscation, argued District Attorney Asher Robbins's letter; it was important "to shield [Cuffe's] character from injurious imputation." A half-dozen such letters lay before the president, who asked for time to consider the request.[9]

Rain filled the muddy carriageways as Cuffe, Hutchinson, and others lobbied for political support. Rhode Island's J. B. Howell promised "that every indulgence will be extended to him & his Case." Cuffe's long-range plans for African civilization reemerged in the Executive Office at noon on Monday. After waiting for an hour, he and Hutchinson met with Albert Gallatin, who had just spoken to the president. "He then told me," wrote Cuffe with relief, "that all of My property Was Remitted or to be Restored to me." The treasury secretary offered a startling proposal: "anything that the Government Could do to Promote the good Cause that I Was pursuing, Consistent With the Constitution, they would certainly be always Ready to Render."[10] Cuffe thanked Gallatin "for his firmness" and pledged that government assistance would be requested "if I should continue my aid towards Africa." He prayed silently that a president who condoned slavery would somehow help Africans on both sides of the sea.

The triumphant Westporter headed home. On the Baltimore stagecoach a "blustering powderhead man" accused him of taking the best seat. "I Was no Starter and Sat Still," recalled the black merchant. Taunts went unanswered. When two women entered the coach Cuffe firmly announced, "We always give way to accommodate the Women." Not until Rhode Island's Senator William Hunter warmly greeted the black Friend at a Maryland tavern did the hostility disappear and insults turn to "Loving" affection. When proprietors at an eating establishment in Baltimore insisted on Cuffe's segregation from the other customers, he refused to eat with the servants. The black traveler recalled later, "not as I thought myself better than the Servants, but from the nature of the Cause." He was determined to stand his ground whenever possible, so "my Enemies Will Become friendly."[11]Humility was not to be confused with weakness.

Cuffe found "friends on Every Side" in Baltimore. Bernard Gilbert took him to meet Quaker druggist Jesse Talbott, one of William Allen's correspondents, and Cuffe was the houseguest of renowned abolitionist Elisha Tyson, a Friend whose dramatic acts of courage had saved countless slaves. Black teachers Daniel Coker and George Collins ushered the visitor through their African School, with over a hundred students. Cuffe took tea with many prominent people of color and conversed agreeably on the best way to aid Africa. These reputable blacks promised him "a correspondence" on the subject and said they would consider enlisting a few emigrants to Africa. A society was formed for that purpose, and Friends Elisha Tyson and Elisha Thomas spread the news.[12]

In the early hours of May 7 the Wilmington stagecoach rumbled northward, leaving a late-arriving, disappointed Cuffe behind. The morning paper provided some consolation, however. "PAUL CUFFEE, the colored man of whom some account was lately published in an English newspaper" was in town. The three-paragraph editorial updated readers as to the celebrity's activities. "Unacquainted with the grabbing and restrictive practices of his native country," the *Traveller*'s owner had been required to petition for release. "This pious and humane citizen has already been of considerable service to many of the Africans, to whom he has carried several teachers" and for whom he seemed willing to continue investing time and money.[13] Cuffe later reached Friend Brian's Wilmington home, then he proceeded on to

Extract of another letter, dated Jan. 31, 1812.

"Report says that Gen Artegas has fallen in with the Portuguese army and destroyed them to a man—say 7 or 9000 men."

Sun rises 1 m after 5—sets 59 m. after 6

FEDERAL GAZETTE:

THURSDAY....MAY 7.

PAUL CUFFEE, captain and owner of the brig Traveller, is now in town. This is the coloured man of whom some account was lately publish d from an English paper. His vessel and cargo were seized at Newport R.I. on his return from Sierra Leone, in Africa.—Captain C had been 18 months absent, and was unacquainted with the *grabbing* and *restrictive* practices of his native country. He went to Washington—and having stated his case to government, was very politely treated, and his vessel and cargo immediately restored. This pious and humane citizen has already been of considerable service to many of the Africans, to whom he has carried several teachers—and for whose further benefit he appears willing to employ many of his days and much of his large pecuniary resources.

—

THE FRENCH.—We wish it to be explicitly underssood as our opinion, that there is no room for *doubt* as to the existence of the French decrees, which the President *says* are off. As some people, however, believe only what Democrats say, we republish the following confessions from the democratic papers of this city.

From the "Whig"

FRENCH AGGRESSION, &c.

The capture of the ship Congress, (owned by major Biays) on her voyage hence for England, by a French vessel, augurs badly. She was

Congress of the United States.

—

Reported for the Federal Gazette.

—

HOUSE OF REPRESENTATIVES:

Wednesday, May 6.

Mr. Bleeker presented a memorial signed by upwards of 700 of the citizens of Albany (New-York) complaining of the hardships suffered in consequence of the Embargo, & praying its repeal or modification.

Mr B. moved to refer the memorial to a select committee.

Mr. Rhea moved to postpone its consideration till the 4th of July

Mr. Gholdson moved that it lie on the table. Lost, 39 to 42.

Mr. Randolph & Mr. Bleeker spoke against the embargo and the war question.

Mr Calhoun, Mr. Johnson, & Mr. Grundy spoke in favor of both Embargo and War. The latter declared that they would be prepared to vote for war by the termination of the Embargo at least.

The question was then taken on Mr. Rhea's motion to postpone the further consideration of the petition till the 4th of July, & carried. 58 to 30 adj'd at half past three.

A sketch of this important debate to morrow.

The Senate have postponed the bill appointing Two Assistant Secretaries at War, till June. [The *go by*.]

ALEXANDRIA, May 7.

BERLIN AND MILAN DECREES.

It is rumored, & we believe there is some foundation for the rumor, that Mr. Monroe, has received a letter by the late arrivel at Boston, stating that the Berlin & Milan Decrees have been again put in full force against American commerce, and that a democratic Senator was heard to say, if this should be the fact, *war would be declared against France in six weeks!!*

News of Cuffe's successful petition to President James Madison filled the national press. Even Federalist papers, which praised the celebrated black Yankee Anglophile, were forced to concede his success despite the Democrats' "grabbing" and "restrictive" practices. Cuffe's subsequent petition would not be so fortunate in evading political prejudice. From the *Federal Gazette and Baltimore Daily Advertiser*, May 7, 1812. Courtesy of The New-York Historical Society.

Philadelphia. Time was set aside there to meet with Ann Mifflin. "It was comforting," Cuffe wrote laconically after their Sunday conversation. They discussed "Keeping the American Side of the Query" open; the result would be "the Passage of many sober Blacks engaged on Principle, to assist in the Civilization of the Natives."[14]

Philadelphia's most prestigious blacks gathered the following evening at six o'clock to hear Cuffe speak. His "account of Africa" enticed many black churchmen and merchants from the 2,000 free people of the city. Cuffe concluded that "Something [was] operating" to indicate "that good Will Come . . . toward Africa." Philadelphia blacks resolved at Cuffe's insistence to gather "for the purpose of aiding, assisting, and Communicating with the Sierra Leone Friendly Society as well as with the African Institution in London for Africa's good."[15] Cuffe talked the next day with Benjamin Rush, of the Pennsylvania Abolition Society, and with Rev. Absalom Jones and James Forten. Friend John James, still hurt and frustrated by his and Cuffe's financial difficulties, nonetheless hosted his black Friend and ushered him about town.

The news of Cuffe's success in Washington was reported all along the East Coast. When he reached New York Quakers flocked to see him, so much so that his sister Freelove Slocum and fellow blacks had difficulty finding him. Less than twenty-four hours after his arrival Cuffe appeared at the African School House, where twenty or so prominent New York blacks, and almost as many Friends, had gathered. A society was formed by representatives from the African Methodist Episcopal Zion Church, the African Society of Mutual Relief, and the African School to unite "with that of Philadelphia, Baltimore, ec. for the further promotion of Africa, . . . of which Sierra Leone at present Seems to be the principal Established Colony."[16]

When two Methodist preachers approached Cuffe on the street to ask sarcastically if he understood English, Cuffe answered: "there Was a part I did not understand (viz) that of one Brother professor making merchandise of, and holding in Bondage his Brother professor. This part I should be glad they Would Clear up to me." The Methodists departed without "any further conversation," but Cuffe refused to drop the matter. He drew up a petition and with Friend Thomas Eddy, his host in New York, went to the Methodist meeting hall. Those present dismissed Cuffe's statement with "Coolness." That evening he called at the home of Methodist Bishop Francis Asbury. Their encounter was brief and to the point: would the Methodist Conference answer Cuffe's query posed to the two preachers? "Merciful Father,"

Cuffe prayed, "I humbly beseech thee that thou would be pleased to enlighten my understanding." Why, he begged "in much love," should Christian brothers merchandize one another.[17]

Before leaving town the celebrity gave a packet of letters to Dr. Ross of Greenwich, to use as the Society of Friends deemed appropriate. As Cuffe sailed out into Long Island Sound some of his New York admirers were busy compiling *A Brief Account of the Settlement and Present Situation of the Colony of Sierra Leone*.[18] That publication, printed by Friend Samuel Wood, initiated the most widely repeated religious explanation of his African visit: "that the inhabitants of the colony might become established in the truth, and thereby be instrumental in its promotion amongst our African brethren." It also purported to contain "some advice to the people of colour in the United States," although neither Cuffe's "minutes on the oppression of Slavery" nor his Methodist query ever did appear.

At Newport, Rhode Island, Cuffe delivered the waiver he had received from Gallatin for the *Traveller* to the customs collector. He was clearly displeased at having to pay what he considered were exhorbitant and unjust fees incurred as a result of the seizure, but he did so and then departed for home after a brief visit with Stephen Gould.[19] He closed his seventeen-month *Traveller* log and journal with a "desire ever to be thankful, world without end, amen."

The African benefactor was home at last. On May 15, 1812, the *New Bedford Mercury* welcomed this "captain and owner, the humane and pious man of colour, Paul Cuffe." English and African goods were stored in Cuffe's Westport sheds and at William Rotch, Jr.'s, countinghouse. Choice Medgely flannels, broadcloth, and cashmeres, plus assorted African hides, palm oil, and peanuts, were delivered to P & A Howards, his sons-in-law's new establishment, which was generously guaranteed one-half of all profits from Cuffe's imported goods. The store sold over $2,000 worth of merchandise, and several other firms also sold goods for Cuffe.[20] He distributed trinkets and gifts throughout the community, and bottles of palm oil went to native Africans living nearby.

Cuffe's appearance of complete well-being was deceiving, however. Privately, he juggled complex factors in an attempt to perpetuate his African scheme. "For the good of our fellow creatures," he wrote to black Bostonians Prince Saunders, Robert Roberts, and Perry Lockes, a vessel would leave in a few months for Sierra Leone. They should duplicate the African institutions begun in Baltimore, Philadelphia, and New York. He hoped to be in the city soon. The Westporter was

ties. *8th mo.* 27, 1812.

P. & A. Howard,

HAVE for ſale—3000 wt. New-Orleans and Havana white and brown SUGARS; 400 wt. Loaf and Lump ditto; beſt Windward Iſland MOLASSES; Hyſon, Hyſon-ſkin, and Souchong TEAS; Coffee, Chocolate, Raiſins, Caſſia, Cloves, Nutmegs, Mace, Allſpice, Pepper and Ginger; beſt Poland Starch, Brimſtone; Meſs Pork, Butter and Cheeſe; Rice, New-Orleans Cotton; Cotton and Wool Cards; 400 wt. Lorillard's bladder SNUFF; Sweet-Oil; Candles, and Soap; Leaf Tobacco.

Alſo—A handſome variety of GLASS, CROCKERY, STONE, and EARTHEN WARE; among which are a good aſſortment of Flower-Pots.

Alſo—An aſſortment of ſuperfine, common, and low priced Broadcloths; Caſſimeres; Ladies' Pelice Cloths, and Flannels. An aſſortment of Men's and Women's Leather and Morocco Shoes; a variety of Ladies' Mock Turtle Hair Combs, and many other articles not mentioned.

☞They preſent their grateful thanks to their friends for the liberality of their cuſtom, and reſpectfully ſolicit a continuance of their favors. *Oct.* 3.

Camwood, Ivory, &c.

FOR Sale, by the Subſcriber, in *Weſtport*, a quantity of CAMWOOD, IVORY, and DRY HIDES; lately imported from Africa.—*ALSO*—

Whole, half, and quarter-blooded MERINO SHEEP—rams and ewes.—

Apply to PAUL CUFFE.

Weſtport, 10th mo. 7.

Clothing Mill.

ough, Vt. about a mile below the V lage, delightfully ſituated on the w bank of Connecticut River, by the Sta road leading to Northfield and Boſt It conſiſts of about 260 acres—180 o is of the beſt intervale. Said Farm well watered and wooded, and has or a well finiſhed painted Houſe, with th ſtack ſof chimneys—two large Barns by 30 each, and about 160 feet of ſhe It is extremely well adapted for raiſi Grain and fatting Cattle—it annua produces about 120 loads of hay, a about 1400 buſhels of corn and grain and is well calculated to pleaſe gent men of agricultural taſte.

Alſo,—Another FARM lying in Ma borough, Vt. about ſix miles weſt Brattleborough, within 60 rods of Turnpike road leading from Brattlebo to Bennington; containing 70 ac moſtly under improvement, with a ho and barn—It is very good land for and paſturing, and is well watered a wooded.

For further particulars enquire of ſubſcriber, who lives in Brattleboro Village; (or of Capt. BERIAH FIT now at Mr. GIDEON SHEPHERD's, N Bedford.)

FRANCIS GOODHUE.

Brattleborough, (Vt.) *Oct.* 20, 1812.

Farm for Sale.

FOR Sale, a FARM, ſituated in North-eaſt Diſtrict of *Fairhave* containing 126 acres—is an excell Farm for corn, grain, and graſs; good Buildings and a good Orchard is well fenced with ſtone-wall, well wo ed and well watered, and under go improvement. For further particula inquire of WILLIAM WING.

Due to the close of Cuffe & Howards prior to Cuffe's departure for Sierra Leone, the returning merchant guaranteed a portion of his imported African cargo to his sons-in-law's new firm. But goods consigned to him by members of the Friendly Society of Sierra Leone, such as camwood, ivory, and hides, had to be sold from Westport. From the *New Bedford Mercury*, Oct. 30, 1812. Courtesy of the American Antiquarian Society.

more pessimistic in writing to William Allen that the unjustified "pretense" offered by the *Sabrina* had been Maxwell's fault and that "trying circumstances" and "very considerable" expenses on both sides of the Atlantic jeopardized his continuing in the African traffic.[21] When the United States declared war on England on June 18, 1812, Cuffe told Boston blacks he foresaw that the war would stand "between us and Africa."[22]

Several articulate and sophisticated black Bostonians expressed eagerness to emigrate to Sierra Leone. Prince Saunders, the teacher at Boston's African School (he had studied at a school adjoining Dartmouth College), rejoiced on hearing that "so many of our African brethren" wanted "to visit the land of our fathers." Cuffe sentimentally addressed black Bostonians as the "Lambs of the African Sierra Leone Benevolent Society."[23] The Boston African Institution's officers—Perry Lockes, Thomas Jarvis, and Prince Saunders—plus others seemed ready to settle in Africa.

Their optimism echoed that of the Friendly Society of Sierra Leone, which now had agents in Freetown to produce, cultivate, and accumulate goods for shipment. William Allen was their agent in London, and a Liverpool agent would be announced soon. Allen agreed with John Kizell that African chiefs needed to receive some form of compensation for stopping the slave trade and that cultivation and commerce had to expand.[24] Friendly Society officers were indebted to Cuffe for his early initiatives and to Allen for his latest promises. "We are not without our fears" that British humanitarians will "be afraid to trust their money with such people as we are," wrote the society's president. For so long people had portrayed them as "very indolent and ignorant." Hence, for the time being, they wished *"no money,"* only articles for local trade or barter.

By July directors of London's African Institution began to follow through on Cuffe's initial proposals. Their *Sixth Annual Report* showed considerable interest in settler affairs. A dozen pages were devoted to growing indigo; ten pages documented John Kizell's importance to the native population; new students from the colony were reported to be studying in London; and three pages recounted Cuffe's intermediary role. The directors resolved to distribute land to Cuffe for prospective passengers and agreed to reimburse him for his earlier expenses in England, to offer "every reasonable encouragement" to lure him permanently to Sierra Leone, and to cover "any reasonable expense" for recruitment of upstanding characters. They also endorsed the establishment of a whaling industry in Sierra Leone. Writing separately for the directors, William Allen and Thomas Clarkson reminded Cuffe that some settlers should be familiar with tropical cultivation and be able to handle certain equipment. Meanwhile, William Wilberforce took Cuffe's request for settler land grants to Colonial Secretary Earl Bathurst.[25]

Cuffe waited and worried, uncertain as to how seriously the war with England would affect his business ventures and his plans for an African trade. Would the King's Privy Council consider granting him a trading license in spite of hostilities between England and the United States? Cuffe informed Allen that he could not settle in Sierra Leone just yet—more would be accomplished by his remaining in America; furthermore, his wife was unwilling to leave.[26] Allen, in turn, confirmed that Cuffe had been correct all along when he insisted that blacks in Sierra Leone were being bilked by European traders. Allen reminded members of Sierra Leone's Friendly Society to report directly to him when obstructed by "envious persons"; to retaliate locally, without influence, would be disastrous. Cuffe, their real advocate, had begun to awaken England to the situation.

Meanwhile, "MEMOIRS OF CAPTAIN PAUL CUFFEE" began to circulate throughout the United States.[27] A Wilmington newspaper initiated the story, then without further mention of the African celebrity quoted a letter from James Wise, clerk of the Friendly Society of Sierra Leone, about former New Yorker James Stephens (he and his family had gone to Liverpool and then to Freetown). Stephens wanted American blacks to know that the governor in Freetown would give land to newcomers and that the local settlers were happy. After twenty years in the United States, Stephens said, he had returned "to his native land to spend the remainder of his days." In spite of this positive account and the growing publicity, Cuffe still feared that a nation entrenched in slavery and fearful of its own black population would not respond favorably to his Pan-African initiatives.

11

WAR BRINGS FURTHER DELAYS

PAUL CUFFE strongly disapproved of the War of 1812 on religious, economic, and philanthropic grounds. The war not only vilified God's spirit among humankind, but it barred international trade and threatened to disrupt the significant progress being made in America and England for the civilizing of Africa. While he yearned to sail for Sierra Leone, where he owned property and had friends, Cuffe instead prepared to wage peace-making diplomacy in Washington as British philanthropists did the same in London. He also tended to family matters, personal business transactions, and commitments to the Society of Friends.

In the first month of 1813 the Westport Monthly Meeting appointed the black merchant to a committee that included Philip Tripp, John Mosher, Josiah Sherman, Prince Wing, and Ebenezer Baker, to consider necessary restorations and estimates for work on their Meeting House. Successive meetings resolved that shipmasters Baker and Cuffe would commence "Cutting Some of the principle sticks" for a completely new building. Along with Prince Wing and four others, they would superintend construction of a forty-five-by-thirty-foot hall with gallery and a sliding divider between the men's and women's meeting rooms. Cuffe agreed to act as the accountant for the construction project; John Moser served as treasurer.

Men, women, and children helped to dismantle the old structure as the summer of 1813 approached. Anything useable—timber, nails, shingles—was salvaged. Lemuel Milk, Pardon Gifford, and Thomas Stoddard delivered hemlock and pine boards from the logging mill, and Pardon Gifford donated nine gallons of cider for the workers. An auction raised a hefty $204 of the $1,200 budgeted for construction. By winter the Friends worshiped in their new Meeting House. Cuffe's ledger showed that the "Whole Cost" stopped short of the

$1,200 figure by $1.92.[1] His contribution amounted to $577.97; the next largest donation was from Thomas Stoddard, at $337.50, followed by Prince Wing, at $70.58. Cuffe's generosity favorably compared to that of Dartmouth's preaching and slaveholding proprietor Peleg Slocum, who over a century earlier had been the largest contributor to the area's first Meeting House.

Meanwhile, the Pan-African continued to search for a way to neutralize the effects of the Anglo-American war on his African scheme. He sought advice from the Rotches and sent letters to Hannah Little and Elisha Tyson of Baltimore.[2] In particular, he asked Friend Little to communicate with her dear companion Dolly Madison in order to reach the president on matters of trade. Madison himself sent Cuffe a mixed message. Through his stepson he impersonally cited the law prohibiting English trade, but when called on by Hannah Little, Madison "appeared very friendly disposed" and recommended a written petition and a lobbying campaign by the black American himself. The "novelty" of the request, Friend Tyson cautiously wrote later, would produce deep reflections on the African cause, regardless of the outcome.

On June 16, 1813, Cuffe composed a petition to the president and the Congress of the United States.[3] Unlike the provocative memorial he and his brother had sent to the Massachusetts General Court during the Revolution, this one studiously tried to avoid controversy. His motives were "dictated by that philanthropy which is the offspring of Christian benevolence"; he intended to benefit "his brethren of the African race, within their native climate." Cuffe sadly acknowledged that Africans were "selling their fellow creatures into a state of slavery for life," and thus wanted to promote "the civilization of the Africans." Some "willing" free blacks were already organized in Baltimore, Philadelphia, New York, and Boston to help the cause, but money was urgently needed. Thus he begged for a license to conduct a "triffling" commerce. The letter-draft went to Elisha Tyson and other Baltimore Friends for review, and they cautiously withheld it until the Congress next convened.

The Westporter told Perry Lockes of Boston's African community that good would come if "We may be favored to Run the race Set before us With patience." Eventually the government would permit him to "pass and repass to and from America and Africa." As he later wrote to Allen, such a "neutral path" would be "for the encouragement of the Civilization of Africa."[4]

Difficulties in Sierra Leone continued to worry Cuffe. He feared that the death of his attorney there, David Edmonds, Sr., would mean the loss of £400 worth of property. Resentful settlers, many associated with the Friendly Society, still refused to comply with the Militia Act. Governor Maxwell continued to lash out at them, citing their "ingratitude" as intolerable. Black merchants were bitter over the refusal of Macaulay and Babington's firm to ship fifteen tons of processed rice for the Friendly Society; the rice lay rotting on the docks, thanks to the persistent and systematic exclusion of blacks by white traders. Settlers couldn't "send anything," John Kizell wrote angrily. He spoke of "*private individuals of consequence*" who had stripped him of a favorite schooner then sold the vessel at auction; even the mayor and the sheriff were in collusion against the settlers. Kizell also charged that Maxwell was guilty of enlisting recaptured slaves "for life." He boldly told Thomas Clarkson about a "riotous set of people" who promoted slanderous remarks about blacks.[5]

Kizell rightly feared a cover-up by the directors of London's African Institution. At the insistence of William Allen—and only as a result of careful maneuvering on his part—a committee was formed to investigate settler complaints. Interviews with Judge Thorpe, who was convinced that European merchants intentionally mistreated settlers, and several others caused the directors some embarrassment—enough so that Allen wrote that "the mystery of poor Paul Cuffe's ill usage is now unravelled." But the findings of the committee were apparently dismissed by the full board of directors. Instead, African Institution *Reports* for 1813 and 1814 lauded Cuffe's "character and merits" and expressed the hope that he would still travel to the colony in spite of the war. Friendly Society President Henry Warren continued to lash out at England's economic imperialism, however, claiming that Britishers came to Africa to reap their fortunes then "bid farewell to the Vertical Sun, under which we poor dispicable wretches breed."[6]

All of the news was not grim, however. A prestigious deputation of directors from the African Institution called at England's Colonial Office in December 1813 "to lay before Lord Bathurst the following particulars concerning a free Black named Paul Cuffee."[7] Secretary Thomas Harrison, Parliament members William Wilberforce and Henry Brougham, and William Allen linked Cuffe with the best interests of British colonial development and settler harmony. Here was one "eminently calculated to promote the best interest of any new Colony, especially those of S.L." Cuffe would excite "a Spirit of Industry" by bringing a sawmill, a ricemill, and exemplary settlers to the community. If he were lured there, surely his best friends would

Council Office, Whitehall
16th Decr 1813.

Sir,

Having laid before the Lords of His Majesty's Most Honourable Privy Council, your Letter of the 15th Inst, with its inclosures, on the subject of a request from the African Institution, that a Licence may be granted to Paul Cuffee, permitting him to trade between Newport in Massachusetts, Sierra Leone & England; I am directed to acquaint You, for Lord Bathurst's Information, that the Lords of the Council, would very willingly have given a favorable consideration to this Application, if they had not thought that by so doing a very inconvenient principle would be established and considerable embarrassment created

Hy Gou
Esqr

The

This letter was written in response to a petition by directors of the African Institution. It states that Lords of the Privy Council, while acknowledging Cuffe's benefits to Sierra Leone, conditionally denied the United States merchant a trading license during the Anglo-American war. Within the month, Cuffe's British admirers would begin their own society to motivate black Sierra Leoneans. From the Colonial Office, Sierra Leone Original Correspondence, CO 267/37. Reproduced by permission of the Public Record Office, London.

The Lords of the Council have no doubt of the merits of the Individual in whose favor the Application in question has been presented to Lord Bathurst by the African Society, nor do their Lordships take upon themselves to question the advantage which might be derived, to the Settlement of Sierra Leone by allowing a vessel under his direction to trade between the United States of America Sierra Leone and this Country: But their Lordships beg to submit to Lord Bathurst's consideration, that Paul Cuffee is a Native and Subject, of the United States of America, now in Hostility with His Majesty, and that the grant of such a Licence as is requested by the African Society would be in direct Violation of every principle upon which the Lords of

the

the Council have invariably felt themselves bound to Act on subjects of this nature. And Their Lordships are further convinced that an acquiescence in this proposal would open the door to every species of Fraud, and lead to the most embarrassing consequences; Their Lordships however feel it to be their Duty to submit these considerations to Lord Bathurst, But if his Lordship should still continue of Opinion, that the Licence in question ought to be granted, and will communicate the same to the Lords of the Privy Council, their Lordships will, notwithstanding their decided repugnance, nevertheless acquiesce in such a requisition.

I am
Sir
Your Most Obedient
humble Servant
Chetwynd

P.S.
I herewith inclose the Papers, according to your request.

follow. The directors requested a trading license for Cuffe "to be employed between West Port, Sierra Leone and England." Permission also was needed for black colonists to sell at "the greatest advantage," and the colonial secretary should consider that the present Militia Act deterred the best settlers from emigrating with Cuffe.

Lord Castlereagh, to whom the deputation proceeded next, and other lords of the Privy Council seemed unimpressed with the directors' logic. Britain was at war, and "Fraud and . . . embarrassing consequences" would result if the license were granted, even though the honorable "Native and Subject of the United States of America" might bring advantage to the colony.[8] Despite the unfavorable response the case was kept open, with an indication that the lords might reverse themselves if the colonial secretary would insist that Cuffe appear before them.

Uncertain that the Privy Council would reverse itself, Allen and Clarkson turned to a project they had been working on for months. Without losing sight of the colonial incentive, they argued among British Friends for a counterpart to Cuffe's Friendly Society of Sierra Leone. George Harrison, Samuel Hoare, Jr., T. F. Forster, B. Forster, and Charles Barclay joined Allen and Clarkson at Plough Court on January 24, 1814, to inaugurate the "SOCIETY FOR THE PURPOSE OF ENCOURAGING THE BLACK SETTLERS AT SIERRA LEONE, AND THE NATIVES OF AFRICA GENERALLY." Its very existence conceded the inadequacies of the African Institution, although every line of the public proclamation stated otherwise.[9] Signed by Clarkson, as the group's chairman, the statement attested to the "fixed determination" of members to avoid commercial speculations in Africa. Yet because the settlers remained very poor they needed a financial stimulus to cultivate and transport produce to Europe. Individuals could join the Society by making a donation of twenty pounds, or two guineas annually.

As in Britain, the success or failure in obtaining a trading license from the U.S. government depended on political alliances. The press attempted to favorably influence the government's decision. Massachusetts Senator Christopher Gore and Representative Leban Wheaton simultaneously had introduced Cuffe's petition to both houses of Congress on January 7, 1814. Very subtle, but racially and politically significant changes had been made within the copied text: emigrants were to be "free" blacks only; they would be "inclined" to emigrate, rather than "willing" to emigrate; and new phraseology played down Cuffe's request for a commercial license.[10] The House of Representatives immediately assigned the memorial to the Committee of Commerce and Manufacturing; the Senate managed hasty action under Gore's direction and assigned it to a favorable committee of three. Just three days later the bill received its first reading: "*Be it enacted by the Senate and House of Representatives of the United States of America in Congress* assembled, That the President of the United States be, and he is hereby authorized, under such regulations and restrictions as he may prescribe, to permit Paul Cuffe and his associates, to depart from the United States with a vessel, not exceeding two hundred tons burden, and cargo, for Sierra Leona, in Africa, and to return to said United States with a cargo, the produce of Africa, any law to the contrary notwithstanding."[11] Gore managed a second reading the following day, at which point Georgia Senator Bibb called for a postponement.

Washington's prestigious *National Intelligencer* reprinted Cuffe's memorial for the national media, "at the request of several subscribers, who probably feel an interest in the success of Mr. Cuffe's expedition." Cuffe confidently headed northward as his supporters gathered along the way to meet him. Media coverage was extensive, and so many black families expressed a desire to emigrate that he sent a request to Washington that the present bill be rewritten to accommodate the larger 268-ton *Alpha*.[12]

Cuffe soon learned that after a brief delay the bill had received its third reading in the Senate, thus assuring its passage there. The anti-Federalist-dominated House Committee of Commerce and Manufacturing, however, after conducting hearings on the measure, declared that at a time of war, when commerce was nonexistent, a proposal to provide supplies to the enemy for a mission, "how benevolently soever conceived," could only be viewed as speculative and inconsistent with the best interests of the nation. The committee viewed the colony of Sierra Leone as a failure, much like the now-defunct Sierra Leone Company; hence, Cuffe's financial venture there was destined to fail as well.[13] Passage of the bill by the House seemed doomed.

On March 18 the matter came before the full House, by which time Cuffe had passed through New York. The *Annals of Congress* delicately reported "a discussion of a very diffuse nature, and of no little length." Proponents, led by Timothy Pickering and Leban Wheaton of Massachusetts, praised Cuffe's excellent character, philanthropy, humanity, and religion. Realizing their desperate need for votes from the opposition, and particularly from slavery sympathizers, the two men pleaded for "the establishment of an institution which would invite the emigration of free blacks, a part of our population which we could well spare, ec."[14] Democratic opponents pointed out that the Yankee merchant in question would have unique rights thus far denied all law-abiding American fishermen and coasters. They derided England's need for a cargo to propagate the Gospel and wondered why a free black should be permitted to carry disloyal slaves to bolster British defenses.

When the vote was finally taken the bill lost by a seven-vote margin. "The Democrats combined against it," Wheaton sadly explained to Cuffe. Although no one ventured "to deface your character, they endeavored to throw the object into ridicule and contempt, and were but too powerful." Free blacks like Cuffe were left to read slanderous references to themselves in the newspapers as full disclosure of the debate swept through Baltimore, Philadelphia, New York, New Bedford, and Boston. Massachusetts's *Weekly Messenger* bitterly pondered "The Case of Paul Cuffee," said to be a "political heretic, a federalist, an enemy of the war, and one of those people called Friends."[15]

News of the congressional debate reached Friend Jesse Kersey in Virginia. On June 1 he questioned the man in the White House to learn whether President Madison had thought about removing "slaves to Africa upon the plan contemplated by Paul Cuffee." "Many objections" remained. As the British forces neared Washington City, arguments prefigured by Ann Mifflin and Thomas Jefferson increasingly linked Cuffe to saving more than civilization in Africa. Some seemed to think he might also save white civilization in America, an argument that would reverberate throughout the nation's capital two and a half years hence.[16] Some months later Cuffe admitted to William Allen that the petitioning had been an "experience to me." Perhaps his scheme "would be like the bread that was cast on the waters, [and] was found after many days."[17]

A black shipowner named John R. Truite wrote to Cuffe from Bridgeport, Connecticut, that nowhere was there "so great an example for the people of color in North America by [*sic*] yourself." He wished to visit Westport to learn how Cuffe had so remarkably avoided white resistance in his own community. Requests came from others as well. A white do-gooder asked to join Cuffe's "company," claiming to be an expert on "savages" from India, Africa, and North America; he also was "*inured to a warm climate*." Even Maryland's former governor, John F. Mercer, applied to Cuffe for advice. He had become guardian for two wealthy offspring of a slave and her deceased master and wanted to know where Cuffe would suggest they be sent because of the "deep-rooted prejudice of our country."[18]

During that summer of 1814 family and local business continued in the midst of the worst rash of British attacks since war had been declared. Washington was burned, Maryland slaves threatened desertion, free black Philadelphians gathered to defend the Quaker City, and fighting broke out near Westport. Friends like Cuffe tried to ignore the war; he concentrated instead on the acquisition of a salt meadow on Horseneck Point, which he purchased in partnership with the aging Michael Wainer, and seventy acres of land.[19] The firm of P & A Howards moved commodities briskly until Peter Howard's death in July.[20] Several family members moved West: nephews Gardner and Michael Wainer, along with son David Wainer, now lived in Cayuga, New York. Sierra Leone apprentice Aaron Richards journeyed westward himself, never to return.

Continued media coverage promoted the African cause. From July through early September, 1814, the Boston *Weekly Messenger* carried a seven-part story boldly entitled "Paul Cuffe's Mission to Sierra Leone," written by evangelical theologians from Andover Seminary.[21] The authors correctly recognized that Cuffe's objective in Sierra Leone was "not exclusively, nor primarily religious"; they summoned the nation to observe his benevolence. They also devoted a number of installments to Christian philanthropy in general.

As the war persisted, barring Cuffe's return to Sierra Leone, frayed nerves on the part of African settlers there showed what can happen when trusted intermediaries are absent. Stephen Gabbidon, a Maroon who was stripped of his land by Governor Maxwell, regretted having ever left Nova Scotia; he and Samuel Thorpe embarked for England to complain to the African Institution. Scotsman Duncan Campbell, who qualified for membership in the Friendly Society of Sierra Leone because of his settler wife, lashed out at whites in general, as well as untutored, negligent Society members. Kizell, Henry Warren's replacement as president of the Friendly Society, pointed to the European "speculators" who cared "not a copper" for the colony and held blacks "below the rank of freemen." Seven settlers requested return passage to their Jamaican homeland, only to be told at year's end by Judge Robert Purdie that they had violated a 150-year-old act of Parliament that prevented "Transfers of land on fraudulent and fictitious vouchers." Lawbreakers would be fined £100 and imprisoned for three months.[22]

Cuffe's demands for a Pan-African scheme escalated as the war drew to a close. He pushed for his black American brethren to begin their own enterprises to aid African descendants. He called on black Bostonians to double their efforts for the "freedom of our Beloved countrymen, the African, who are yet in bondage" in America, and he asked their African Institution to lay down a little money in "common stock" to build a 200-ton vessel for the purpose of "regular commercial intercourse between America and Africa." Cuffe asked James Forten of Philadelphia the same question and was assured that he would discuss "building a ship for the African trade" at Philadelphia's upcoming African Institution meeting.[23]

Finally, the Treaty of Ghent, signed on December 24, 1814, ended the war with England. That news brought Cuffe more requests for passage "to visit our brethren in Sierra Leone." A relieved James Forten declared that war no longer separated "us from Africa." As the aging Pan-African looked toward the sea, he may have recalled the eloquent words written at the outset of the war by Liverpool's Rathbone brothers: "We look forward with hope and confidence to the time . . . when the ships of Africa, owned by Africans, and manned by them will carry their produce to different countries, and return bearing with them comfort and the knowledge of what may be gained by industry. We trust they will also have the blessings of the Christian religion . . . bright examples of its real influence which may lead to humble and instruct some of their white brethren."[24] Paul Cuffe shared their hope and confidence. The coming of peace might make those dreams a reality.

12

RENEWED OPTIMISM

PAUL Cuffe's postwar ambitions were similar in principle to those of his countrymen but also reflected his African perspective. Many Americans yearned to civilize the territory west of the Allegheny Mountains, while others—New Englanders in particular—channeled their energies into expanding manufacturing enterprises, resuming the China trade, and whaling in the Pacific. Cuffe's objectives were to spread humane, civilizing principles eastward to Africa by promoting settlement there, as well as stimulating tropical cultivation, international trade, and an African whaling industry.

As the frozen harbors along Buzzards Bay thawed in early March 1815, Cuffe was optimistic that his dreams would be realized. Now that the war with England had ended, he reopened correspondence with William Allen in London. "My mind is impressed with the duty I owe to my [African] countrymen," he told Allen. He was determined to establish some settlers in Africa but needed the assistance of Allen and other supporters. Passage would cost approximately a hundred dollars per person, and land grants and provisions would be needed on arrival. Increased numbers of applicants would make it necessary to finance the construction or purchase of a vessel larger than the *Traveller*. Moreover, Cuffe required a British trading license "to defray [my] expenses." Finally, he told Allen that he planned to leave in October 1815.[1]

The black Westporter was depending on family as well as British connections to aid his African cause. Nephew Michael Wainer negotiated with Nantucketers Peleg and George Folger, who were interested in buying the African leather Cuffe had transported to America to sell for the Friendly Society of Sierra Leone. Michael's brother Paul began the task of renovating the *Traveller* for another African voyage.[2] Numerous local craftsmen worked on her until June, when

Paul accepted his uncle's appointment as captain. Alexander Howard, having ceased business after his brother's death, reopened the family store as soon as maritime trade resumed, once again providing a ready outlet for African goods.

The family suffered a severe blow in early summer with the death of Michael Wainer, who had been such an integral part of Cuffe's early maritime successes. The locus of authority among the next generation now shifted decisively to the New Bedford branch of Cuffe's family. There, Alexander and Ruth Howard courted the business expertise of Richard Johnson, an up-and-coming black entrepreneur who would eventually become Ruth's second husband. By late 1815 the shingle for the family store read Howard & Johnson.

The Westporter's plans for continued commercial success depended on the *Traveller* alone, since the bark *Hero* had been condemned as unseaworthy in Chile and the ship *Alpha,* his only other vessel, still represented a drain on financial resources due to ongoing disagreements with John James. Unpaid debts on that ship amounted to $1,000, but Cuffe refused to pay his share until the vessel was sold; James held out for a higher sale price because of his own financial difficulties. James Forten of Philadelphia lamented the "infinite and irreparable hurt to the good cause" for Africa that might result unless Cuffe and James resolved their business problems, and Cuffe's attorney, Samuel R. Fisher, almost gave up mediating between the two. Eventually, James somehow obtained sufficient funds to buy Cuffe's share of the *Alpha,* thus ending their business dealings.[3] Back at the New Bedford customs office Cuffe registered the 109-ton *Traveller,* to reenter commercial service with a Passamaquoddy-to-Wilmington run.

In July evangelical pastor Samuel J. Mills wrote to Cuffe to urge him to visit Andover Seminary, whose students had written about him in the *Weekly Messenger* the previous summer. Mills had just returned from distributing Bibles throughout the Southwest and wanted a conference with the Friend "on the general subject relative to what can be done in this Country in aid of our object." In particular, Cuffe's admirer wished to know more fully about the "contemplated Mission to *Sierra Leone*." There was no "establishment" to help people of color in America, he vaguely asserted, although "the prospect is becoming more favorable."[4] Mills also sent news about Thomas Paul, the preacher at Boston's African Baptist Church, who was journeying to England to collect a $150,000 bequest.[5] He suggested that Cuffe might approach Paul about providing some funds for his African scheme.

African issues again attracted the public's attention in England, but the publicity further exposed the weaknesses of the African Institution and its directors, particularly when contrasted to the less orthodox settler-advocates working out of Plough Court. Cuffe's unlikely successor to convey settler grievances to England from Sierra Leone was Vice-Admiralty Court Judge Robert Thorpe, who thoroughly discredited the African Institution and made the colony's affairs look very bleak—so much so, in fact, that Cuffe's old friend Prince Saunders opted instead to relocate in Haiti, and Bostonian Thomas Paul followed suit.

Thorpe exploited Cuffe's image as he lambasted the African Institution. Beneficial plans intended by the long-defunct Sierra Leone Company had never been implemented, he asserted. Now, cotton seeds and machinery sent by William Allen either had rotted or been thrown into the river. Three hundred boys were not being educated, as the Institution claimed, and seeds and plants were far from "flourishing." "I saw Mr. Cuffe in Sierra Leone," wrote Thorpe. "He appeared a man of truth and observation, and I know he constantly lamented . . . the dreadful state of deprivity into which it was sunk." He was certain that Cuffe "never gave such incorrect information" as reported by African Institution directors. He cynically dubbed Zachary Macaulay, Cuffe's earliest consultant on the colony, "the great shopkeeper of the colony . . . , lately Secretary and always Director." Thorpe claimed that he had "expected nothing, and was not disappointed."[6] William Allen, who along with Cuffe and John Kizell were the only persons to escape Thorpe's scathing criticism, said that he could not tolerate Thorpe's "spirit of malevolence," yet he also refused to "contradict the whole."[7]

Maroons Stephen Gabbidon and Samuel Thorp, newly arrived in England from the colony, confirmed Judge Thorpe's charges. They helped Allen to compile for the *Philanthropist* a detailed property plan of Freetown to explain black discontent. The plan listed all landowners along with the designations Nova Scotian, Maroon, European, or American. Property was described and given an approximate value, and confiscated land was labeled as well. The *Philanthropist* also published sweeping grievances against the Militia Act oath, mismanagement in general, and quit-rents, and it made a point of announcing that Cuffe, the Friendly Society's founder, soon would be sailing for Sierra Leone with "a few Black families" trained in cleaning rice and managing cotton.[8] Allen and Thomas Clarkson skillfully worked behind the scenes of the African Institution and the Society to Encourage the Black Settlers of Sierra Leone to link Cuffe's expected arrival in the colony with solutions to many of its problems.

On May 27, 1815, Allen asked Earl Bathurst, the colonial secretary, to accept Cuffe's American commerce in both the colony and England as if he were a British subject, speculating that in a very few years Cuffe's tropical expert settlers would raise sufficient cotton to end British dependency on North America for that particular commodity. But, he emphasized, the settlers would only go to Sierra Leone provided they were granted sufficient land, and those grants must "forever remain unquestionable." Six days later Clarkson reiterated to Bathurst that new settlers denied land tenure were powerless and would not remain. Furthermore, settlers already in the colony were vehemently opposed to the Militia Act oath and were degraded by unwarranted quit-rents. Both of these letters were followed by a formal petition from Allen to the Privy Council, clearly stipulating that Cuffe needed "special protection of the Governor."[9] Earlier requests also were repeated.

The Privy Council acted slowly. Clarkson withdrew to Paris, where Cuffe's name may have come up in antislavery discussions with Tsar Alexander I of Russia.[10] Allen wrote to the new Sierra Leone governor as though speaking for the colonial secretary. The Quaker philanthropist insisted that Lt. Col. Charles MacCarthy give Cuffe every conceivable economic advantage on his arrival, noting that the black American earlier had been ill used by white merchants. In a separate letter he advised the Friendly Society of Sierra Leone to consult with Cuffe about building their own vessel. While Allen's letters were en route to the colony he was informed that the Privy Council had rejected his petition on the grounds that the lords feared for Cuffe and the safety of his black company in slave-trading waters.[11]

In America, Cuffe's preparation for another African voyage proceeded on the false assumption that Britain would grant the trading license. Careful planning, coupled with full warehouses, ready cash, and his own popularity, eased the final stages before embarkation. On the brig *Traveller*'s run to Wilmington, the black merchant bid farewell to Friend James Brian, whose current involvement with Wilmington's African School Committee matched Cuffe's schooling interests in Westport and Sierra Leone. Captain Paul Wainer ordered 200 barrels of flour to be loaded for Freetown, and the brig then sailed on to Philadelphia for a load of tobacco. Cuffe's success in appealing to Philadelphia's free black American elite was publicized on September 20 in *Poulson's American Daily Advertiser*, just as supplies purchased

O rbem disturbavit;
L ibertatem oppressit;
E cclesiam distraxet;
O mnia esse voulit,
N ihil erit.

In translation, the order of letters peculiar to the Acrostic, cannot be expected:

He was nothing;
He became Emperor;
He conquered nations;
He disturbed the world;
He oppressed liberty;
He distracted the church;
He wished to be every thing;
He shall be nothing.

The last line was as prophetic as the others were true; and the prophecy is fulfilled.

Description of Algiers.

As Commodore Decatur in the course of a few weeks, with the first squadron alone, has succeeded in humbling the Algerine buccaneers, we publish the following account of these desperadoes from the Saratoga Journal, that our readers may know what kind of an enemy our Yankee boys have so speedily conquered.

[*Boston Patriot.*

The mole, or mound of earth, which connects Algiers with an island before it, and forms the defence of the city, is the fruit of the unremitted labor of *thirty thousand Christian Slaves for three years.*

It was completed in the 16th century by Hayradin, who succeeded Horuck Barbarossa in the government of Algiers.

It was this Hayradin who when about to meet the army of the emperor Charles V. proposed to murder *ten thousand* of his Christian slaves, for fear of their rising. His officers however rejected the proposition, and Charles soon liberated them.

In this expedition he was successful, but, soon after this he undertook another against them with 120 ships, 20 gallies and 30,000 men, almost all of which were destroyed. He was landing his troops, and the senate or dowan, were proposing to submit, when a disciple of the prophet of Medina, rushed in as a prophet and told them to hold out, and that in a few days their foes would be destroyed—the prediction was verified—a violent tempest arose after Charles had landed his army and before either provisions or tents could be brought on shore, which scattered and destroyed his fleet.——His troops without shelter or provisions, most of them, who could flee from the sabre of their enemy, perished in the storm—and Charles, the "sovereign of Spain, Germany and the Indies," returned with the miserable remnant of so large a fleet and army, without effecting any thing against the enemy.

Some years after this the French went against them with 50 sail—and took and destroyed or dispersed their fleet. In this battle the Algerine admiral *sunk his own ship—himself and crew going down to the bottom rather than surrender.*

In 1685 admiral Duquesne bombarded the city with a French fleet, and set it in flames. While this was doing, the Algerines *butchered the French prisoners, seized the French Consul, placed him alive before the mouth of a cannon, and discharged it towards Duquesne's squadron.*—The admiral, however, left not the harbor till their city was a heap of ruins, and all their fortifications and shipping destroyed. This for once humbled the pirates—they sued for and obtained an abject peace.

try. This is a most serious evil, which should be strictly watched, and the penalties enforced. We hope an example may soon be made; the penalty by 23d Geo. II. chap. 13, is 500 pounds for the first offence, and 1000 pounds for the second.

[*Birmingham paper.*

Almanack.

1815. SEPTEMBER.	☉ Rises	☉ Sets	High Water.	Moon's Phases
20 Wednesday,	5 56	6 4	3 34	New ◐ 3 0 9 om. D. H. M.
21 Thursday,	5 57	6 3	4 8	First ☽ 10 5 5pm.
22 Friday,	5 58	6 2	4 52	Full ☉ 18 14 15m.
23 Saturday,	6 0	6 0	5 40	Last ☾ 26 2 10m.
24 Sunday,	6 1	5 59	6 31	
25 Monday,	6 2	5 58	7 24	
26 Tuesday,	6 3	5 57	8 21	

Federal Conferees.

THE Committees appointed by the Federal Conferees in the CITY AND COUNTY OF PHILADELPHIA, AND COUNTY OF DELAWARE, for the purpose of nominating a Candidate for Congress, are requested to meet at the house of William Elliot, No. 43 north Third street, on Thursday 21st inst. at 4 o'clock, P. M.

VOYAGE TO AFRICA.

WHEREAS Capt. PAUL CUFFE, a citizen of the state of Massachusetts, made application to the Congress of the United States, at the session of 1814, for permission to make a voyage to Africa, for the purpose of aiding in the civilization and improvement of the inhabitants of that country; and also to promote this desirable object, to take with him a few sober, industrious families, the situation of publick affairs at that period being unfavorable to the design, his proposition failed of success; but now under the blessing of Divine Providence, the causes of obstruction are removed, and he is again preparing to prosecute his voyage, accompanied, by two families of this city, who have agreed to visit Africa and settle there.

The African Institution of Philadelphia, established for the promotion of this plan, feel it to be a duty to state, that it cordially unites with Paul Cuffe, in his disinterested and benevolent undertaking, and recommends the families of Anthony Survance and Samuel Wilson to the Friendly Society of Sierra Loan, as persons of good moral character, having satisfactorily settled their outward affairs as far as appears.—The Institution likewise solicits on behalf of the adventurers, the friendly notice of all those among whom they may come.

Signed on behalf of the African Institution of Philadelphia.

James Forten, *Pres't.*

RUSSEL PARROTT, *Sec'ry.*

N. B. The brig Traveller is now at Philadelphia, from whence she will sail about the 20th inst. for New Bedford, she will there be joined by the residue of her company and proceed towards Africa about the last of the 10th month (Oct.) Further information may be obtained by applying to the African Institution of Philadelphia, or to Capt. Paul Cuffe, at Westport, Massachusetts.

sept 20

Spanish & American Dollars.

THE highest price given for Spanish and American Dollars. At No. 145 Market street, between Third & Fourth streets.

sept 20 1ot

Mason to get hold of the main-cross trees and made himself fast below the Frenchman, over whom I should judge the sea broke at least half the time. About 9 o'clock the next morning, the Frenchman resigned his soul to HIM who gave it, and with nothing but a shirt and handkerchief on him, fell into the water. I neither heard nor saw any thing of any other one who was on board, after the vessel went down.—About 10 o'clock, we were discovered by the inhabitants of Cohasset, who very humanely dispatched a boat with five men to rescue Mr. Mason and myself from a watery grave.

Port of NEW-YORK, Sept. 18.
Monday Noon.

Arrived, The sloop Ocean, Baldwin, 4 days from Newbern.

The sloop Hiram, 12 days from Porto Rico, (mentioned in our last) left schr. Merchant of Baltimore, to sail in 9 days; and schr. Sylvia-Ann, of *Philadelphia,* going in pursuit of a market.

Brig Orleans.

The following letter from a passenger in this brig, was yesterday received by the sloop Ocean, from Newbern:

Extract of a letter from a passenger in the brig Orleans, from this port bound to Charleston, dated Beaufort, Sept. 11.

"I have the pleasure to inform you that I am still alive, when many of my fellow acquaintances are in eternity. We have had one of the most severe gales that I or any other man ever experienced. After getting within one days sail of Charleston, we lost our masts, spars, sails and rigging of every description, and afterwards, by the assistance of Divine Providence, we got into Beaufort, North Carolina. We lost Hart, a seaman, overboard."

Port of WILMINGTON, (N. C.) Sept. 9.

The Storm.

During the night of Sunday last and the morning of the following day a most dreadful Storm of Wind and Rain was experienced in this place. The wind which had prevailed at North East for three or four days continued to increase gradually in violence till Sunday Morning, when it was accompanied with frequent showers with a violent gale which by the evening had increased to a storm. The rain continued so abundant as to drive into the most secure Dwellings, during Sunday night the wind gradually changed to North and then early on Monday morning to N. West, increasing in violence with every change from 8 to 10 o'clock; it increased to its utmost violence, during its change from North West to West. About 10 o'clock it gradually came round to the South West, when the rain began to cease and the wind to come in puffs with intervals of 4 or 5 minutes—from this time it gradually ceased in violence and by 3 o'clock P. M. the rain ceased altogether. The effect of the Storm have been visibly marked by a general prostration of fences and trees.

The Chimneys of the Cape Fear Bank, of the large House lately owned by Wm. Giles, Esq. deceased, of Mr. Robert Mitchell, of the Stores occupied by Mr. Jennett and Messrs. M'Ree and Gorrie were blown down and the Roof of the last mentioned Store was carried away.—The Wharves have been somewhat injured, a Sloop from Bermuda sunk, and a brig forced from the wharf and driven some distance below on the shore of Mr. Campbell's Plantation.—Fortunately no lives have been lost nor have we heard of personal injury received by any one in the Town. But along the Sound the devastation has been wide spread and ruinous. The tide

Unlike later nineteenth- and early twentieth-century appeals for blacks to apply for passage to Africa, this news item carried the endorsement of America's most prominent black spokesmen, in this case James Forten and Cuffe. Here Forten, a prosperous Philadelphia sailmaker, publically endorses Cuffe's Pan-African scheme, an endorsement Forten would never withdraw. From *Poulson's American Daily Advertiser,* Sept. 20, 1815. Courtesy of the American Antiquarian Society.

from James Forten and others were loaded on board the *Traveller*. The paper reported that black Philadelphians had approved of Captain Cuffe's attempt in 1814 to help civilize and improve Africa with "a few sober, industrious families," and that now the city's African community had endorsed two families to go with Cuffe and settle in Africa: "The African Institution of Philadelphia, established for the promotion of this plan, feel it to be a duty to state, that it cordially unites with Paul Cuffe, in his disinterested and benevolent undertaking, and recommends the families of Anthony Survance and Samuel Wilson to the Friendly Society of Sierra Leone, as persons of good moral character, having satisfactorily settled their outward affairs as far as appears." Further information could be gotten "by applying to the African Institution of Philadelphia, or to Capt. Paul Cuffe" at his home.

Some months later James Forten and Russell Parrott wrote to William Allen at "the request of the 'African Institution of the City of Philadelphia,'" to inform him that their members represented "People of Colour in this country" who were impressed with Allen's noble and disinterested zeal in helping "victims of the petty tyranny of mankind." Cuffe, their "common brother" and "indefatigable friend and countryman," had suggested that African Institutions be established in various cities in the United States to facilitate "your benevolent intentions." Their Institution selected useful persons "from among those who have applied for passage to Africa" and who were "persons of good report, united with a knowledge of cultivation of produce familiar to the African climate, or those useful branches of the mechanic arts. . . ." Forten and Parrott both expressed approval of "an assylum for the oppressed" in Africa.

These black Philadelphians also wished to promote emigration and African-American trade, so they asked Allen "what privilege" Britishers would grant "to such as may hereafter emigrate to the colony of Sierra Leone." They inquired about unspecified exemptions should the African Institution of Philadelphia "embark in any commercial enterprise desireable for the purpose of Civilizing Africa."[12] Clearly, they anticipated future emigration and black-operated transatlantic commerce. But like Cuffe they would not agree to such an undertaking without British cooperation.

The Pan-African departed Philadelphia and sailed northward to continue gathering a list of those who would be leaving to settle in Sierra Leone. Charles Columbine, a Senegalese native, and his wife were endorsed by the New York African Institution. In Boston, where

REPORT AND MANIFEST

of the Cargo, laden at the Port of Westport on board the Brig^t Traveller, Paul Cuffee Master, bound for Sierra Leona

Marks.	Numbers.	PACKAGES, or ARTICLES in BULK. N. B. Articles to be arranged alphabetically.	Contents or quantities.	Value at the port of exportation.
B.T.	1 @ 11	Eleven Hogsheads Tobacco	12169 lb Tabacco	$2239.62
B.T.	1 @ 145	One hundred forty five barrels Flour	145 bbls Flour	1305. —
B.T.	1 @ 62	Sixty two barrels pilot Bread	62 bbls Bread	284. "
W Rotch J^r	1 @ 22	Twenty two boxes Sperm^t Candles	22 boxes Sperm^t Candles	267.40
A. Cook	1 @ 30	Thirty boxes Soap	30 boxes Soap	122.42
B.T.	1 @ 200	Two hundred kegs of Crackers	200 kegs Crackers	100. "
— —	1 @ 15	Fifteen hundred weight Bar Iron	15 cwt bar Iron	100. "
— —	— —	Three M lumber	3 M Lumber	40. "
Gifford	— —	Ninety four axes $105 / 100 & 30 hoes $15	94 axes & 30 hoes	118.67
B.T.	1 @ 4	Four kegs Wage Tobacco	4 kegs tobacco	100. —
— —	1 @ 6	Six Iron bars	6 Iron bars	20. "
B.T.	1	One box of Hats	1 box Hats	17.50
B.T.	1 @ 2	Two rolls of Leather	2 Rolls Leather	20. "
B.T.	1 @ 3	Three casks of Nails	3 cask Nails	45. —
W	1	One Small Box & eighty five pair loose shoes	Shoes	90. —
—	1	Saw Mill utensils & Iron work	Saw mill utensils &c	107
— —	1 @ 2	One Waggon $50 & one plow $4.50	Waggon & plow	54.50
				$5031.11

District of New Bedford December 2nd 1815.

I Paul Cuffe Master or Commander of the Brig Traveller bound from the port of New Bedford to Sierra Leona do solemnly, sincerely and truly affirm, that the Manifest of the Cargo on board the said Brig now delivered by me to the Collector of this District, and subscribed with my name, contains, according to the best of my knowledge and belief, a full, just and true account of all the goods, wares and merchandise now actually laden on board the said vessel, and of the value thereof; and if any other goods, wares, or merchandise shall be laden or put on board the said Brig previous to her sailing from this port, I will immediately report the same to the said Collector. I do also affirm, that I verily believe the duties on all the foreign merchandise, therein specified, have been paid or secured, according to law, and that no part thereof is intended to be re-landed within the United States, and that if by distress, or other unavoidable accident, it shall become necessary to re-land the same, I will forthwith make a just and true report thereof to the Collector of the Customs of the District wherein such distress or accident may happen. And I further affirm, that according to the best of my knowledge and belief, the Certificate hereunto annexed contains the whole quantity of salted Beef on board the said vessel, and that no salted Beef is shipped on board said vessel for the ship's company, on freight, or on cargo, but what is inspected and branded according to the Law of this Commonwealth.

Paul Cuffe

his manifest lists the *Traveller's* African-bound cargo, ranging from tobacco, axes, and elt hats, to wagon, plow, and sawmill parts. Forty-six persons came aboard the crowded eventy-foot brig, including a ship's company of eight plus emigrants ranging in age rom sixty years to eight months. From the Inward Manifests, Bureau of Customs, New edford, 1805–25. Courtesy of the Boston branch of the National Archives Center.

correspondents had pleaded since 1812 to be Cuffe's first settlers, Dr. Jedediah Morse blessed Cuffe's recruitment campaign and guaranteed recommendations for all. To him, however, qualifications for those familiar with tropical cultivation were less important than character references to please antislavery Claphamites. The families of Perry Lockes, Thomas Jarvis, William Guinn, Samuel Hughes, Peter Wilcox, and Robert Rigsby were endorsed, adding thirty-two more passengers.[13]

The rapidly accelerating series of events leading up to the departure for Africa turned the quiet Acoaxet shore community of Westport into a beehive of activity. Thirty-eight passengers, ranging in age from eight months to sixty years, descended on the Cuffe farm with their meager belongings. Area workmen finished preparing makeshift bunks in the cramped quarters below the *Traveller*'s deck while crew members stowed the remaining cargo. Butter, salt, soap, spermaceti candles, and crackers were stacked next to iron for a sawmill, a wagon, ninety-four axes, thirty hoes, a plow, three casks of nails, and a box of Prince Wing's black felt hats.[14] Log paper, a pair of dividers, and Nathaniel Bowditch's indispensable navigational guide were stowed in the captain's cabin.

Paul Cuffe, approaching his fifty-seventh birthday, paused in the midst of farewell celebrations to reflect on his current situation. A $5,000 cargo lay in the hold of his ship, and unpaid passenger expenses now exceeded $2,900. Yet only one American had contributed $100 toward his passage, despite promises from many philanthropists that money was forthcoming. How much would the London African Institution contribute, he wondered uneasily? Would a British trading license await him in Sierra Leone? Would his new settlers be welcomed, provided with town lots, and given sufficient land for cultivation?

"The brig *Traveller*, Captain Paul Cuffe, it is expected, will sail this day from Westport, for *Sierra Leone*," announced the local *Mercury* on December 8, 1815, "with several coloured families, . . . who intend to form a settlement there." Two days later the *Traveller* slipped past Horseneck Beach and into Buzzards Bay, as friends of various religious denominations, the families of those aboard, and well-wishers bid them good-bye.[15] Thus began the first black-initiated emigration movement from the Western Hemisphere to the shores of Africa, later to be known as the back-to-Africa movement.

13

ESTABLISHING AFRICAN HOMESTEADS

UNDER the command and protection of Captain Paul Cuffe and his crew of seven, eighteen adults and twenty children, crammed aboard the seventy-foot brig, headed for their new African homesteads. For half of the transatlantic crossing they endured gale-force winds and excessive seasickness, but they eventually reached the coast of West Africa otherwise unharmed. As the *Traveller* approached the Cape of Sierra Leone the humbled shipmaster noted that all gathered to give thanks.[1] He ordered the brig's anchor set off Freetown, praying that his pioneer mercantile-emigration scheme would be equally fortunate.

Almost immediately, however, the rugged view of Sierra Leone discouraged the shaken would-be settlers, despite their yearning for life ashore after such a rough passage. Discontent grew as the boarding customs officer bluntly refused permission for the U.S. vessel to anchor for more than a few hours. Cuffe himself was distraught to find that a British trading license had not been issued. Then, when the governor refused the *Traveller*'s entire cargo, he dejectedly wrote to his New Bedford mercantile friend William Rotch, Jr., "If nothing favorable appears in a few days, I shall leave Sierra Leone for America."[2] The entire voyage would be a failure in the absence of a favorable commercial climate.

Governor MacCarthy quickly changed his tone, however, when he read the letters of endorsement carried by Cuffe. William Allen's frank letter of August 10 imploring trade concessions for Cuffe reached Freetown, as did Bathurst's official request to soften those trade restrictions the Privy Council had failed to overturn in Cuffe's favor. Colonial governors since T. P. Thompson increasingly had been irritated by the disproportionate trade allowed from America. While MacCarthy conceded that Cuffe was not simply another interloper, as governor he was entirely within his rights to charge the full tariff on foreign vessels levied the previous August. Moreover, he noted later, the financial "interest of an English trading House" had to be considered.[3] A governor's word was law in a crown colony, at least in the absence of a Privy Council order to the contrary.

MacCarthy thus granted some concessions despite the lack of a British trading license, although they were of little consolation to Cuffe, who felt that the goods he had transported were being seriously undervalued. At one point customs officers refused tobacco, soap, candles, and naval stores amounting to $2,600, and the colonial government later lowered the negotiated prices on bar iron and flour. Taxes and port duties added up to $290. Before departing from Sierra Leone some months later, Cuffe wrote to Samuel Fisher, "My not being permitted to make trade in Sierra Leone with much of my cargo" was like "trading on Sufference in Africa." The governor's story differed considerably: "Captain Cuffe was permitted to sell every article except some tobacco and Naval Stores" which he traded a short distance from the colony.[4]

While in Sierra Leone Cuffe tactfully avoided offending anyone who might obstruct his ultimate goal as an African civilizer. Friendly Society members, churchgoers, and laborers were the people with whom he associated. The trading part of his mission employed members of the black cooperative trading society whenever possible, and he extended credit to them just as England's Society to Encourage the Black Settlers of Sierra Leone had done. Business transactions involved Stephen Gabbidon, George and Anthony Davis, Pompey Young, David Edmonds, Jr., James Wise, and Duncan Campbell.

Cuffe's most obvious success derived from securing homesteads for his black American brethren. James Wise, secretary of the Friendly Society, clerk for the Governor's Council, and the government printer, noted on February 26, 1816, that "the following persons who had arrived in the Colony in the *Traveller*, Cuffee, from America, to settle, received a town lot each family, and arrangements were made for putting them in possession of their quantities of country land," after which he listed the names of seven settlers and their families.[5] Along with former crew members Samuel Hicks and Prince Edwards, they now joined Cuffe as African homesteaders. Charles Columbine and Anthony Survance, two of the settlers who arrived with Cuffe, eventually returned to their native Senegal and Congo regions.

The efforts of this civilizing mission soon paid off. Cuffe's imported industrial tools—axes, hoes, a plow, a wagon, and sawmill parts—

permitted newcomers to help the local population, among whom they distributed these implements. Samuel and Barbara Wilson, along with the five Boston families, began a slash-and-burn process in the country before trying to raise tobacco. William and Elizabeth Guinn, and their seventeen-year-old daughter Nancy, went to work on MacCarthy's extensive plantation. When Perry Lockes complained about being selected for jury duty, Cuffe told him that black emigrants from America should welcome such civic responsibilities.

Official declarations recognized Cuffe's achievements. John Mesier, Governor MacCarthy's clerk, commended Cuffe for his choice of settlers and recognized a $432.62 initial advance to promote the settler's "present comfort and future advantage," plus a full year's deposit made by Cuffe toward the settlers' provisions. MacCarthy felt certain that the entire amount would be reimbursed by London's African Institution. James Wise handed over the Friendly Society's certificate of approval, which confirmed that all nine families "brought from America by Capt. Paul Cuffee, have arrived in the colony of Sierra Leone, and are now residing therein."[6]

The colony itself showed some progress, although of a halting nature. Business opportunities were increasing for black entrepreneurs, thanks to the Friendly Society and its British counterpart, and confiscated lands were being returned to original owners. Racial and political rivalry appeared less evident, and schools seemed sound. Corrective action was being taken with regard to problems such as imported liquor, but local slave trading still persisted to some degree. The Friendly Society even planned a "factory" at Port Loko to foster the exchange of indigenous commerce there.

Homesteading and other successes notwithstanding, Cuffe faced enormous expenses that would not be offset by the trading aspect of his mission. His outstanding debts in regard to both old and new settlers probably amounted to more than $8,000.[7] Much of this expense could have been avoided if he had had a trading license from Britain. In April of 1816 he wrote to William Allen that it appeared he would not be able to undertake a yearly voyage from America to Africa. Nevertheless, he knew that commerce, the prerequisite for Africa's growth, could not falter because American "trading stock" might disappear. He continued, "I much approve that of Employing a vessel from London to Sierra Leone. . . . I hope thee may not Lose sight of the subject . . . , for it ever was my mind & I see nothing that I think would have a tendency of doing so much good for the Inhabitants of Sierra Leone as that plan." Now, the Pan-African concluded, he must return to "the great family of Africa . . . in our region." American brethren "ought not to be neglected."[8] The founder of one of America's most successful black maritime enterprises clung to his belief that black maritime trade was essential for the advancement of Africa.

On April 4, 1816, forty-one black American and indigenous African émigrés, including crew member Edward Cook, gathered to bid farewell to their aging benefactor. Some may have maneuvered about in escort craft. The scene "was like a father taking leave of his children, receiving the tokens of their overflowing affection, and with pious admonition, commending them to the protection of God."[9] With the captain and his crew of four went a cargo of squirrel skins, elephant "teeth," barrels of fruit and peanuts, woven mats, and baskets.

That same day in London the members of the African Institution met and continued to perpetuate their deceptive contribution to Cuffe's civilizing mission. Directors generalized at length on their antislavery and Sierra Leone accomplishments, portraying picturesque black settlers as differing "very little from that of the generality of English villagers" and falsifying the record by boasting that the government had provided Cuffe all he needed in Sierra Leone.[10] Unknown to the departing black captain and his supporters, Britishers henceforth would ignore Cuffe's civilizing mission, and thus their portion of his costs for carrying industrious settlers to Sierra Leone.[11]

Preceded by appealing religious propaganda in New York, Cuffe stepped onto the city's busy South Street docks and immediately seized the opportunity to speak out against the continuing—although outlawed—Atlantic slave trade. That day, May 28, the *Commercial Advertiser* routinely announced his arrival, then added: "Capt. Cuffee informs us that the schooner *Rebecca*, Hathaway belonging to New York, had been captured, and sent to Sierra Leone, and was there condemned." The captain noted six additional vessels "all engaged in the slave trade."

Almost immediately Cuffe's disclosures provoked outrage in the state capital. Within a few days the editors of the *Albany Daily Advertiser* expressed indignation over the devious, inhumane conduct of fellow New Yorkers: "We should hope that no inhabitant of that city could be so lost to all justice and humanity, so monstrously cruel and depraved, as to be concerned, directly or indirectly, in that horrid and murderous traffic." They declared that every ship so engaged should be destroyed and all involved individuals, from owners to mariners, should be ruined. During the next two weeks, more than a dozen

These documents, reprinted in the national press, became public proof that the first black emigrants who traveled with Cuffe were welcomed and cared for in Sierra Leone. They illustrate his effectiveness in opening a channel of communication between the government of Sierra Leone, the settlers' society of black merchants, and the African Institution in New York. From the *New York Commercial Advertiser,* June 11, 1816. Courtesy of The New-York Historical Society.

Extract from the minutes of the "New-York African Institution."

June 6, 1816.—The Society met for the purpose of obtaining information from Captain PAUL CUFFEE, respecting certain individuals and families of colour, whom he carried from the United States in December last.

After an examination of various documents which he produced relative to these persons, and the general state of the people of Sierra Leone, the following resolutions were adopted:

Resolved unanimously, That the Society is well satisfied that the intentions of Capt. Cuffee in taking those persons on board his vessel, were the most pure, honorable, and benevolent; and that he has done every thing in his power to make their emigration advantagous to them.

Resolved unanimously, That for the information of the friends of those persons, and of all others who may feel interested in the subject, it is expedient that the sense of the society, as expressed in the foregoing resolution, be published; and also the following certificates of the landing of these persons at Sierra Leone.

(COPY.)

Free Town, Sierra Leone, April 4, 1816.

This is to certify, that Perry Locks, Samuel Hughes, Robert Rigsby, Peter Wilcox, Thomas Jarvis, William Guim, Samuel Wilson, Antonio Savanee, and Charles Columbine, and their families, brought from America by Capt. Paul Cuffee, have arrived in the colony of Sierra Leone, and are now residing therein.

JAS. WISE, Sec'ry. to the Friendly Society.

To all whom it may concern.

(COPY.)

Sierra Leone, March 21, 1816.

To Capt. Paul Cuffee, brig Traveller.

SIR—I am directed by his excellency Gov. M'Carthy, to acknowledge the receipt of your note enclosing certificates, from various respectable persons in the United States, of the good characters of the people whom you have lately brought to this colony as settlers.—His excellency has observed, with much satisfaction, their steady and sober conduct since the time of their arrival; and feels fully convinced that the certificates you have forwarded for his examination, were well deserved by the respective parties to whom they were given. With respect to the sum of 432 dollars and 62 cents, which you have kindly and humanly advanced to the settlers since they landed, his excellency assures you that he will take every means to procure a repayment of the sum from his majesty's government, as he entertains no doubt but that the same privileges will be extended to them as were granted to the Nova Scotians in 1792. It appears by the letter of Mr. W. Allen to you, that application had been made for a years provisions for all the passengers you might bring out as colonists; and there is little doubt, but that request is already acceded to. The money you have advanced being intended to promote, as far as possible, their present comfort and future advantage, does away the necessity of any further supples of that nature. His excellency will take the earliest measures to get the amount paid to any person whom you may point out as your agent authorised to receive it.

JOHN MESIER.

Signed in behalf of the New-York African Society.

ABRAHAM THOMPSON, Pres't.

New York papers hailed the celebrated captain who dared to reveal the names of slave traders and their vessels. From the nation's capital to Boston, the reading public learned of Paul Cuffe's attack on those who continued to illegally enslave his African brethren.

The publicity surrounding Cuffe included coverage in the *Commercial Advertiser* of a June 6 meeting of the New York African Institution, whose members had been summoned to hear the black captain's account of his recent voyage. Extracts of Peter Williams, Jr.'s, minutes defended the black American's "intentions . . . as the most pure, honorable, and benevolent," noting that Cuffe had "done everything in his power to make the emigration [to Sierra Leone] advantageous" for the settlers.[12] On June 12 Boston's *Recorder* came out with an article on "Our Black Countrymen at Sierra Leone" to satisfy local curiosity. Letters brought back by Cuffe confirmed the governor's generous distribution of land and the settlers' contentment. The only complaint seemed to involve immense numbers of African ants that devoured "all the serpents that fall in their way." Black Philadelphians, and people from Richmond to Cincinnati, also read these glowing reports in their local papers.

The Westporter finally rejoined his family in mid-June after a six-month absence. Almost immediately he was asked to visit Philadelphia "to clear up many unfavorable reports" spreading among the people of color concerning his mission, even though several of them still wished to emigrate. Instead, Cuffe urged Peter Williams, Jr., to correct the misinformed, saying that documents now in the possession of the New York African Institution would "give every information necessary."[13] He considered the rumors insignificant and was more concerned with the lack of equality for the new black settlers and former crew members now in the African colony. Peter Williams and James Forten, leaders of the two remaining U.S.-based African Institutions, similarly bemoaned that inferiority based on race. But who could afford to carry more settlers to Africa to increase their number and possibly help them gain majority status? After the expenses of his last voyage, it was clear that Cuffe could not.

14

PERILOUS TIMES IN AMERICA

IN the months ahead Paul Cuffe's defense of his African brethren would assume a new urgency. Just as he welcomed the conciliating spirit of white abolitionist societies and the urban missionary movements, he felt strongly that churchmen, both black and white, were mistaken in their belief that the nation would abolish chattel slavery. By mid-summer of 1816 Cuffe shuddered over the possibility of perpetual American slavery. Such thoughts ignited the passions of one already committed to emigration on commercial and philanthropic grounds. He was determined to find some means of saving the great family of African brethren now in America.[1]

At first Cuffe tried to retreat from the media to the security of the family compound in Westport. He watched son-in-law Alexander Howard and Richard Johnson fill the New Bedford store with local produce, Havana sugar, and Chinese tea. Incoming goods arrived via Johnson and Wainer's sloop *Resolution of Troy* and Cuffe's brig *Traveller;* both vessels made frequent trading runs to the Canadian line.[2] Cuffe enjoyed intimate gatherings at the family homestead, and he also helped his wife, Alice, care for nieces Almira and Alice Howard, who had been living there since their parents' deaths. The black Friend resumed as well various responsibilities of the Westport Monthly Meeting.

But news of increasing racial tension in the United States and abroad brought Cuffe out of seclusion. He read in the *New Bedford Mercury* of a slave insurrection in Barbados that threatened "an extermination of the whites." The following month the *Mercury* carried news of a Fourth of July insurrection in Camden, South Carolina, where slaves had nearly succeeded in turning the guns in Camden's arsenal on the white master class.[3] Various papers also published news of increased immigration to America from Ireland and England, as though European settlers might yet "save" American civilization.

This upsurge of racial animosity had a far-reaching effect, triggering Cuffe's deepest fears. In letters to Samuel J. Mills and Samuel Aiken he wrote: "I learn by the public paper that the Southern Slaveholders are much alarmed on account of the African's rising. I have thought it . . . prudent for them to have Early Seen" that brutality could destroy masters as well. Proponents of slavery blinded themselves to potential destruction; they had already prepared "instruments for their own execution."[4] He agonized over the continuing transatlantic slave trade; despite laws to the contrary, traders persisted in seizing Africans who then were forced to bear slave children in America. These were indeed "perilous times."

This son of an African father and an American Indian mother felt deeply "his twoness—an American, a Negro; two souls, two thoughts, two unreconciled strivings."[5] His solution to the dilemma now before him reflected his complex relationship with America. First, the United States must *effectively* abolish the transatlantic slave trade. Second, the lives of his African brethren enslaved in America had to be saved. This goal for survival would replace a desire for racial harmony. Slaves should be freed and colonized "either in America or in Africa, or in both places," as long as the choice was theirs. Third, perhaps slaveowners should give slaves "their plantations on a Lay," just as shipmasters paid shares to their crews.[6]

In August 1816 Cuffe forthrightly declared that blacks "might rise to be a people" in Africa, something they could not do in America. Africa is "just Such Country as we the people of Color Stand in need of," he informed black Bostonian William Harris. New York's Peter Williams, Jr., concurred: he realized "the advantages which the African race, dispersed through the countries belonging to the whites, would enjoy on a return to their own soil." Most, if not all, black Americans stood in need of fulfillment in Africa.[7] Having found personal gratification in Africa, Cuffe dearly wished the same for his oppressed brethren in the United States.

Cuffe pleaded with white antislavery evangelicals and Friends for help. Samuel J. Mills became his staunchest defender and would now serve the same role in America that William Allen had once served in England. "When the right time Comes And the Way opens," Cuffe wrote to Mills, "I hope Always to be ready to Forward Any Views that you may have in Contemplation for the improvement of the human race." Cuffe's priority for "the benefit of the African Nation" continued to differ from white and black evangelical intentions, however. His pragmatic Pan-African civilizing scheme was "for the good of that people universally." He endorsed "a circular route from Africa to England and to America" that would lead to economic and social improvement in Africa and perhaps stimulate new international involvement in this just cause. If "religious Characters" wished to visit Africa they could gain passage there, but his Quaker-influenced civilizing mission remained one of promoting a way of life, not a religion.[8]

The Westporter expanded his advocacy role via letters to black American brethren. Eager would-be emigrants unexpectedly knocked on Cuffe's farmhouse door, and Sierra Leone news continued to appear in the papers and generate requests to emigrate. Peter Williams, Jr., reported many inquiries about banking and sailmaking opportunities in the colony and the highest civilian posts held by black settlers. He enthusiastically promoted a black "Trading fund" to underwrite Cuffe's scheme for a transatlantic "mercantile line of business." Philadelphian James Forten, who approved of the fund, was asked to seek out rice cultivators and a sawmill operator for Sierra Leone; similar requests went to black Savannah merchant Simeon Jackson.[9] Prospective settlers were told to rid themselves of intemperance.

That summer's ambitious letter campaign included brethren in Africa as well. Cuffe discussed family matters with Sierra Leone's Edward Cook; business concerns with Anthony Survance, Samuel Thorp, James Wise, and John Kizell; and Sierra Leone–English trading missions with former maritime apprentice George Davis. He informed James Wise of the Friendly Society that many settlers had not paid their debts, for which they should be taken to court. Wise should also take on the colonial government, since Governor MacCarthy had not repaid Cuffe for the new settlers' expenses, as promised. Plainly, no future trips would occur until trading losses were recouped and trade barriers lifted. But whether he returned or not, the Pan-African reminded Friendly Society members to maintain respectability before man and God, praying that they would become "more and more Known among The Nations of The Earth." He warned that the Society's failure would be "a deadly blow to Africa" and that commercial pursuits would determine her "National advancement."[10]

The rising tide of black militancy and white retaliation in America drove Cuffe to request that John Kizell, living south of Freetown on Sherbro Island, investigate a nearby site for mass emigration of black Americans. He also asked Friend Stephen Gould for his counsel: did Gould think the U.S. government could ever "be prevailed upon to

Settle a Colony in Africa?"[11] Cuffe would soon receive an answer, although not from Gould.

Meanwhile, troublesome Westport affairs occupied Cuffe's time. Serious problems included a charge by spinster Prudence White that William, his youngest son, had caused her to bear a son, "which child has been born a bastard."[12] Next came disputed land claims involving his Wampanoag relatives at Gay Head on Martha's Vineyard; acquisitive whites had conspired to seize ancestral lands.[13] Business prospects fared little better, with the unsold African cargo from his last voyage still in New York, New Bedford, and Westport warehouses. The black captain complained of a stagnant commerce.

Cuffe did, however, join forces with Job Gifford in the construction of a forty-five-ton vessel to be used for southern trade routes. She went up for sale at Cuffe's shipyard on October 4, 1816. The brig *Traveller* was also listed for sale or charter. The customary careful management of Cuffe's mercantile empire was noticeably lacking. Partly in an effort to recoup trading losses, Cuffe shifted his interest to black merchants in Santo Domingo and Haiti and decided to send the *Traveller* to the Caribbean.[14] A letter to Peter Williams, Jr., asked if he and other members of the New York African Institution would take an interest in the *Traveller* and in Caribbean trade until the way was reopened for voyages to Africa.

The Pan-African, having not heard from William Allen in some time, sadly regretted his esteemed Friend's long silence.[15] Undaunted by past setbacks, he resolved to make one final offer to Allen and the directors of London's African Institution. In seeming desperation he volunteered to visit England the following year to join them in preserving "the little seed" at Sierra Leone. No sooner was that letter mailed than Cuffe's prayers for assistance in the colonization of Africa appeared to be answered. Local newspapers told of a national colonization movement that was prevailing on the U.S. government to settle a colony in Africa.[16] Elaboration of that scheme came from the Reverend Samuel Mills, followed by a barrage of questions from the Reverend Robert Finley, the new American Colonization Society's founder.

Public disclosures plus personal correspondence signified that well-meaning white Americans now sought government approval and financial backing to transport free people of color to Africa "with their own consent." At first Cuffe had no reason to question Finley's sincerity, nor the overall goal of giving "an opportunity to the free people of color to rise to their proper level"—to which Finley added an incentive to end the transatlantic slave trade as well as to spread civilization and Christianity to Africa. The new organization needed statistics on Sierra Leone, its "prospects of happiness," the geography and productivity of the Guinea coast, and locations of slave factories and European settlements. Would the Westporter explore the Guinea coast for a colonization site if requested to do so by "the General Government"?[17]

It soon became obvious that this national plan for African colonization publicly catered to racist Americans; thus it made more sense, at least to Cuffe, for blacks to leave altogether. Articles in the *National Intelligencer* and the *Daily National Intelligencer* boasted that Henry Clay, Speaker of the House of Representatives, defended the rights of slaveholders and that he wanted "to rid our country of a useless and pernicious, if not dangerous portion of our population"—namely, the free blacks. Maryland's Francis Scott Key reiterated that the American Colonization Society must protect slavery as an institution. Virginia's John Randolph added that the Society "must materially tend to secure the property of every master in the United States over his slaves." Only Elias B. Caldwell, Finley's brother-in-law and head of Washington's American Bible Society, called for a "national atonement for the wrongs" to Africa.[18]

The Society's benefits to the confirmed black emigrationist were clear, but so was the organization's most serious, if not fatal, flaw. Cuffe immediately advised Mills and Finley of their mistake. A master of subtlety, the Pan-African stressed that a successful national colonization movement designed to attract free black emigrants would have to "be guided by Wisdom's best means." Years later, when blacks broadly lambasted the American Colonization Society, Cuffe's friend James Forten would make the same point to William Lloyd Garrison: "Colonization principles, abstractly considered, are unobjectionable; but the means employed" determined the difference.[19] Cuffe and Forten both were making a very important point—that colonization schemes must be responsive to and executed in cooperation with free people of color; otherwise, they would fail.

Despite serious objections Cuffe promised to do everything possible to promote an enterprise that would ultimately lead to "the liberation of the African race." The organizers of the American Colonization Society needed to contact members of the New York and Boston African Institutions, who advocated communication, trade, and emigration to Africa. Cuffe felt that Peter Williams, Jr., should lead the government's survey team to Africa. The navigable Sherbro Island region south of Sierra Leone, John Kizell's territory, would be ideal for a new colony, but the U.S. government also should explore the fertile Gambia River delta, the Congo River basin, and, finally, the expansive Cape of Good Hope area, "could it be obtained." Promoters should have an alternative settlement location available in the United States as well, so that freed slaves would truly have a choice.[20]

These perilous times took their toll on Cuffe's pioneering Pan-African scheme. Blacks in America had "a need of" Africa where they could "rise to be a people," but that might only be possible in view of the new society. No longer could he single-handedly orchestrate and finance his own plan. Cuffe's enthusiasm nearly matched that of Mills and Finley, who privately prophesied a new day for African descendants. Those who had petitioned for passage aboard the *Traveller* could anticipate free emigration. Manumission would increase as white masters freed their slaves in the absence of local restrictions. Ultimately, the family of Africa would be free, if only the new society adhered to "Wisdom's best means."

15

COLONIZATION AND A QUIET PASSING

As Paul Cuffe approached his fifty-eighth birthday he faced perplexing and monumental questions about racial harmony in America and the survival of his black brethren. He would maintain a steady course, set years earlier, as a Pan-African concerned with the best interests of the whole African family, a perspective that literally transcended national boundaries. White racism threatened Africans across the Atlantic, where Englishmen monopolized commerce in Sierra Leone and throttled black industry there; it also seemed to rule the American South, where enslaved brethren appeared doomed to perpetual bondage. The national debate on colonization consumed the country and drained Cuffe of the energy he needed to conclude his fight for dignity and self-determination.

The Westporter sadly came to realize that the American Colonization Society was using him to promote racial separation in America. But the alternative—death or never-ending servitude for his black brethren—was for him the greater evil. The national debate ostensibly began when Robert Finley asked, "What shall we do with the free people of color?" Many whites felt that no place in North America was suitable as a colony for former slaves because they might join with the Indians and treat whites as their "enemies." Finley's *Thoughts on the Colonization of Free Blacks* stated that slaves should only be freed "on condition" that they be colonized; he told Cuffe the opposite, however, that blacks would leave "with their own consent."[1]

Two days after the first meeting of the American Colonization Society free blacks from Georgetown, Virginia, gathered to express mixed emotions about colonization. Lewis Hillery had opened the solemn meeting, claiming that America was "his native soil"; his parents had lived and died there and he wanted to do the same. Many others like him favored racial separation, yet they also wanted government protection and a guarantee of certain rights under the law. Joseph Moore guessed that not one out of a thousand blacks would choose Africa or the Pacific coast but would prefer that a colony be established, say, along the banks of the Missouri River. The meeting's secretary, Christopher McPhearson, heartily agreed, and Thomas Williams added that brethren like himself had fought with "undaunted courage" in past wars for American protection, and thus were an integral part of the nation.[2]

The election of slaveholding managers for the American Colonization Society prompted Joseph Adams, who had gathered with the Georgetown blacks, to declare that "it had now become actually necessary" for free men of color to form into a strong "social compact." Moore quickly added that his goal was "peace, love and harmony, throughout our beloved Union," but he nonetheless discussed a provocative black national "body politic." Joseph Moore suggested a universal association of blacks. When reports of the Georgetown meeting appeared in the *Messenger*,[3] the editors received angry protests from frightened white readers who wanted them to stop publishing news that had incited these "riotous proceedings."

No mention was made of this black protest against the American Colonization Society in the *New Bedford Mercury*. Cuffe continued to write suitably humanitarian sentiments to both Samuel Mills and Robert Finley while sides were being drawn up elsewhere. Readers of the *New York Courier* (Jan. 13, 1817) were subjected to articles such as the following, in a contrived black dialect:

> Misser Printer: I understand, dere be great fuss in e city of Washington, for make people of colour go back to he own country, wat he nebber see. *Misser* Clay and Misser Randolf, he berry sorry poor people of colour can't marry wite gal. . . . But *Misser Clay* say, color people muss go to Africa den he berry happy; den he marry wite gal, if he find him. . . .
>
> Now, I ax *Misser Clay* small question. *Misser Clay,* how you like leave Kentuck, and go lib in Africa? Not berry well, I tink . . . , de sun be verry hot—and he ole country full of wile negger . . . you don't care much were he go, if he only go away.

The Society's first rebuttal to uppity protestors, both black and white, attempted to use Cuffe's reputation, and that of others tied to the Society, to strengthen its cause. "A Brief Sketch of Sierra Leone" appeared in the Washington papers and swept the country, noting that Paul Cuffe clearly had made things happen.[4] The article gave details such as the Friendly Society of Sierra Leone's commercial credit of £1,200 and its members' trade and correspondence between Britain and the United States. Other published pieces expressed pride that former President George Washington's nephew Bushrod was president of the American Colonization Society and that he had signed the Society's petition to the U.S. Congress. Robert Finley's meritorious contributions as founder of the Society were recognized in Georgia, which awarded him the presidency of its state university.[5]

For weeks James Forten and other leading figures in Philadelphia uneasily listened to the new Society's repeated insults to free persons of color. They saw outrage grow among the 3,000 free blacks in the city, many of whom had migrated from the South and who still had relatives in bondage. On January 8 Forten summoned the members of the city's African Institution to discuss the issue. At a subsequent mass gathering at Richard Allen's AME Bethel Church, all those present—reportedly the entire black community—called for the condemnation of the American Colonization Society.

> WHEREAS our ancestors (not of choice) were the first cultivators of the wilds of America, we their descendants feel ourselves entitled to participate in the blessings of her luxuriant soil, which their blood and sweat manured. . . .
>
> RESOLVED, That we view with deep abhorrence the unmerited stigma attempted to be cast upon the reputation of the free People of Colour by the Promoters of this Measure, "that they are a dangerous and useless part of the community," . . .
>
> RESOLVED, That we never will separate ourselves voluntarily from the slave population in this country. . . .
>
> RESOLVED, That having the strongest confidence in the justice of God, and philanthropy of the free states, we cheerfully submit our destinies to . . . Him who suffers not a sparrow to fall without his special Providence. . . .[6]

The negative vote was unanimous in condemning the Society's goals. Eleven people were appointed to a committee and instructed to communicate these sentiments to Washington legislators.

The blacks of Philadelphia had spoken, but how genuinely did the resolution represent the established black leadership? The "whole continent seems to be agitated with alarm," Forten wrote to Cuffe. Robert Finley, who met with the committee from Philadelphia, claimed to have made a surprise visit "to satisfy them of the purity of our designs." According to him all the committee members had wanted separation from whites, and eight had selected Africa as the preferred location for a colony.[7] In reality that committee had expressed views consistent with Cuffe's Pan-African scheme. Some, including Forten, agreed with Cuffe that the Society, although seriously flawed, could be useful.[8]

In the midst of this turmoil it was reported that an imposter, who at various times posed as a bishop's son, as Paul Cuffe, and as Cuffe's brother-in-law from New York, had been arrested for stealing money and horses in cities throughout the East.[9] Cynics thereby justified their argument that free blacks could not be trusted by pointing to this imposter. The Pan-African responded to a preposterous personal appeal for freedom from the prisoner, who had addressed him as "Dear Father."

> If the Great evil that thou hast embarked upon, were only against me as an individual . . . I should not have to lament the Cause so much. But this is a national Concern. It is a Stain to the Whole Community of the African race. Wilt thou consider, oh thou imposter, the Great number that thou hast lifted thy heal against. . . .The manumission of 1,500,000 Slaves depends upon the faithfulness of the few who have obtained their freedom. Yea, . . . but the Whole Community of the African race, which are according to best accounts 30,000,000.[10]

In Cuffe's mind both colonization critics and this imposter failed to consider the best interests of the whole African family.

Early in February 1817 Cuffe suffered a "Severe Attack," which he endured for eight hours; "all circulation of blood was stagnated," he reported. Openly content "to experience that glorious Resurrection with our Lord and Saviour Jesus Christ," he now cautioned black colonization opponents to be silent: "Amen to it" if the slightest benefit emerged for the African cause. He clearly equated colonization with a means for greater freedom, and he concurred with Forten that the plan would only survive if acceptable to God.[11] His Westport activities slowly resumed, but the aging merchant never fully recovered from the attack. In addition to overseeing the construction of a saltworks, he supervised his brig *Traveller*'s departure to North Carolina, from where she would sail to Santo Domingo.[12]

Encouraging letters and the publication of *A View of Exertions Lately Made for the Purpose of Colonizing the Free People of Colour . . .* ,[13] lifted Cuffe's sagging spirits. President James Madison was urged to accomplish "an entire and immediate abolition" of the slave trade and, significantly, to promote colonization of free persons in West Africa "with their own consent." Samuel Mills recalled Cuffe's British and African successes and asked if he still envisioned favorable prospects for an American agent in London and on Sherbro Island. Would the British reject a mass migration of former slaves to the colony, as they had earlier? Peter Williams, Jr., also praised the black humanitarian, certain that God had preserved him for a purpose. He asked if Cuffe had heard additional information from his British or American supporters.

The national press continued to write of blacks and whites as being destined for separation. The *Richmond Enquirer* published excerpts of a January 21, 1811, letter that detailed the procolonization sentiments of former President Thomas Jefferson, who was actually responding to questions posed by Friend Ann Mifflin, one of Cuffe's admirers.

> Sir—You have asked my opinion on the proposition of A M to make measures for procuring, on the coast of Africa, an establishment to which the people of color of these states might from time to time be colonized. . . . I have ever thought it the most desirable measure which could be adopted for gradually drawing off this part of our population most advantageously for themselves as well as for us. . . . And the proposition should be made with all the prudent caution and attention requisit to reconcile it to interests, the safety, and the prejudices of all people. . . . (April 11, 1817)

What the newspaper failed to mention was that neither Cuffe nor Jefferson expected their respective races to wholely accept a full-scale African removal in the foreseeable future.

Cuffe's mail accumulated in Westport. Nephew Thomas Wainer wrote from western New York for funds. Unsold African camwood was a cause for concern, as was the dissolution of Howard & Johnson's.[14] Correspondents wanted to know where black schoolchildren in Charleston, South Carolina, might find a black teacher; whether the Gabon River area had ebony wood for trade; what Cuffe's prospects were for sailing soon to Sierra Leone; whether the Westporter would testify for a man named Cuffe Johnson, now a slave in Philadelphia; and what could be done for 300 Virginia slaves manumitted by the will of Samuel Grist, a Richmond planter.[15] Moreover, James Forten, Absalom Jones, Richard Allen, and their African Institution painfully recognized the need for an asylum.

By the time Forten's July 25 call for a black refuge reached Massachusetts, the American Colonization Society's white proponents had fatally alienated the entire Philadelphia free black community. The Society published an erroneous statement by Robert Finley to the effect that the black committee appointed earlier had secretly withdrawn their opposition to colonization, and it further claimed that James Forten and Russell Parrott now recognized the American Colonization Society as an extension of Cuffe's scheme.[16]

On August 10 black Philadelphians gathered with Forten and Parrott and resolved to bury the manipulative slaveowner's society that was unconcerned with "Wisdom's best means." They declared that the ultimate abolition of slavery was progressing under "a just God"; and they fervently disclaimed "every connection" with a plan to exclude them from these advantages—to do otherwise would be to condemn brethren to "perpetual slavery and augmented sufferings." But they "emphatically" denied opposition to "all plans of colonization,"[17] thus avoiding the slightest criticism of Cuffe's Pan-African scheme.

Thoughts of pending death, not the fatal severance of black support for the American Colonization Society, hung over the Westport farm. Following his sister Lydia's death on July 4 an ailing Paul Cuffe drew closer to his own end. His excessive sweating, chills, and coughing worried everyone. Anxious friends and admirers gathered to seek final advice, among them Samuel Mills, who would carry the sentiments to Thomas Clarkson and William Allen in England, then to John Kizell at Sherbro Island, south of Sierra Leone. Newport's Dr. Hazard rushed to Cuffe's bedside.[18] On August 27 Cuffe summoned his family and "bid all farewell" in the presence of the Lord. "It was as broken a time as was ever known amongst us," recounted John, his early mentor and loyal brother. Neighbors of Cuffe's color, "the special object of his concern," assembled in the room to hear prayers to the Heavenly Advisor. At 2:00 A.M. on September 7 Paul Cuffe uttered, "Let me pass quietly away," and died.[19]

The next afternoon a solemn procession made its way from the Cuffe family farm to Westport's South Meeting House, just a short distance away. Inspired eulogies extolled the virtues of the black Friend, who humbly had accumulated an estate of nearly $20,000. Prayers arose to the God who "made of one blood all the nations of men." Interment followed in a far corner of the Friends' burial ground, an area separated from the graves of white Friends. Even in death racial separation seemed unavoidable. Across the nation, in England, and in Sierra Leone, newspapers bore the news of Cuffe's passing.[20]

Paul Cuffe's Pan-African scheme represented the interests of blacks on both sides of the Atlantic, unlike the scheme of the American Colonization Society. Yet Cuffe had been convinced that the Society represented the only feasible channel by which imperiled brethren could be transported willingly to Africa; certainly, implementation of that plan required more than his own meager capabilities.

At this crucial turning point in black American history, many blacks refused to consider African colonization. Reluctantly, Cuffe had persisted in the belief that blacks would be better off in Africa, where they could "rise to be a people." Eventually, his dream of a new African "historian nation"—Liberia—became a reality.

NOTES

1. COFFE SLOCUM MISTER

1. Holder, *Quakers,* p. 321; Ricketson, *New Bedford,* pp. 37, 183, 185; Slocum, *History,* pp. 1, 11–12, 27–29, 45; Lowry, "Quakers," pp. 8, 12; H. H. Edes Papers, Jan. 30, 1732/33, letterbox, n.d.–1776, MHS.

2. Imported slaves persisted in using the name "Kofi," although spellings varied widely; that name dotted the New England landscape. Hugh Hall, a Boston slave merchant, sold a man named "Cuffee" in 1728, and another named "Cuffy" from Barbados the following year (see Hugh Hall Papers, MHS; Donnan, *Documents,* 3:32, 34; Greene, "New England Negro"; Greene, *Colonial New England,* pp. 146, 158, 173). The *Columbian Museum and Savannah Advertiser* for Aug. 13, 1798, listed a "Cuffee Town"; and Benjamin Franklin entrusted money to his "Cuff" in England (Eddy, "Account Book," p. 114).

3. Miers and Kopytoff, *Slavery,* pp. 3–24; Priestly, *West African Trade,* pp. 17–18; Wilks, "Mossi and Akan States"; Rattray, *Ashanti,* pp. 47, 119, 124, 161, 170–71, 173, 175–77, 200, 211; Elkins, *Slavery,* p. 96.

4. Slavetraders from England, Massachusetts, and Rhode Island usually left their cargoes in the West Indies, but some carried them on to New England (Du Bois, *African Slave Trade,* pp. 27–29; Hedges, *Browns,* 1:70; Donnan, *Slave Trade,* 3:1).

5. Horatio P. Howard, a descendant of Paul Cuffe, believes that Kofi arrived in 1728 (*Self-made Man,* p. 5). See also Holder, *Quakers,* p. 72.

6. Bill of Sale, vol. 4, Paul Cuffe Manuscript Collection (hereafter Cuffe MSS), NBPL.

7. Drake, *Quakers,* pp. 17–18, 30–45; Drake, "Elihu Coleman"; Ricketson, *New Bedford,* p. 38; Donnan, *Documents,* 3:115–16; Davis, *Slavery in Western Culture,* pp. 291–332, 483–93.

8. Ruth Cuffe, granddaughter of Kofi Slocum through David, told James B. Congdon that a Mr. Hull's father had bought Kofi and then released him. Mr. Hull relayed to her an intriguing tale about a squire's arrival at breakfast time, Kofi's astonishment and fright when told that he was to be freed, and

his master's offer to employ Kofi until he earned some money. Ruth's sister wrote a shorter account (Feb. 12, 1851, vol. 16, Cuffe MSS) to the effect that sisters Bathsheba and Hannah Hull married Ebenezer and Captain Holder Slocum, respectively, raising the possibility of a sale within the extended family (Slocum, *History,* pp. 66–67; *Monthly Repository of Theology and General Literature* 2:221).

9. Intentions of Marriage, Jan. 31, 1745, Cuffe MSS; *Monthly Repository* 2:221; Harris, *Paul Cuffe,* p. 15; Starbuck, *American Whale Fishery,* 1:11–17, 43, 119; Ricketson, *New Bedford,* pp. 20, 22, 58, 148.

10. Slocumb, *History,* pp. 67, 72, 89; Haskell, *Cuttyhunk,* pp. 14–17; Salvador, *Paul Cuffe,* p. 11; Exercise Book, vol. 2, Cuffe MSS.

11. *Monthly Repository* 2:337. Ricketson, *New Bedford,* p. 41; Tabor, "Social Life among Friends," p. 15; Salvador, *Paul Cuffe,* pp. 8–15.

12. Exercise Book, vol. 2, Cuffe MSS.

13. The farm bordered property owned by Jonathan Soule, Rachel Wilbur, Enos Gifford, and Phillip Allen (Cuff Slocum Deed, David Brownell's note of Dec. 11, 1766, Exercise Book, S. Smith's survey of Apr. 12, 1769, vols. 2, 5, Cuffe MSS).

14. Exercise Book, vol. 2, Cuffe MSS.

2. THE STRUGGLE FOR INDEPENDENCE

1. Ricketson, *New Bedford,* pp. 22–23, 332; Ellis, *New Bedford,* p. 232; Bullard, *Rotches,* pp. 11–13, 31; Stackpole, *Forgotten Man,* pp. 11, 22.

2. Jonathan's name appears only a handful of times in the Cuffe MSS, and these very early. He is prominently listed among three signators of Gay Head Indians on Martha's Vineyard for 1798. The earliest memoir refers to at least one brother living on the Elizabeth Islands during the War for Independence; he may have been David. Neither older brother was living at home, thereby avoiding taxation and involvement in the lengthy petitioning process to follow. See List of Indian Children to the Gospel Society of Boston, May 14, 1798, MHS; *Monthly Repository* 2:222, 285; Coffe Slocum Exercise Book, vol. 2, Cuffe MSS.

3. Cuffe to Ann Bouthron, Sept. 4, 1811, vol. 6, Cuffe MSS; Starbuck, *American Whale Fishery,* 1:11, 15, 23, 31, 43–51, 54–56, 90; Ricketson, *New Bedford,* pp. 22–23, 59, 252; Woodson, "Negroes and Indians"; Langley, "Negro in the Navy"; Greene and Woodson, *Negro Wage Earner,* p. 7; Board of Trade, *New Bedford,* pp. 18, 25–29; Bullard, *Rotches,* pp. 11–13. The history of upward mobility for blacks and Indians through maritime commerce deserves much more serious attention than it has yet received.

4. Starbuck, *American Whale Fishery,* 1:57; Tower, *American Whale Fishery,* pp. 36–37; Morgan, *Naval Documents,* 5:234, 252; *Monthly Repository* 2:222. Benjamin Quarles states that the *Charming Polly* was seized in 1777 with

William Cuffe, Prince Hall, and Cuff Scott aboard, all from Massachusetts coastal towns (*American Revolution,* p. xii).

5. Paul's signature never appears with the Slocum surname, but the case is quite different for John, who used random notations, some barely legible. Ricketson (*New Bedford,* p. 254) states that the Cuffes used a form of their father's name out of pride for Africa. Two of the sisters recalled that the white Slocums forced the change (Feb. 12, 1851, n.d., vol. 16, Cuffe MSS; see also Quarles, *Black Abolitionists,* p. 20). The Slocum surname was retained by Paul's mother, his brother Jonathan, and Freelove, his youngest sister.

6. *Monthly Repository* 2:222; Exercise Book, vol. 2, Cuffe MSS. Marriage records generally support later contentions that Michael Wainer was an Indian. However, the record of his marriage to Paul Cuffe's sister Mary reads: "Michel (Waner) married Mary Slocum, "Mulattoes of Dartmouth, October 11, 1772" (New England Historic Genealogical Society [hereafter NEHGS], *Vital Records of Dartmouth,* 2:523). A list of Indians at Dartmouth, dated Aug. 25, 1763, includes John, Isaac, and Mary Pequet (Miscellaneous Bound, 1761–65, MHS).

7. Moore, *Slavery,* pp. 191, 196; Hart, *Commonwealth History,* 3:115–16, 184–85; *Continental Journal and Weekly Advertiser,* June 18, 1778.

8. Crapo, "Villages of Dartmouth." Ricketson (*New Bedford,* p. 74) estimates the damage at $422,680.

9. *Monthly Repository* 2:336–37; Sherwood, "Paul Cuffe," pp. 162–66. Executor rights to the Coffe Slocum estate went to John in 1783, but property rights were not transferred to John and Paul until 1796 (vol. 1, Cuffe MSS).

10. *Monthly Repository* 2:222, 285; Starbuck, *American Whale Fishery,* 1:68; Macy, *Nantucket,* pp. 92–93.

11. *Monthly Repository* 2:222, 285; Macy, *Nantucket,* pp. 88–97, 107–10; Pease, *Samuel Rodman,* p. 5. Edouard Stackpole speaks of "British refugee privateers" raiding seaside communities (*Sea-Hunters,* p. 87; *Nantucket,* pp. 61–80). In her diary, now at the Peter Folger Museum, Kezia Coffin Fanning, one of Nantucket's notorious Tories, frequently mentioned British privateers, destroyed vessels, and lost crews during the war.

12. Dec. 5, 1779, vol. 1, Cuffe MSS; Stackpole, *Sea-Hunters,* p. 87, and *Nantucket,* pp. 81–98; Ellis, *New Bedford,* p. 142.

13. Mar. 6, 22, Apr. 14, June 25, 1780, General Court Petitions, 186:116–17, 139–43, 174, 263–65, MSA.

14. General Court Petitions, 186:134–36, MSA; petition, Feb. 10, 1780, vol. 1, Cuffe MSS. This petition restated the inconsistency of seeking freedom while perpetuating American slavery. Davis points out that the inconsistency was rarely expressed publicly (*Slavery in the Age of Revolution,* pp. 225–86; see also Quarles, *American Revolution,* pp. 42–43).

15. Petition, Feb. 10, 1780, vol. 1, Cuffe MSS. Proceedings for the Massachusetts House of Representatives and the Council (second legislative

chamber) are missing, although all acts and resolves which were passed by the legislative body have been printed. I wish to thank Mr. Leo Flaherty for his patient and thorough assistance in this matter.

16. Two petition drafts exist in the Cuffe MSS, dated Feb. 10, 1780. The more lengthy copy represents, with only a few alterations, the original sent to Boston's General Court. The legislative table of contents for retained petitions notes the "Interesting Petition." The reverse side of the archives copy states ". . . [Representative] Wm Davis knows they are taxed March 16, 1780 Mr. Wm Stickney, Mr. Benj. Thomas, Capt. Seth Sumner." General Court Petitions, 186:134–36, MSA; *Acts and Resolves,* 21:3–5; Ellis, *New Bedford,* p. 158.

17. The printed petitions from Massachusetts blacks for 1773, 1774, and 1777 appear in MHS *Collections,* 5th ser., vol. 3, pp. 432–37. See also letters and documents regarding slavery, ibid., pp. 375–431; General Court Petitions, 212:132, MSA; Hart, *Commonwealth History,* 3:191, 347–48, 351.

18. Brig. Gen. Jedediah Preble's journal for June 13, 1777, and George Moore's Jan. 25, 1869, letter to the editor of the *Historical Magazine* explain that John Adams stopped a provocative message, inspired by the blacks' petition, from reaching the Continental Congress (Moore, *Slavery,* pp. 182–83, plus inserts in Moore's book, MHS).

19. House of Representatives General Court Records, Apr. 10, 18, 21, 1780, General Court Petitions, June 25, 1780, vol. 142, MSA; legislation of Mar. 25, 1780, in *Acts and Resolves,* 21:401; Moore, *Slavery,* pp. 202, 222; Thorpe, *Constitutional History,* 1:209, 294, 485.

20. Ellis, *New Bedford,* p. 142. Sherwood ("Paul Cuffe," pp. 162–63) thoroughly researches the petition to the Taunton judiciary.

21. Sherwood, "Paul Cuffe," pp. 162–65; Oct. 28, 1780, Revolutionary Resolves, 229:442, MSA.

22. *Continental Journal,* Feb. 1, 1781; petition Jan. 22, 1781, and notations, Dec. 23, 1780, Feb. 20, 1781, vol. 1, Cuffe MSS; Sherwood, "Paul Cuffe," pp. 164–65.

23. Five drafts exist, each being slightly different; three are dated April 22, one the 21st, and one the 24th. At the bottom of the latter are the words: "A true copy . . . to have all free Negroes and mulattoes to be entered equally with the white people. . . ." An unexplained notation shows Edward Pope acknowledging 24*s* from John Cuffe (vol. 1, Cuffe MSS; Sherwood, "Paul Cuffe," pp. 164–65).

24. Sherwood, "Paul Cuffe," p. 165; June 11, 1781, vol. 1, Cuffe MSS.

25. June 5, Aug. 19, Nov. 16, 19, 1781, June 26, 1782, Feb. 19, 25, 1783, marriage receipt, Feb. 25, 1783, Cuffe to William Harris, Aug. 10, 1816, vols. 1, 3, 21, Cuffe MSS; *Monthly Repository* 2:285; Ellis, *New Bedford,* p. 158; NEHGS, *Vital Records of Westport,* p. 35.

3. RISING PROSPERITY AND AFRICAN AWARENESS

1. Historian John Hope Franklin asserts that the Negro's search for independence at the turn of the nineteenth century was a "struggle to achieve status in the evolving American civilization," and that Cuffe typified those "Negroes . . . who were searching for economic independence and group self-respect" *(Slavery to Freedom,* pp. 108, 113).

2. Cuffe's earliest biography speaks of his moving from a farm, perhaps the family farm, to a rented shoemaker's shop on the Acoaxet River. The recorded deed of June 2, 1789, locates him next to the Sowles, presumably near Hix Bridge on the west branch of the Acoaxet, where he later owned property. However, a town survey of Oct. 11, 1790, shows a "Cuff" living along the northeast border of Westport (*Monthly Repository* 2:286; deed, June 2, 1789, NBRD; *Field Notes,* n.p., NBPL). A 1790 census lists both "Paul Cuff" and "John Cuff" living in Westport (*Heads of Families, 1790,* pp. 58–59).

3. The crime-control law passed on Mar. 26, 1788, the same day the state outlawed citizen participation in the Atlantic slave trade. Negroes, mulatoes, and even Indians were evicted twelve years later under this law, after Virginia's infamous Gabriel Revolt. The law eventually was rescinded in 1834 (*Perpetual Laws,* pp. 407–9, 411–13; Moore, *Slavery,* pp. 59, 299–341). Cuffe repeatedly encountered what Winthrop Jordan correctly cites as a trend toward exclusion (*White over Black,* pp. 403–26, 472).

4. Rotch Family Papers, letters, 1785–95, MHS; Pease, *Samuel Rodman,* p. 5; Rotch, *Memorandum,* p. 68; Nantucket Society of Friends, "Births, Deaths, Removals," Apr. 28, 1788, Oct. 22, 1795, PFM; Ricketson, *New Bedford,* p. 23; Stackpole, *Rotch,* pp. 7, 28; Bullard, *Rotches,* pp. 31, 74.

5. Worth, "Heads of Westport," p. 19; Bullard, *Rotches,* pp. 31, 36, 71, 254–63; Rotch, *Memorandum,* pp. 36–68; *Mercury,* Sept. 26, 1794; William Rotch, Jr., to Radcliff Monthly Meeting in London, June 23, 1787, to Monthly Meeting in Canterbury, Aug. 27, 1787, manuscript portfolio no. 17, pp. 123–25, FHL.

6. Davis and Boulding both analyze these characteristics (Davis, *Slavery in Western Culture,* pp. 328–29, and *Slavery in the Age of Revolution,* pp. 233–42; Boulding, "Economic Life," pp. 43–49). At least two local Friends, William Gifford and Lemuel Milk, lost out to the consuming power of the Rotch empire.

7. Kezia Fanning's original Nantucket diary no longer exists, but based on the copy at the Peter Folger Museum, it is possible that the quoted extract refers to Paul Cuffe.

8. Unless Cuffe met the Rotches on Nantucket during the war, the prominent whaling merchants probably first heard of the Westporter on moving to the mainland in late 1787 or early 1788. The Rotches played an important role in Cuffe's life, but they were certainly not alone in this regard. Too few sources exist on early Rotch activity, not to mention so many other unnamed Cuffe associates. See Bullard, *Rotches,* p. 72.

9. *Monthly Repository* 2:285–86; "Memoir of Captain Paul Cuffee," *Liverpool Mercury,* Oct. 4, 11, 1811; memorandum from John Wainer to James B. Congdon, n.d., John Wainer to James Congdon, n.d., vol. 21, Cuffe MSS. The Cuffe's first daughter, Naomi, was born on Mar. 8, 1783, followed by Mary on Oct. 5, 1785, Ruth on Aug. 10, 1788, and Alice on Sept. 10, 1790. Thomas Wainer was born Jan. 27, 1773, followed by Gardner on Oct. 1, 1774, Paul on Oct. 17, 1776, Jeremiah on July 10, 1778, David on Mar. 19, 1780, and John on Jan. 27, 1782 (NEHGS, *Vital Records of Westport,* p. 99).

10. Works Progress Administration (hereafter WPA), *Ship Registries of New Bedford,* 1:xiv; John Wainer to James Congdon, n.d., vol. 21, Cuffe MSS; Morison, *Maritime History,* pp. 157–58; Albion and Pope, *Sea Lanes,* p. 93.

11. *Monthly Repository* 2:286–87 carried the peculiar whaling story without naming the craft and misdating the episode.

12. Customs documents correct tonnage estimates for the *Sunfish* and *Mary* suggested by Abner Davis and John Wainer to James Congdon (n.d., vol. 21, Cuffe MSS; Tonnage Book [1790–1802], entries Nov. 26, 1792, Mar. 20, 1793, Newport Bureau of Customs, FRC; see also *Newport Mercury,* Dec. 10, 1792).

13. *Newport Mercury,* Nov. 19, 1793, Nov. 11, 1794. Donnan cites sixty-two departures for Africa between Jan. 1796 and July 1800, "probably a small proportion of the Rhode Island vessels engaged in the slave trade at this time" (*Documents,* 3:335–79; "New England Slave Trade"; "Agitation").

14. *Medley,* Nov. 27, 1792; *Monthly Repository* 2:287, 335; *Ranger* permanent certificate of registry, Mar. 15, 1800, no. 6, and *Hope* permanent certificate of registry, May 9, 1800, no. 9, French Spoliation Claims, NA; WPA, *Ship Registries of New Bedford,* 1:1472, 2643. Never during her fourteen years and some eighty entrances and various registries and enrollments did the *Ranger*'s ownership exclude Cuffe or his extended family, and she was not commanded by an outsider until 1810. She became the training vessel for all the Wainer seamen and sometimes for suitors to the Cuffe daughters as well, as in the case of Capt. Alvin Phelps. Cuffe remained captain of the family crew until 1800. *Monthly Repository* 2:335 notes final details of her preparation for sea in 1795 or 1796.

15. Albion and Pope, *Sea Lanes,* pp. 74–75; Dookhan, *West Indies,* p. 41. Davis claims that Georgia was the only state legally importing slaves from Africa in 1793, but Du Bois includes South Carolina (Davis, *Slavery in the Age of Revolution,* pp. 26–29; Du Bois, *African Slave-Trade,* pp. 71–74, 86–88).

16. *Monthly Repository* 2:335. See also Stump, *Blackwater and Nanticoke,* pp. 53, 96, 101–2, 225–26.

17. WPA, *Maryland,* p. 377; Stump, *Blackwater and Nanticoke,* pp. 53, 102; Jordan, *White over Black,* pp. 375–82, 406–8; Du Bois, *African Slave Trade,* pp. 70–72; Franklin, *Slavery to Freedom,* pp. 150–51.

18. Jones, *Dorchester County,* p. 88. See also *Monthly Repository* 2:335–36.

19. Morison, *Maritime History,* pp. 173–74; *Monthly Repository* 2:336; Sharf,

Delaware, 2:750; Porter, *Wilmington and Brandywine,* p. iii; Federal Writer's Project (hereafter FWP), *Delaware,* p. 51.

20. Certificates of enrollment were for coastwise use; registries for coastwise and foreign trade. The *Ranger*'s permanent registry of Mar. 15, 1800, no. 6 (see n. 14), listed the preceding enrollment no. 31 for Aug. 18, 1798 (New Bedford Bureau of Customs, NA). For his probable business dealings on Nantucket in 1798, see Kezia Coffin Fanning Diary, PFM.

21. Forty acres of Eddy property were bought for $1,000 on Feb. 6, 1799; the land bordered the Acoaxet River. Another 100 acres bought that day involved a homestead farm, for $2,500, the same property sold to Wainer on Mar. 17, 1800. Presumably, it abutted the 40-acre tract since it also bordered the Acoaxet. The day before Wainer bought his homestead farm, Lemuel and Mary Sowle added to the deal sixteen rods along the river at a dollar each. Ruth Cuffe's 100-acre farm had been divided between John and Paul Cuffe in 1796 (NBRD documents; July 23, 1796, vol. 1, Cuffe MSS).

22. The estimate of Cuffe's worth is based conservatively on one-half the value given by a report of Cuffe's holdings seven years later (letter to John Parrish, Aug. 9, 1807, Cox, Parrish, and Wharton Papers, 5:85, HSP).

23. For early Rotch contacts, see Benjamin Rotch to Elizabeth Rodman, Aug. 20, 1785, and other letters through 1786, Rotch Family Papers, MHS; Rotch, *Memorandum,* pp. 36–51; Bullard, *Rotches,* pp. 213–63.

24. Letters, 1741–95, and "Miscel. Writings and Negro Colonization," William Thornton Papers, LC. Samuel Hopkins and Moses Brown were skeptical concerning some of Thornton's claims. See Hopkins to Brown, Mar. 7, 1787, in Park, *Hopkins,* 1:139–40; Hopkins to Brown, Aug. 13, 1787, box 6, p. 11, Moses Brown Papers, RIHS.

25. Members from these meetings attended Rhode Island's Yearly Meeting and frequently visited one another (Minutes, Westport Monthly Meetings, 1766–97, RIHS).

26. African Petition, no. 2358, Jan. 4, 1787 (committed Feb. 5, 1787), Journal of the House of Representatives, Commonwealth of Massachusetts, vol. 7 (May 1786–May 1787), p. 381, MSA. See also William Rotch to Moses Brown, Nov. 8, 1787, in Drake, *Quakers,* p. 102; Rotch to Brown, Dec. 1, 1787, Asa Gray to Brown, Feb. 2, 1788, box 6, pp. 19, 27, Moses Brown Papers, RIHS.

27. Thornton to John Lettsom, May 20, 1787, in Pettigrew, *Lettsom,* pp. 516–20.

28. *Heads of Families, 1790,* pp. 58–59.

29. Hopkins to Moses Brown, Apr. 29, 1784, Hopkins to Granville Sharp, Jan. 15, 1789, and other letters, in Park, *Hopkins,* 1:119–41, 157; Hopkins to Pennsylvania Abolition Society, Jan. 27, 1789, Letter Book, p. 3, Pennsylvania Abolition Society Papers, HSP. See also Ferguson, *Hopkins,* pp. 82–88, 176–82; Quarles, *American Revolution,* pp. 34–35. Newport's African

Union Society was founded in 1789, and the nation's second African Masonic lodge was established in Newport in 1799 (Bartlett, *Slave to Citizen*, pp. 35–36; Douglass, *First African Church*, pp. 25–28).

30. See Martin Benson to Brown, Benson, & Ives, Aug. 9, 1794, box 1794–95, Brown, Benson, & Ives Papers, JCBL. Fyfe, *Sierra Leone*, pp. 110–11. Anglo-American communications by the turn of the century stressed commercial aspects as well as settlement conditions in Sierra Leone. The American press published pamphlets from the Sierra Leone Company (Pennsylvania Abolition Society to Samuel Hopkins, Mar. 9, 1789, Letter Book, p. 4, Pennsylvania Abolition Society Papers, HSP; *Delaware Gazette*, Dec. 15, 1794). Hopkins idealistically preached on the prospect of commerce (in Park, *Hopkins*, 1:146).

31. Kraus, "Slavery Reform," p. 54; Turner, "First Abolition Society"; Davis, *Slavery in Western Culture*, pp. 483–93; Davis, *Slavery in the Age of Revolution*, pp. 213–16; 1796 American Convention of Abolition Societies, Pennsylvania Abolition Society Papers, HSP; *Aurora General Advertiser*, Jan. 18, 1796.

32. Du Bois, *Philadelphia Negroes*, pp. 12–22; Douglass, *First African Church*, pp. 15–17, 28–29; Bragg, *Allen and Jones*, pp. 1–2; Bracey, Meier, and Rudwick, *Black Nationalism*, pp. 1–10, 18–21; Bracey et al., *Afro-Americans*, pp. 143–56. Benjamin Rush's diary and letters suggest his pivotal role in facilitating separate African churches. However, he also emphasized that colonization was the logical extension of such reasoning: "who knows but it may be the means of sending the gospel to Africa. . . ." Two summers later he proposed a plan to John Nicholson: "I wish to suggest to you an idea of offering 10,000 or more acres for sale on moderate terms, and on a credit for a few years, to *Africans only* who have been brought up as farmers. The attraction of color and country is such that I think the offer would succeed, and thereby a *precedent* be established for colonizing them, in time, all the Africans in our country" (in Butterfield, *Rush*, 1:600–602, 608–9, 2:636, 754–55, 786; see also Corner, *Rush*, pp. 202–3, 228–29).

33. Glocester, *Forten*, pp. 18–24; Billington, *Forten*, pp. 13–14; Absalom Jones, Wm. Grey, and Wm. Gardner to Granville Sharp, Nov. 25, 1793, in Hoare, *Sharp*, pp. 254–55; Robinson, *Philadelphia*, n.p.; Minton, *Negroes in Business*, pp. 15–16; Ritter, *Philadelphia*, pp. 33(map), 36, 46, 135, 142; William Dillwyn to James Pemberton, Mar. 12, 1795, 4:141, Pennsylvania Abolition Society Papers, HSP.

34. Calvert, "Abolition Society," pp. 295–300, 309–10; Sharf, *Delaware*, 2:750–52; FWP, *Delaware*, pp. 50–51; Porter, *Wilmington and Brandywine*, pp. iv-v, 67; Moses Brown to James Phillips, Feb. 23, 1797, 157:109, Spriggs Manuscript Collection, FHL; *Delaware Gazette*, Dec. 15, 1795. By Mar. 1801 James Brian was convening Wilmington antislavery meetings at his home (Minutes of the Acting Committee, Mar. 18, 1801, Delaware Abolition Society Papers, HSD).

35. Mifflin was one of the forerunners in the American antislavery movement. He founded Delaware's first abolition society in 1788. His wife, Ann Emlen Mifflin, was an important figure in Paul Cuffe's future as an African civilizer (Justice, *Mifflin,* pp. 39, 60–61; Warner Mifflin correspondence folder, HCAL).

36. *Monthly Repository* account of this school offers no date for its establishment; the 1811 *Liverpool Mercury* account suggested 1797. Henry B. Worth notes the exasperating lack of evidence about early Westport schools ("Heads of Westport," p. 20). Members of the Society of Friends were very skeptical of formal education, particularly in Puritan New England, where home training was very common (Tabor, "Social Life among Friends," p. 15; letter to John Parrish, Aug. 9, 1807, Cox, Parrish, and Wharton Papers, 5:85, HSP). Quaker schooling in the Westport area followed the example of Cuff's School. The New Bedford Academy opened on May 1, 1800, under the auspices of the New Bedford Meeting, and Westport Friends considered opening their own school (*Columbian Courier,* Apr. 25, 1800; May 16, 1801, Minutes, Westport Monthly Meeting, 1797–1836, p. 50, RIHS).

4. FEDERALIST SHIPPING MERCHANT

1. Albion and Pope, *Sea Lanes,* p. 93; Morison, *Maritime History,* pp. 173–86.

2. *Columbian Courier,* Feb. 27, 1801, Apr. 23, June 25, 1802, June 3, 1803, Mar. 2, Aug. 10, 24, 1804. This weekly was the only paper for New Bedford, Dartmouth, and Westport from Oct. 18, 1799, when John Spooner's *Medley* ceased publication, to Mar. 1, 1805 (Brigham, *Newspapers,* 1:370).

3. Naomi was now eighteen, Mary was two years younger, and Ruth had just entered her teens. The younger children were Alice (eleven), Paul (nine), Rhoda (six), and William (two). Ages are computed as of 1801 (NEHGS, *Vital Records of Westport,* pp. 35–36).

4. Entrances, May 23, 1801, Inward Vessels, 1800–1802, Philadelphia Bureau of Customs, NA; *Mirror of the Times,* July 18, 22, 1801; schooner *Hope,* permanent certificate of registry, no. 9, Apr. 13, 1801, French Spoliation Claims, NA; WPA, *Ship Registries of New Bedford,* 1:1472; *Mirror of the Times,* May 23, July 25, Aug. 1, Oct. 10, 1801. The Aug. 26, 1801, and Apr. 25, 1804, issues of Wilmington's paper discuss the shipment and usefulness of plaster of paris for farmers in the Middle Atlantic states.

5. The two earliest published biographies indicate that one-quarter of the brig was owned "by persons not related to the family." Cuffe held one-half and Thomas Wainer one-quarter, not Cuffe's "brother" as the sources suggest (*Monthly Repository* 2:221–22, 235–38, 285–87, 336; *Liverpool Mercury,* Oct. 4, 11, 1811, reprinted in *Memoir of Cuffee,* p. 10).

6. Brig *Hero,* permanent certificate of registry, no. 5, Jan. 25, 1802, New Bedford Bureau of Customs Registries, 1802–3, NA; WPA, *Ship Registries of New Bedford,* 1:1434. At one time the Maritime Historical Association of

Mystic, Conn., had a bond in Cuffe's name dated Jan. 25, 1802, but it has since been lost.

7. *Mirror of the Times,* June 5, Aug. 11, 18, 21, Sept. 15, 1802.

8. The name "Cuff" or "Cuffe" appears in records of the Delaware Abolition Society for Sept. 24, 1802, and Nov. 15, 1804. The slave child mentioned had been born in 1798 (Minutes of the Acting Committee, 1802–7, n.p., Original Minute Book of Proceedings, 1801–4, n.p., Delaware Abolition Society Papers, HSD).

9. Thomas Wainer commanded the *Hero*'s first two European voyages. An unexplained name, Manchester, appears as the brig's master on her return from Spain (*Columbian Courier,* Apr. 29, Sept. 9, 23, 1803, June 29, 1804). At least once Jeremiah Wainer sailed the *Ranger* from Wilmington to Philadelphia during his New Brunswick voyages (*Mirror of the Times,* July 27, Sept. 3, 7, Nov. 9, 1803). The estimate of $5,000 may be too conservative if the *Ranger* actually netted $1,000 on each of two coastal runs from Massachusetts to the Chesapeake in 1796 (*Monthly Repository,* p. 336).

10. Starbuck, *American Whale Fishery,* 1:200–206; schooner *Ranger,* permanent certificate of registry, no. 18, Apr. 14, 1804, and brig *Hero,* permanent certificate of registry, no. 35, July 14, 1804, New Bedford Bureau of Customs, Registries, 1804–5, NA; WPA, *Ship Registries of New Bedford,* 1:1435, 2644; *Columbian Courier,* July 20, Nov. 23, 1804. Cuffe still owned the *Ranger* with Jeremiah and his father Michael Wainer; the *Hero* remained in the hands of Cuffe, Thomas Wainer, and the two Corys.

11. Samuel Tobey's promissory note of June 8, 1805, on behalf of Paul Cuffe, transferred payment through William Rotch, Jr., to Tristram Folger and then Obed Coffin. This and James Brian's Dec. 3, 1805, letter to Cuffe tying their business to the firms of Stockton & Craig and Baltimore's Jones & Passmore, represent the earliest business receipt and incoming correspondence in the Cuffe MSS held by the New Bedford Public Library. Cuffe to Mr. Fisher, Feb. 28, 1805 (letter, vertical file, MdHS) is the earliest of Cuffe's handwritten letters known to exist.

12. Bark *Hero,* permanent certificate of registry, no. 25, June 9, 1806, New Bedford Bureau of Customs, Registries, 1806–7, NA; WPA, *Ship Registries of New Bedford,* 1:1436; Starbuck, *American Whale Fishery,* 1:206; bark *Hero* accounts, n.d., Nov. 19, 20, 1811, Cuffe MSS. Wainer's 157-page log notes sightings of right, sperm, and humpback whales (International Marine Archives Collection, ODHS, cited with permission of private owner Gale M. Blosser, Millbrae, Calif.). Benjamin Lindsey began New Bedford's third newspaper on Aug. 7, 1807, more than two years after the *Columbian Courier* ceased publication. News of the *Triton, Hero,* and *Acushnet* appeared on its pages on Oct. 23 and Dec. 11.

13. Apr. 11, 1805, vol. 1, Cuffe MSS. The log for the *Ranger*'s Guadaloupe voyage is also owned by Gale M. Blosser, Millbrae, Calif.

14. Cuffe to Freelove Slocum, Oct. 30, 1805, vol. 1, Cuffe MSS. For

accounts of the African Methodist Episcopal church, see Rush and Collins, *African Methodist Episcopal Church,* pp. 9–23; Moore, *African Methodist Episcopal Church,* p. 16; Frazier, *Negro Church,* p. 28.

15. Details of this incident are in Ricketson, *New Bedford,* p. 254; see also a letter from an unknown individual to John Parrish, Aug. 9, 1807, Cox, Parrish, and Wharton Papers, 5:85, HSP.

16. Starbuck, *American Whale Fishery,* 1:206; schooner *Ranger,* permanent certificate of registry, no. 14, Apr. 11, 1806 (canceling enrollment no. 61, Nov. 1, 1805), New Bedford Bureau of Customs, Registries, 1806–7, NA; WPA, *Ship Registries of New Bedford,* 1:2645. The schooner *Hope* had been temporarily registered in Washington, N.C., before her permanent registry on May 23, 1806, no. 21, New Bedford Bureau of Customs, Registries, 1806–7, NA; WPA, *Ship Registries of New Bedford,* 1:1472. See also *Aurora General Advertiser,* July 11, Sept. 8, 1806.

17. Cuffe owned three-quarters and Milk one-quarter of the ship (ship *Alpha,* permanent certificate of registry, no. 38, New Bedford Bureau of Customs, Registries, 1806–7, NA; WPA, *Ship Registries of New Bedford,* 1:78. See also *Monthly Repository* 2:336; *Memoir of Cuffe,* p. 10.

18. Parrish letter, Aug. 9, 1807, Cox, Parrish, and Wharton Papers, 5:85, HSP. The Parrish letter is supported by marriage statistics in NEHGS, *Vital Records of Westport,* p. 145. Compare Friend Ann Mifflin's strikingly similar portrayal of the Rotches as a family surrounded with every genteel convenience yet possessing "a pattern of true and unaffected humility." She likened "Wm Rotch & Wife to a King and Queen, in a mere Palace of a house, & his children round him in buildings little inferior, to young Princes." Of course, she hastily added, they remained "lowly & humble" within Christ. Ann Mifflin to Ann Emlen, diary entries, June 22, 30, 1801, Emlen Papers, HSP.

19. Once again, Parrish's unnamed correspondent and Ricketson both note Cuffe's reluctance to sit at the table with white visitors in his home (Parrish letter, Aug. 9, 1807, Cox, Parrish, and Wharton Papers, 5:85, HSP; Ricketson, *New Bedford,* p. 255), although both sources contain information not recorded by the other. The letter to Parrish, an advocate of racial separation, confirms what we already know—that Cuffe preferred black crews, mostly black partnerships, and black sons-in-law.

20. Shipping arrangements are mentioned in the *Monthly Repository* 2:336–37.

21. Cuffe to Barker, Aug. 26, 1806, miscellaneous letters, PFM. The *Alpha* embarked after Cuffe wrote to Barker, contrary to information in *Narrative of Cuffe,* p. 3, and Harris, "Cuffe's White Apprentice," p. 194.

22. Calvert mentioned the Delaware origins of the Cuffe memoir but erroneously believed that it first appeared in England in 1811 ("Abolition Society," esp. p. 309, n.53).

23. Du Bois, *African Slave Trade,* pp. 85–92; *Columbian Museum and Sa-*

vannah Advertiser, Dec. 13, 20, 24, 27, 31, 1806, Jan. 3, 1807; Jordan, *White over Black,* pp. 408–9.

24. Since the beginning of the century, Ladd had been master or agent for the ship *Eliza* and the schooner *Edward.* He sailed to Philadelphia, Savannah, Kingston (Jamaica), and St. Augustine. *Savannah Advertiser,* Feb. 28, July 11, 22, 1800, June 6, 1804; *Georgia Republican,* Feb. 25, Dec. 2, 1806; Pinney, "Ladd"; Beals, "Ladd"; Beckwith, *Ladd,* pp. 1–5.

25. Black Savannah proprietor Simon Jackson offered insight into the bittersweet fruits of free status in the South. He would soon default on his taxes and then be injured by a bat hurled through his shop window, offering a double reward should a white man rather than a black be caught and convicted. Jackson may have been the Georgian through whom Cuffe ordered 709 sacks of rice for the *Alpha.* Cuffe corresponded with Jackson years later. See *Republican & Savannah Evening Ledger,* Nov. 5, 1808, Apr. 4, 1809, Mar. 8, Apr. 3, Aug. 4, 1810, Feb. 29, Aug. 1, Dec. 15, 1812; Cuffe to Simeon and Susannah Jackson, Oct. 20, 1816, vol. 3, Cuffe MSS.

26. Newspapers fail to show the *Alpha*'s departure date, but *Narrative of Cuffe,* p. 4, states that the ship remained in Savannah for three months; on July 21, 1807, the *Savannah Advertiser* confirmed her European arrival from that city. Jefferson signed legislation on Mar. 2, 1807, banning the involvement of United States citizens in the trade and importation of slaves after Jan. 1, 1808 (Du Bois, *African Slave Trade,* pp. 107–8.

27. Massachusetts Colonization Society (hereafter MCS), *Proceedings,* pp. 2–3. John L. Thomas claims that Ladd went along "to study the Negro character" (*Garrison,* p. 50). There is every reason to believe that Cuffe's original intent was to sell his Savannah cargo to the Liverpool firm owned by William and Richard Rathbone, where he and William Rotch, Jr., conducted business some five years later. The Rathbone's interest in cotton began earlier in the century (Marriner, *Rathbones,* pp. xi, 1–5).

28. Registered cargo landed at Göteborg in May included 251 bales of cotton, 709 sacks of rice, 22 tons of redwood, and 1 bale of cork (*Göteborges Stads Huvudbok,* 1807, Landsarkivet, Göteborg, Sweden). I am indebted to Borje and Wolly Thorsell of that city for this information. Alfred W. Crosby's study provides a superb picture of conditions Cuffe encountered in the Baltic (*America,* pp. 40–56, 84–102).

29. *Narrative of Cuffe,* p. 4; Crosby, *America,* pp. 16, 31. As Ladd later commented, in reference to Cuffe's respectability, "Cuffe was an able shipmaster, an honest, virtuous, and philanthropic man, and was esteemed in Europe as much, at least, as the supercargo" (MCS, *Proceedings,* p. 3). The indenture was approved later by selectmen (Westport selectmen's agreement to Rodin-Cuffe indenture, May 7, 1808, Cuffe MSS).

30. Crosby, *America,* pp. 102–3; *Freeman's Journal and Daily Advertiser,* Sept. 21, 1807; *Poulson's American Daily Advertiser,* Sept. 21, 1807; *United States Gazette,* Sept. 21, 1807; *Aurora General Advertiser,* Sept. 22, 1807; Entrance,

Sept. 21, 1807, Inward Volume, 1806–10, vol. 2, Philadelphia Bureau of Customs, NA; Albion and Pope, *Sea Lanes,* pp. 85–87.

31. Cuffe may have waited in Philadelphia for the *Ranger* until November 7, but that seems unlikely considering the *Traveller's* near completion. He did leave the *Alpha* there. *Mercury,* Sept. 18, 1807, Jan. 1, 29, 1809; *Freeman's Journal,* Nov. 7, 1807; Cuffe financial receipt from New Bedford, Dec. 7, 1807, vol. 8, Cuffe MSS; brig *Traveller,* permanent certificate of registry, no. 28, Dec. 11, 1807, New Bedford Bureau of Customs, Registries, NA; WPA, *Ship Registries of New Bedford,* 1:3042; ship *Alpha,* proof of ownership, Dec. 28, 1807, record group 41, New Bedford Bureau of Customs, NA.

5. INTERNATIONAL FRIENDS OF AFRICAN CIVILIZATION

1. See Thomas, "Memoirs."

2. *Monthly Repository* 2:219–21; African Institution, *Committee Report,* p. 65; Fyfe, *Sierra Leone,* pp. 95–98, 105. See Curtin's discussion on the spread of "civilization" (*Africa,* pp. 142–43, 157–58, 253, 259–61). Less critical works referring to the African Institution's beginnings include George, *British West Africa,* pp. 152–54; Griggs, *Clarkson,* pp. 95, 112.

3. African Institution, *Committee Report,* pp. 9, 15–16, 65–71; *Philanthropist* 1 (Jan. 1810): 45–49; *Eclectic Review* (pt. 2, Dec. 1810): 642–43; Thomas Clarkson Papers, microfilm no. 958, p. 1, RHC.

4. *Life of Allen,* 1:60–64.

5. *Monthly Repository* 2:221.

6. William Sancho was the son of Ignatius Sancho, whose *Letters* appeared in 1782, the first work by an African to be published in England (see Fyfe, *Sierra Leone,* p. 13).

7. Subtitled *A Brief Account of the Proceedings of the Committee Appointed in the Year 1795 by the Yearly Meeting of Friends of Pennsylvania, New Jersey, ec. for Promoting the Improvement and Gradual Civilization of the Indian Nations.* The Baltimore Yearly Meeting spoke of a prospect "truly gladdening to the enlightened Christian mind, to survey the hastening of that day, when this part of the human family, weaned from savage habits, and allured by the superior advantages of civil life, shall exchange the tomahawk and scalping knife for the *plough* and the *hoe* so that the advantages of LIGHT and KNOWLEDGE" might be spread among them.

8. James's study shows that correspondence between the Permanent Indian Committee of the Philadelphia Yearly Meeting and those directly in contact with the Indians "simply ignored the whole subject" of preaching the gospel. The committee's policy was to avoid offending the Indian's religion (*People,* pp. 93, 286, 299–315, 332).

9. African Institution, *Committee Report,* pp. 24–26.

10. Clarkson, *African Slave-Trade,* 1:202; Pemberton to Logan, Jan. 1, 1805, Logan Papers, 5:57, HSP; Dillwyn to Pemberton, Oct. 20, 1804, Jan. 30,

31, Feb. 14, Mar. 15, July 1, Oct. 2, 1805, May 20, June 4, Dec. 1, 1806, June 5, 11, Pemberton Papers, 56:58, 76–77, 79, 84, 93, 99, 115, 118–19, 126–27, 142, HSP; Dillwyn to S & S Emlen, Jan. 25, Feb. 4, 1807, Emlen to Dillwyn, Feb. 26, 1807, Dillwyn MSS, vol. 4 (1807–11), LCP; Dillwyn to Pemberton, July 9, Aug. 12, 1807, Pemberton Papers, 56:152, 158, HSP; Emlens to Dillwyn, Feb. 26, 1807, Dillwyn MSS, vol. 4 (1807–11), LCP.

11. *Poulson's American Daily Advertiser,* Sept. 21, 22, 23, Oct. 20, 1807. Williams, *Oration;* Quarles, *Black Abolitionists,* p. 118; Morse, *Discourse;* Elsbree, "Missionary Spirit," p. 304; *Mercury,* Mar. 3, 11, 18, July 22, 1808.

12. Forten's home became the center of black abolitionist activity in Philadelphia. See Quarles, *Black Abolitionists,* pp. 3, 5, 9, 12, 19, 24, 27, 33, 180; Billington, "Forgotten Abolitionist."

13. Cuffe to Samuel R. Fisher, Jr., Feb. 28, 1806, vertical file, MdHS. Cuffe's letter of June 9, 1809, addresses John James and Alexander Wilson as acquaintances (vol. 6, Cuffe MSS). See Samuel Emlen to Dillwyn for Alexander Wilson's familiarity with the transatlantic correspondence, Dec. 15, 1807, vol. 4, Dillwyn MSS, LCP. Mifflin's letters between 1801 and 1807 catalogue her travels (letters and documents, Emlen Papers, HSP).

14. Evidently, publications from the Institution's July meeting did not reach Pemberton until after his visits with Cuffe. Existing records do not explain why the Cuffe memoir failed to arrive in Delaware and Philadelphia by September, or the following spring for that matter.

15. Mifflin to Dillwyn, Feb. 8, 1811, Cuffe to John James and Alexander Wilson, June 10, 1809, Pemberton to Cuffe, June 8, 1808, vol. 6, Cuffe MSS.

16. Dillwyn to Pemberton, Dec. 11, 1807, Pemberton Papers, 56:160, HSP; Pemberton to Jefferson, May 30, 1808, Jefferson Papers, 178:31503, LC; Pemberton to Cuffe, June 8, 1808, vol. 6, Cuffe MSS.

17. Pemberton to Cuffe, June 8, 1808, vol. 6, Cuffe MSS.

18. Dillwyn to Pemberton, June 1, July 6, Aug. 22, 1808, Pemberton Papers, 56:166, 169–70, HSP. Thompson assumed his duties as governor on July 27, 1808 (Colonial Office Sessional Papers, 270/11:1, PRO).

19. Men's Minutes, Feb. 13, Mar. 25, Apr. 16, and Women's Minutes, Mar. 19, 1808, Westport Monthly Meeting, RIHS.

20. Cuffe to Pemberton, Sept. 14, vol. 1, Cuffe MSS.

21. Pemberton to Cuffe, Sept. 27, 1808, vol. 6, Cuffe MSS. See also James, *People,* pp. 305–6.

22. Stephen Wanton Gould Diaries, June 14, 1804, Aug. 18, 1807, Jan. 12–Nov. 17, 1808, vols. 3, 9, RHC; see also Bartlett, *Slave to Citizen,* p. 35.

6. ECONOMIC AND PHILANTHROPIC PARTNERSHIPS

1. *Mercury,* May 20, June 3, 17, July 1, 8, Aug. 19, 1808.

2. Morison, *Maritime History,* p. 208.

3. *Mercury*, Jan. 20, Mar. 17, Apr. 7, 1809; William Rotch to George Logan, Jan. 9, 1809, Logan Papers, 5:88, HSP; Cuffe to John James and Alexander Wilson, June 10, 1809, vol. 6, Cuffe MSS.

4. *Traveller*, permanent certificate of registry, no. 31, May 15, 1809, New Bedford Bureau of Customs, Registries, 1808–9, NA.

5. *Mercury*, May 19, 1809.

6. Cuffe to James and Wilson, June 10, 1809, vol. 6, Cuffe MSS.

7. Rotch Family Papers, 1785–92, MHS; Rotch Papers, 1785–92, ODHS; Bullard, *Rotches*, pp. 36, 230; Rotch, *Memorandum*, pp. 33, 38, 45–68.

8. Starbuck, *American Whale Fishery*, 1:208; log of the bark *Hero*, Apr. 16–May 5, 1809, International Marine Archives Collection, ODHS.

9. Pemberton stated the following to some friends less than two weeks before his death: "I wish thee after I am gone to write to Wm Dillwyn, & relate to him the cause of my long delay. . . . I would have thee to keep up a correspondence with him: it may be very useful to thee on many occasions" ("Biographical Sketch of J. P.," handscript, James Pemberton Papers, HCAL). James and Wilson conveyed Cuffe's letter to England on June 21, forwarding a copy of their letter to Westport (vol. 6, Cuffe MSS).

10. July and August ads in the *Mercury* read "Cuff & Howards," then were corrected to Cuffe's preferred spelling.

11. *Mercury*, Apr. 28, May 26, July 7, 1809; *Traveller* manifest, May 22, 1809, *Ranger* manifests, June 15, 29, July 1, 1809, Miscellaneous Manifests, 1809–24, New Bedford Bureau of Customs, FRC; Jan. ?, May 13, 1809, Minutes of the Westport Monthly Meeting, pp. 122, 128, RIHS.

12. *Mercury*, July 28, Aug. 4, 1809.

13. *Mercury*, Oct. 27, Nov. 3, 10, 17, 24, Dec. 15, 22, 1809; *Ranger* manifest, Sept. 28, 1809, Inward Manifests, New Bedford Bureau of Customs, FRC; Abner Brownell financial statement, Oct. 8, 1809, vol. 10, Cuffe MSS.

14. *Mercury*, Jan. 12, Feb. 16, Mar. 2–June 22, Nov. 3, 1810. James to Cuffe, Nov. 8, 1809, June 30, 1810, vol. 6, Cuffe MSS; *Ranger* manifest, Feb. 5, 1810, Inward Manifests, New Bedford Bureau of Customs, FRC. For the first time in her fifteen years of service, the schooner *Ranger* failed to have a family captain—she sailed under the command of a man named Gifford, presumably Sylvester Gifford of Little Compton, R.I., who subsequently took the *Traveller* to Lisbon (*Mercury*, Mar. 9, 1810).

15. *Hero* manifest, Feb. 24, 1810, Inward Manifests, New Bedford Bureau of Customs, FRC; *Hero* receipts, Mar., Apr. 1810, vols. 8, 13, Cuffe MSS; log of the bark *Hero*, Nov. 3, 1808–Feb. 22, 1810, International Marine Archives, ODHS; *Mercury*, Mar. 2, 1810.

16. Macaulay to Dillwyn, Aug. 29, 1809, vol. 6, Cuffe MSS; Fyfe, *Sierra Leone*, pp. 48–77, 92–98, 105–10; Peterson, *Province of Freedom*, pp. 22–23; Curtin, *Africa*, pp. 98, 108, 142; Booth, *Macaulay*, pp. 17–24, 45–58, 72–81, 191.

17. African Institution, *Third Report*, pp. 1–33; Wilberforce and Wilber-

force, *Correspondence,* 2:50–52; Curtin, *Africa,* p. 69; Johnston, *Jay,* 4:320–22, 331; Macaulay to Rush, Aug. 1, 1809, 6:218, 224, and Letter Book, 1794–1809, pp. 109–14, Pennsylvania Abolition Society Papers, HSP.

18. Davis superbly places Allen within the context of British philanthropy and Quaker thought (*Slavery in the Age of Revolution,* pp. 242–49). See also Chapman-Huston and Cripps, *Allen & Hanbury's,* pp. 47–60; Allen, *Life and Labors,* pp. 8–20; *Life of Allen,* 1:1–84.

19. *Life of Allen,* 1:85–86; Allen to William Rotch, Jr., Nov. 14, 1809, vol. 21, Cuffe MSS.

20. Ricketson described the visit to Cuffe by Rotch and some English travelers in *New Bedford,* p. 255. The letter to John Parrish, although probably predating the event, helps to explain Cuffe's behavior (Aug. 9, 1807, Cox, Parrish, and Wharton Papers, 5:85, HSP). Clarkson's work had been advertised and promoted in the United States since late 1807 (Jefferson-Pemberton correspondence, June 21, Nov. 22, Dec. 7, 1808, Thomas Jefferson Papers, 178:31588, 182:32406, 183:32509, LC; *Poulson's American Daily Advertiser,* Oct. 20, 1807; *Mercury,* Apr. 21, 28, Dec. 29, 1809). Cuffe's reference to Clarkson's work appears in a log entry on the brig *Traveller,* Feb. 13, 1811, vol. 24, Cuffe MSS.

7. EMBARKING ON A CIVILIZING MISSION

1. Cuffe to [John James and Alexander Wilson], June 3, 1810, in *Life of Allen,* 1:100; James and Wilson to William Dillwyn, June 16, 1810, vol. 6, Cuffe MSS.

2. Cuffe's experience with the African Institution revealed its vast social and political potential, its use of antislavery propaganda, and its influence on Englishmen, Americans, and Sierra Leoneans in particular. But its inadequacies would plague Cuffe and many others. Generally, the Institution has received low marks from historians who have evaluated its effectiveness. Fyfe offers the most articulate political treatment of this organization (*Sierra Leone,* pp. 105–23). Peterson calls it "almost absolutely useless" for the indigenous African (*Province of Freedom,* p. 65). Curtin considers it one of several "important but distinct pressure groups" for British commitment to the Sierra Leone area and notes its later shift of focus to West Indies affairs (*Africa,* pp. 17, 142–43).

3. James and Wilson to Dillwyn, June 21, 1809, vol. 6, Cuffe MSS; William Allen to Thomas Haughton, [Feb. 1, 1810], Business Account Letter Book, 1805–15, William Allen Papers, A&H; Tolles, *Logan,* pp. 288–90; *Life of Allen,* 1:89–90; African Institution, *Fourth Report;* George Harrison to Robert Barclay, [July 18, 1810], William Wilberforce to Logan, July 20, 1810, Logan Papers, 5:112–13, HSP.

4. African Institution, *Third Report,* pp. 30–33; Harrison, *Some Remarks,*

pp. 3–8; Roscoe to the Duke of Gloucester, n.d., no. 1758, Roscoe Papers, LPL; *Life of Allen,* 1:91; Dillwyn to James Pemberton Pa[rker], Aug. 10, 1810, Pemberton Papers, 57:4, HSP; *Philanthropist* 1(1):16–21; Davis, *Slavery in the Age of Revolution,* n.51, 248.

5. *Life of Allen,* 1:92.

6. Stephen Wanton Gould Diary, June 11, Sept. 21, Oct. 26, 1810, vol. 10, RHC; L. H. Eddy to John Hartshorne, May 18, 1812, Moorland-Springarn Collection, HUL.

7. Westport Monthly Meeting Minutes, Sept. 15, Oct. 13, 1810, RIHS; Rathbones to Cuffe, Dec. 14, 1810, vol. 3, Cuffe MSS.

8. Property sale, Nov. 13, 1810, NBRD; Paul Cuffe to John Cuffe, Nov. 17, 1810, vol. 1, Cuffe MSS. See also announcements of closure and notices to debtors and creditors in the *Mercury,* Dec. 7, 14, 21, 28, 1810, Jan. 4, 11, 1811.

9. *Mercury,* Nov. 23, 1810; John Cuffe to Freelove Slocum, Jan. 5, 1811, *Traveller* log, Nov. [24], 25, 1810, Dec. 4, 1811, vols. 1, 24, Cuffe MSS; NEHGS, *Vital Records of Westport,* p. 243.

10. *Political and Commercial Register,* Dec. 5, 1810; *Freeman's Journal* and *Aurora General Advertiser,* Dec. 6, 1810. Cuffe's account of proceedings during his travels are recorded on fragmentary pages of the *Traveller*'s log. Two omissions are suspect, the first being for events in Philadelphia when he disagreed so heatedly with John James; the second is discussed later in note 29. Accounts for Dec. 4, 1810–Jan. 13, 1811, are missing as are those for Apr. 8–May 11, 1811 (vol. 24, Cuffe MSS).

11. Rhoads's account of Cuffe's moving testimony at the Arch Street Meeting House is not dated, but Cuffe's entry loosely dated Dec. 4 mentions approval by that meeting (Rhoads, "Yearly Meeting," p. 94; *Traveller* log, Dec. 4, 1810, undated testimony, vols. 19, 24, Cuffe MSS).

12. Rush recommendation, Dec. 27, 1810, vol. 6, Cuffe MSS. See also *Freeman's Journal,* Dec. 17, 27, 1810; *Aurora General Advertiser,* Dec. 18, 1810.

13. *Traveller* log, Jan. 14–Feb. 28, 1811, vol. 24, Cuffe MSS.

14. The *Traveller* log continues as Cuffe's journal during his stay in Sierra Leone (Mar. 1, 1811, vol. 24, Cuffe MSS). Physical descriptions of the scene also come from United States merchant Samuel Swan, who arrived on Mar. 12 of that year, and missionary George Warren, who sailed from England with Cuffe in Nov. (Bennett and Brooks, *New England Merchants,* p. 72; George Warren to Dr. Thomas Coke, Dec. 1, 1811, in *Methodist Magazine* 9:797; Mar. 1–30, 1811, log for the *Crocodile,* Captain's Logs, Admiralty Office Papers, 51/2198, PRO).

15. *Traveller* log, Mar. 2–4, 1811, vol. 24, Cuffe MSS; Feb. 12, 1810, Feb. 20, Apr. 30, 1811, Governor's Council, Colonial Office Sessional Papers, 270/11:55, 207, 270/12:8, PRO; Fyfe, *Sierra Leone,* pp. 106–13; Peterson, *Sierra Leone,* pp. 56–57.

16. *Traveller* log, Mar. 2, 5–11, 1811, Cuffe to William Allen, Mar. 24, 1811, vol. 24, Cuffe MSS; Mar. 12, 1811, *Crocodile* log and Governor's Council, Oct. 3, 1810, Colonial Office Sessional Papers 270/11:202, PRO; Fyfe, *Sierra Leone,* pp. 101, 105, 113–14, 116, 118; Bennett and Brooks, *New England Merchants,* pp. 47–48. Since 1794 American traders increasingly frequented Sierra Leone on African trading runs. In Mar. 1809, Governor T. P. Thompson told Lord Castlereagh, "I have no hesitation in declaring to your Lordship my conviction that this has hitherto been an American and not a British colony." Columbine and his successors opposed the arrival of United States' vessels (Brooks, *Yankee Traders,* pp. 52, 61, 64; Bennett and Brooks, *New England Merchants,* p. 58; Fyfe, *Sierra Leone,* p. 111.

17. Peterson (*Province of Freedom,* pp. 28–32, 45–47, 55–56) convincingly argues that England's paternalism prevented Nova Scotians from exerting themselves to the colony's benefit. Cuffe's experiences in the colony definitely confirm that view. Governors Thompson and Columbine were just the most recent to suppress settlers' energies; only John Clarkson, who first brought Nova Scotians to West Africa, was supportive of their efforts. Yet Clarkson's misrepresentation of the quit-rent policy involving payments later expected from settlers laid the seeds for lasting friction between the settlers and the colonial administrations. See Fyfe, *Sierra Leone,* pp. 28–42, 101, 104; Cuffe to Allen, Apr. 22, 1811, vol. 24, Cuffe MSS; Fergusson, *Clarkson's Mission.*

18. Shortly after Cuffe's arrival the Governor's Commission of Inquiry estimated that 1,917 persons lived within the walls of Freetown, but the census overlooked settlers from the Province of Freetown, the Kru, Europeans in the garrison, and about 1,000 liberated Africans (Colonial Office Sessional Papers 267/29:152–53, 270/12:3, PRO; Fyfe, *Sierra Leone,* p. 114, Fyfe, *Inheritance,* pp. 153–54; George, *British West Africa,* pp. 162–64; Crooks, *Royal African Corps,* p. 83).

19. Presumably the "letter of advice" was identical to that printed in England and New York (*Traveller* log, Mar. 13, 1810, printed enclosure in Paul Cuffe to John Cuffe, Aug. 12, 1811, vols. 1, 25, Cuffe MSS; *Brief Account of Sierra Leone,* p. 9).

20. *Traveller* log, Mar. 14, 18, 19, 31, 1811, Cuffe to Allen, Apr. 22, 1811, vol. 25, Cuffe MSS.

21. Holsoe, "Vai," pp. 293–95; MacCormack, "Sherbro," pp. 191–96; *Traveller* log, Mar. 5, 6, 9, 1811, vol. 24, Cuffe MSS. Smith, the defunct Sierra Leone Company's storekeeper, remained in the colony to trade and was appointed to the Vice-Admiralty Court by Columbine (Fyfe, *Sierra Leone,* p. 116).

22. *Traveller* log, Mar. 11, 12, 15, 1811. Henry Warren had broken away from the orthodox Methodist Church some time earlier and was preaching at Christ Chapel (Coke, *Narrative,* p. 33; Cuffe to Allen, Apr. 22, 1811, vol. 24, Cuffe MSS).

23. *Traveller* log, Mar. 26, 1811, vol. 24, Cuffe MSS.

24. Cuffe's journal entry for Apr. 7, the last daily notation to survive for the remainder of his first stay in Sierra Leone, reads as follows: "This forenoon went on board accompanied by Thomas Wainer, John Kizell ec Where We Stated a sketch of a Petition to Lay before the People for their approbation" (*Traveller* log, vol. 24, Cuffe MSS). Kizell was Cuffe's counterpart in Freetown, an ambitious trader, worshiper, and leader in the community (African Institution, *Sixth Report,* pp. 133–53; *Philanthropist* 2(7):293–97; Fyfe, *Sierra Leone,* pp. 62, 96, 113; Kizell to Thomas Ludlam, Apr. 6, 1807, in Donnan, *Documents,* 2:658–59).

25. A summary of Allen's letter appears in Cuffe's reply (Cuffe to Allen, Apr. 22, 24, 1811, copy of the Privy Council petition, July 27, 1811, vols. 6, 24, Cuffe MSS; Dillwyn to Emlens, Jan. 28, 1811, vol. 5, Dillwyn MSS, LCP; Wilberforce to the Admiralty Office, July 18, 1811, Admiralty Office Papers, 1/5080, PRO; Kizell to Allen, Feb. 9, 1812, "African Correspondence," pp. 3–6, William Allen Papers, A&H.

26. John Kizell claimed "a Society to be called 'the Friendly Society' . . . was proposed by me and others . . . prior to Capt Cuffee's departure from Sierra Leone for Europe" (Kizell to Allen, Feb. 9, 1812, "African Correspondence," pp. 3–4, William Allen Papers, A&H).

27. Governor's Council, Feb. 12, 1811, Colonial Office Sessional Papers 270/11:206–7, Mar. 9, Apr. 29, 1811, Colonial Office Sessional Papers 270/12:3, 7, PRO; Proclamation, vol. 24, Cuffe MSS.

28. Enclosure in Reinhold Nylander to the secretary of the Church Missionary Society, May 7, 1811, CAI/E2, no. 47, letters and journals, CMS.

29. Governor's Council, Mar. 30, 1811, Colonial Office Sessional Papers 270/12:9, PRO. With four Macaulays locally active in trade and/or politics, Smith clearly felt confident in channeling his attack on Cuffe through Zachary Macaulay in London (see Allen to Clarkson, July 15, 1811, in *Life of Allen,* 1:102). The suspicious absence of Cuffe's journal entries may have been related to provocative encounters since the day he met merchants aboard the *Traveller,* when entries stopped. They resumed once he was at sea.

30. *Crocodile,* Captain's log, May 10–22, 1811, Admiralty Office Papers, 51/2198, and Governor's Council, May 2, 10, 1811, Colonial Office Sessional Papers, 270/12:9, PRO; Cuffe to Thomas Wainer, n.d., and *Traveller* log, May 12, 1811, vols. 11, 24, Cuffe MSS; Fyfe, *Sierra Leone,* p. 113.

8. TAKING HIS MISSION TO ENGLAND

1. Cuffe's log entry shows that the harbor pilot came aboard at two o'clock in the afternoon, yet the brig did not tie up until four o'clock the next morning (*Traveller* log, July 12, 1811, vol. 24, Cuffe MSS). L. H. Eddy's information from both an American Friend, presumably Stephen Grellet, and an English newspaper spoke of people lining the shore (Eddy to John

Hartshorne, May 18, 1812, Moorland-Springarn Collection, HUL; *Edinburgh Review,* 18:321n; *Times* [London], Aug. 2, 1811).

2. Grellet probably reached Liverpool after Cuffe (Emlens to Dillwyn, June 7, 1811, Dillwyn to Emlens, July 27, 1811, vol. 5, Dillwyn MSS, LCP; Seebohm, *Grellet,* 1:171).

3. Dow, *Slave Ships,* pp. 111, 183–85; Williams, *Liverpool Privateers,* pp. ix, 678; Donnan, *Documents,* 2:48–49.

4. The *Liverpool Mercury* listed both entrances on July 19, 1811. The Rathbones assigned 118 bales of cotton from the *Alpha*'s cargo to J. Richardson (Minutes, July 15, Nov. 30, 1811, American Chamber of Commerce for the Port of Liverpool, pp. 154–56, Minutes, July 3, 1811, Committee Book, p. 146, African Company of Merchants Trading from Liverpool, LPL; Henderson, "Liverpool," p. 2, 3, 38, 56, 58. See also *Traveller* log, June 30, July 12–13, 1811, vol. 24, Cuffe MSS).

5. *Traveller* log, July 12–16, 1811, vol. 24, Cuffe MSS; *Times* (London), Aug. 2, 1811.

6. Allen to Thomas Clarkson, Allen to Thomas Thompson, July 15, 1811, in *Life of Allen,* 1:101–2 (most of Allen's diary pertinent to Cuffe appears in this book).

7. *Life of Allen,* 1:102; Wilberforce to Rt. Hon. Chat Yorke, July 18, 1811, Admiralty Office Papers 1/5080, Croker to William Hamilton, July 24, 1811, Admiralty Office Papers 2/666, p. 313, PRO; Allen to Henry Woollcombe, July 24, 1811 (summary from National Registry of Manuscripts and Archives, London; Dorothy S. Woollcombe of Plymouth informed me by letter dated July 30, 1972, that Allen's letter had been lost).

8. Wilberforce to Croker, July 18, 1811, Admiralty Office Papers 1/5080, PRO; Allen to Woollcombe, July 24, 1811, National Registry of Manuscripts and Archives (see note 7); Clarkson to Thompson, July 24, 1811, Spriggs MSS, 157:89, FHL; *Life of Allen,* 1:103.

9. Mifflin had explained her ideas for "colonizing some of the Blacks on the coast of Africa." The plan to establish American "returning Societies" would succeed if "a benevolent Company in England would join hands in the measure, and received subjects for it from this Country." She recalled having advocated the measure to Dillwyn "a few years back, showing my letter first to our friend James Pemberton, who approved, and said thou would immediately open the matter to Granville Sharp" (the earlier letter either preceded or referred to the one she had sent in late 1807). Mifflin then asked George Logan "in Congress" to discuss the plan with President Jefferson; Logan's final session had been in Mar. 1807. Sometime afterward, she learned of the society "promoting the civilization of the Africans." The Cuffe MSS copy does not list an intended recipient of Mifflin's letter (vol. 6, Cuffe MSS). For a sample of the Jefferson-Logan correspondence, see May 11, 1805, in Ford, *Thomas Jefferson,* 8:351–53. Curiously, Ann Mifflin's

exuberance in advocating the return of freed slaves to Africa has been ignored by historians of the subject.

10. *Traveller* log, July 20–22, Aug. 21, 1811, vol. 24, Cuffe MSS; Emlens to Dillwyn, Feb. 19, May 8, July 13, Aug. 20, 1811, and Dillwyn to Emlens, Jan. 28, May 1, Sept. 4, 1811, vol. 5, Dillwyn MSS, LCP. Dillwyn's May 1 letter reiterates how much he did to prepare for Cuffe's arrival, suggesting his disappointment with the outcome of the long-awaited meeting with the black Friend.

11. *Traveller* log, July 26–29, 1811, vol. 24, Cuffe MSS; Fyfe, *Sierra Leone*, pp. 31–51, 55, 63, 122–23; Peterson, *Province of Freedom*, pp. 28–32; Fergusson, *Clarkson's Mission*, pp. 8–29.

12. *Times* (London), Aug. 2, 1811; *Liverpool Mercury*, Aug. 9, 1811; *Traveller* log, July 26, 28, 30, Aug. 9, 13, 1811, vol. 24, Cuffe MSS. See also *Commercial Advertiser*, Oct. 17, 1811; *Mercury*, Oct. 18, 1811, quoting the *Boston Palladium;* excerpt of an unnamed English newspaper in the Rotch-Wales Papers (SCFL); *Monthly Repository* 6:509; copy of Felony Act and settlers' epistle in Paul Cuffe to John Cuffe, Aug. 12, 1811, vol. 1, Cuffe MSS.

13. *Traveller* log, Aug. 7, 1811, vol. 24, Cuffe MSS; Roscoe to Clarkson, Jan. 13, 1811, Macaulay to Roscoe, Apr. 10, 27, Aug. 8, 1811, Roscoe to Macaulay, June 19, 1811, and related correspondence, Roscoe Papers, nos. 861, 2482–86, LPL.

14. *Traveller* log, Aug. 2–17, 1811, Cuffe to Thomas Wainer, July 27, 1811, Cuffe to John Cuffe, Aug. 12, 1811, vols. 1, 24, Cuffe MSS.

15. Davis's (*Slavery in the Age of Revolution*, pp. 227–28, 233–49) searching study of Allen's "inner conflicts" raises many points which apply to Cuffe. The late-eighteenth-century Quaker revival involved the two overlapping phases of quietism and evangelism, and Allen encompassed both outlooks. He searched for truth in natural sciences as well as religion. He considered possession of a Bible equal to possession of a job, and found "serious" religion. Social reform was a "spiritual" outlet to him but it was secular by traditional standards. Similarly, quietism and evangelism overlapped in Cuffe's outlook on social reform. His extended success in maritime commerce only recently had allowed him to seek a balance with philanthropy, which increased with his mission to Africa and England. Friends James Pemberton and William Dillwyn always had stressed a "civilizing" mission rather than an evangelizing one; their appeal substantially differed from Samuel Hopkins's traditional evangelical appeal. Cuffe's future cooperation with Christian missionaries reinforced his theory of a holistic civilizing approach, something Allen surely approved of. Hence Cuffe, like Allen, was a secular social reformer by standards of orthodox Christianity.

16. *Traveller* log, Aug. 21, 23, 26, 28, 29, 1811, Mary Cropper to Cuffe, Aug. 23, 1811, vols. 6, 24, Cuffe MSS; *Life of Allen*, 1:104.

17. *Philanthropist* 2:43; Wilberforce to Macaulay, Aug. 6, 1811, William Wilberforce Papers, WPL; Wilberforce to Allen, Aug. 10, 1811, manuscript

portfolio no. 27, p. 38, FHL; Wilberforce to Battel, Aug. 24, 1811, loose letters, William Allen Papers, A&H; *Traveller* log, July 25, 26, Aug. 26, 1811, vol. 24, Cuffe MSS; *Life of Allen,* 1:104. Cuffe had not gone to England simply to acquire land allotments, as Quarles suggests (*Black Abolitionists,* p. 130).

18. *Traveller* log, Aug. 27, 1811, rough notes from Aug. 27, 1811, vols. 6, 24 Cuffe MSS; Resolution of the African Institution, "African Correspondence," pp. 56–57, William Allen Papers, A&H, and vol. 6, Cuffe MSS. Cuffe's image of "African improvement" meant much the same to essayist Leigh Hunt after their meeting: "an excellent specimen of what freedom and instruction can do for the outcastes of color" (in Dykes, *English Romantic Thought,* p. 89).

19. Cuffe's entry notes what he heard the directors say and what he felt himself (*Traveller* log, Aug. 27, 1811, vol. 24, Cuffe MSS). Allen's immediate entry lacked the skepticism reported later in *Philanthropist,* but his published position was consistent with his opening probe to John Kizell a few days later (*Life of Allen,* 1:104; *Philanthropist* 2:41–43; African Institution, *Sixth Report,* pp. 26–28).

20. The extraordinary collection of letters that resulted are in a 225–page leatherbound volume labeled "African Correspondence," William Allen Papers, A&H. The letters involving Allen, Cuffe, and the settlers illustrate the triangular communication system initiated during Cuffe's meetings.

21. *Traveller* log, Sept. 2–6, 8, 9, 15, 16, 1811, vol. 24, Cuffe MSS; Cuffe to Allen, Sept. 9, 1811, loose letters, William Allen Papers, A&H; Cuffe to Thomas and Frances Thompson, n.d., George Stacey Gibson Collection, 1:71, FHL; Fyfe, *Sierra Leone,* p. 113. Russian Tsar Alexander I's eventual proposal for a Holy Alliance to end wars came after meeting William Allen and fellow British Quakers in 1814. Twice Cuffe's entry refers to an international "mutual path" on Africa's behalf (*Life of Allen,* 1:143–47; Allen, *Life and Labors,* pp. 22–35; Davis, *Slavery in the Age of Revolution,* p. 227).

22. *Liverpool Mercury,* Sept. 6, 13, 1811; *Traveller* log, Sept. 7, 10, 11, 14, 1811, various *Traveller* accounts, vols. 6, 10, 24, Cuffe MSS.

23. *Traveller* log, Sept. 18–20, 1811, vol. 24, Cuffe MSS. Bishop Coke could not say enough to commend the "pious Quaker" acquainted with the sea and Sierra Leone. "The ship is wholly manned by American sailors of the same description and complexion with the Captain; the first, in all probability that ever entered into, or sailed from, an English port. And what tends to render the circumstance still more remarkable is that we have reason to believe there was not a seaman on board who did not fear God" (Coke, *Narrative,* pp. 20–21; Candler, *Coke,* p. 253).

24. The Oct. 4 and 11 issues stated that the biography was "written for the *Liverpool Mercury.*" The separate 1811 printing of the "Memoir of Captain Paul Cuffee, A Man of Color" pushed the *Mercury* deeper into self-serving—and false—acclaim, stating that the memoir was "Written ex-

pressly for, and originally printed" on its pages. (Until I discovered evidence of the earlier [1807] version [see chap. 5], this 1811 biography was considered by historians to be the earliest memoir of Cuffe [see, e.g., Harris, *Paul Cuffe,* p. 52].) The *Mercury*'s 1811 printing simply eliminated reference to Cuffe's seizure by the British during the War for Independence and his two whaling voyages, and replaced the *Monthly Repository*'s ending with a few paragraphs updating events since 1806. Quaker publisher William Alexander of York added the Sierra Leone epistle at the end (1811, 1812), and affixed Allen's name as a codistributor. See also *Christian Observer,* 10:825–31; *Philanthropist* 2(5):32–44; *Universal Magazine* (n.s.) 17:146–48.

9. THE FRIENDLY SOCIETY OF SIERRA LEONE

1. Warren to Francis Collier, Dec. 6, 1811, *Methodist Magazine* (n.s.) 8:316–17; *Traveller* log, Oct. 4, 1811, vol. 24, Cuffe MSS.

2. *Traveller* log, Nov. 12, 1811, vol. 24, Cuffe MSS; Warren to Collier, Dec. 6, 1811, *Methodist Magazine* (n.s.) 8:317; Fyfe, *Sierra Leone,* pp. 103–4. Alexander Smith's interim appointment as a judge advocate ended when Robert Thorpe arrived. Zachary Macaulay had written Smith from England; Cuffe had asked Thomas Wainer to send "love to Judge Smith" (Fyfe, *Sierra Leone,* p. 116; Cuffe to Wainer, July 24, 1811, vol. 1, Cuffe MSS).

3. Minutes of Governor's Council, July 1, 10, 17, 1811, pp. 10–11, Colonial Office Sessional Papers 270/13:9–10, Maxwell to Earl of Liverpool, July 29, 1811, Letters to Secretary of State, Public Record Office 30 26/102 and Colonial Office Sessional Papers 267/30, PRO.

4. After nearly a month of local trade Cuffe sent fifteen letters and financial accounts by way of the HMS *Thais* (*Traveller* log, Nov. 13–16, 18–23, 25–30, Dec. 4–6, 1811, vol. 24, Cuffe MSS). Two epistles to Allen were passed on to William Dillwyn; they said "little of his [Cuffe's] future prospects, or of any Cause of Discouragement" (*Life of Allen,* 1:105–6; Dillwyn to Emlens, Feb. 5, 1812, Dillwyn MSS, LCP; William Rathbone to Cuffe, Nov. 30, 1812, vol. 24, Cuffe MSS).

5. *Traveller* log, Nov. 25, 1811, vol. 24, Cuffe MSS. George Warren's letters and diaries provided almost daily details of meetings with settlers, Englishmen, and natives. He gave a lengthy description of the meeting with King George and then spoke of the "young Mulatto man, a native of Cape Coast Castle," who had been educated in England. They were told that twice every Sunday "a black clergyman" held services at the Cape Castle (Warren to Dr. Coke, daily journal beginning Nov. 13, 1811, Warren to Francis Collier, Dec. 6, 1811, *Methodist Magazine* [n.s.] 8:316–18, 636–39, 795–96; *Traveller* log, Nov. 25, 1811, vol. 24, Cuffe MSS).

6. Affixed to a New York Quaker publication, *Brief Account of Sierra Leone* (1812), was an "Address To my scattered brethren and fellow countrymen in Sierra Leone." "Grace be unto you and peace be multiplied from God

our Father," began the sermonette. The text earnestly recommended "the propriety" of assembling together for worship. Worshipers were to monthly "consult with each other" for their mutual good; monthly meeting records were to be kept. The address closed by calling for their "temporal and spiritual welfare." This document represents the Friend's strongest appeal to convert Africans.

7. "That Captain Cuffe was anxious to promote the object of our mission," wrote Bishop Coke, "may easily be gathered from the various occasions on which he has been introduced" (*Narrative,* p. 47).

8. *Traveller* log, Dec. 1, 2, 1811, vol. 24, Cuffe MSS. The colony's chaplain grew more dejected as he awaited the new Church Missionary Society recruits. On Dec. 9 he moaned, "if we neglect Bullom Shore, they [the Methodists] will take it." John Wilhelm and Jonathan Klein reached Freetown in time for a very depressing Christmas. First, Cuffe brought the unpleasant news that the Methodists had Arabic Bibles and were sending missionaries to Bulom. Then the newcomers watched how "the natives were the whole night feasting and firing and dancing, in celebration of Christmas." Leopold Butscher, another CMS missionary, arrived on Jan. 4, 1812 (Klein and Wilhelm letter-journals to CMS Secretary, Oct. 3, 16, Nov. 20, 23–25, Dec. 31, 1811, Nylander to Secretary, Dec. 9, 1811, Butscher to Secretary, Jan. 11, 1812, letters and journals, CAI/E2, nos. 101, 108, 110, 113–16, 119–20, CMS).

9. The provocative preamble to the Militia Act called for protection against "all Enemies, Pirates, and Rebels, both at Sea and Land . . . in, or out of the limits, of the said Colony." The oath put settlers at the mercy of their officers: "I A.B. do sincerely promise and swear, that I will be true and faithful, and bear true allegiance to His Majesty King George; and that I will faithfully serve in the Militia of this Colony, for the defence of the same, until I shall be legally discharged. So help me God" (Colonial Office Sessional Papers 269/1, 270/13:33, Wm M Caulay [*sic*] to Maxwell, Jan. 15, 1812, Colonial Office Sessional Papers 267/34, PRO; Fyfe, *Sierra Leone,* pp. 118–19).

10. Erroneous assertions about the Friendly Society became popular on Cuffe's return to the United States. For example, he was quoted as stating that a body of Sierra Leoneans had been formed "some time since for the further promotion of the christian religion" (*Brief Account of Sierra Leone,* p. 6). That claim, if it refers to the Friendly Society, is not justified (*Traveller* log, Dec. 11, 18, 1811, vol. 24, Cuffe MSS; Warren and Wise to Allen, Feb. 4, 1812, Kizell to Allen, Feb. 9, 1812, "African Correspondence," pp. 3–10, William Allen Papers, A&H; see also chap. 10). Fyfe's contention, with which Harris agrees, that the Society was formed from one of the Methodist congregations, is simply incorrect. While many of the settlers were Methodists, Baptists John Kizell and Warwick Francis had been major forces since the original movement for settler unity (see chap. 7). But even without the Allen and Hanbury material, Fyfe accurately describes the reality of "a co-

operative trading society to break the European merchants' monopoly" (*Sierra Leone,* p. 113; Harris, *Paul Cuffe,* p. 55).

11. Governor's Council, Jan. 4, 1812, Colonial Office Sessional Papers 270/13:44, PRO; Fyfe, *Sierra Leone,* pp. 18–19.

12. *Traveller* log, Jan. 1, 3, 4, 6, 1812, vol. 24, Cuffe MSS. The lease on the East Street property, purchased during his first visit, would take effect after Cuffe left for America. William Henry Savage, the leasee, agreed "not to keep bad house, such as frolicking, drinking, or harboring bad company" (lease copy, Jan. 1, 1812, *Traveller* log, Feb. 8, 1812, vol. 24, Cuffe MSS). Savage received twenty-five pounds a year as clerk of the court of requests; later he succumbed to slave trading (Colonial Office Sessional Papers 270/13:13, PRO; Fyfe, *Sierra Leone,* p. 142).

13. Allen's Aug. 29 letter is discussed in chapter 8. Initially, Cuffe refused any more apprentices for fear they would be seized at sea. Many more applied as he searched about for local business opportunities (*Traveller* log, Jan. 7, 10, 16, 20, 24, Feb. 1, 4, 5, 1812, vol. 24 Cuffe MSS).

14. *Traveller* log, Jan. 16, 18, 23, 26, 27, Feb. 1, 2, 4, 5, 1812, vol. 24, Cuffe MSS; Warren and Wise to Allen, Feb. 4, 1812, Kizell to Allen, Feb. 9, 1812, "African Correspondence," pp. 3–10, William Allen Papers, A&H.

15. Kizell to Allen, Feb. 9, 1812, "African Correspondence," pp. 3–6, William Allen Papers, A&H. The *Philanthropist* (2:201) summarized Cuffe's letter to Allen, dated Feb. 8, 1812.

16. Cuffe spoke with Maxwell twice before leaving. The governor's written confirmation assured "every protection and encouragement will be given to persons of industrious habits who will remove to the Colony" (*Traveller* log, Jan. 24, Feb. 10, 1810, Maxwell to Cuffe, Feb. 8, 1810, vols. 6, 24, Cuffe MSS). Arguments with Smith lasted to the end (Jan. 9, 22, 28, 30, Feb. 4, 6, 7, 1812, vol. 24, Cuffe MSS). The African Institution's investigation of Smith's earlier complaints concluded in early 1814 that Cuffe had been ill-used (*Life of Allen,* 1:138).

17. Drake speaks of Cuffe's "Pan-African sentiments" ("Negro Americans," pp. 673–75). Lynch casts him within "Pan-Africanism and Pan-Negro nationalism" ("Pan-Negro Nationalism," pp. 42, 46–48; *Blyden,* pp. 6–9). See also Legum, *Pan-Africanism,* p. 14; Shepperson, "Negro American Influences," pp. 192–207.

18. Contee, "Du Bois," p. 48.

10. A PAN-AFRICAN RETURNS

1. *Life of Allen,* 1:107–8.

2. Allinson, "Cuffee," p. 268. See also *Traveller* log, Feb. 19–Apr. 8, 1812, vol. 24, Cuffe MSS.

3. *Traveller* log, Apr. 9–21, 1812, vol. 24, Cuffe MSS; *Poulson's American Daily Advertiser,* Apr. 14, 1812; *Columbian,* May 1, 1812. The public papers

were filled with outrage over the latest series of embargo laws, the most recent being on Apr. 4, 1812 (see *Columbian,* May 1, 25, 1812; *Evening Post,* May 20, 1812; *United States Gazette,* Apr. 23, 1812; *Mercury,* Apr. 24, 1812; Treasury Department Circular, Apr. 4, 1812, Letters Received from the Secretary of the Treasury, Newport Bureau of Customs, NA).

4. Brig *Traveller* manifest, Feb. 10, 1812, Inward Manifests, *Traveller* Entry of Merchandise, May 29, 1812, Coasters Manifests, New Bedford Bureau of Customs, FRC; *Traveller* accounts, n.d., vol. 6, Cuffe MSS; Greene, *Colonial New England,* pp. 30, 58; *Traveller* log, Apr. 22–24, 1812, vol. 24, Cuffe MSS; Stephen Wanton Gould Diary, Apr. 21, 22, 24, 1812, vol. 10, RHC. Cuffe was accused of violating the Non-Importation Act (Moses Brown to William Thornton, Apr. 27, 1812, vol. 4, William Thornton Papers, LC).

5. *Traveller* log, Apr. 24–27, 1812, vol. 24, Cuffe MSS; L. H. Eddy to John Hartshorne, May 18, 1812, Moorland-Springarn Collection, HUL. Cuffe later paid Robbins for his services (*Traveller* receipt, June 11, 1812, vol. 6, Cuffe MSS). Judge Constant Tabor had been a slave merchant (Greene, *Colonial New England,* pp. 57–49). Martin and Champlin, the latter coming from a prominent slave-trading family, may have given Cuffe their recommendations in Providence (Eddy to Hartshorne, May 18, 1812, Moorland-Springarn Collection, HUL; Greene, *Colonial New England,* pp. 29–30, n.86; *Mercury,* July 7, 1809). Dr. Walter Channing may have heard of Cuffe when studying in London hospitals during 1811. He had just returned from Europe and joined the staff of the Harvard Medical School in 1815 (Eaton, "Medicine," p. 67; *Weekly Messenger,* Nov. 2, 1815). Cuffe already knew of Varnum (*Mercury,* June 2, 1809).

6. *Traveller* log, Apr. 27, May 1, 8, 1812, vol. 24, Cuffe MSS.

7. Brown, *Free Negroes,* pp. 11, 15; *Spectator,* May 6, 1812; *Traveller* log, May 2, 1812, vol. 24, Cuffe MSS; Drake, *Quakers,* p. 124.

8. Madison had endorsed the location of a settlement in Africa on the grounds that it "might prove a great encouragement to manumission in the Southern parts of the U.S. . . . This [freedom] is rendered impossible by the prejudice of the whites, prejudices which proceeding principally from the difference of color must be considered as permanent and insuperable" (quoted in William Thornton to Etienne Claviere, 1788, vol. 14, Miscellaneous Writings of Negro Colonization, William Thornton Papers, LC). In 1814 Madison reportedly wanted blacks to remain in the United States (see chap. 11); five years later the president proposed a plan for removing all blacks to Africa (Madison to Robert J. Evans, June 15, 1819, in Fendell, *Madison,* 3:133–38; "Madison's Attitude Toward the Negro," *Journal of Negro History* 6 [Jan. 1921]: 74–102; Jordan, *White over Black,* pp. 552–53). For Madison's hesitation to endorse removal of slaves "upon the plan contemplated by Paul Cuffee," see chap. 11.

9. The previous day Madison had granted special permission for a vessel

to carry Stephen Kingston from Philadelphia to Havana "for the sole purpose of landing him and his baggage at that place." In contrast, 538 Boston merchants were turned down after petitioning for protection of their returning vessels (*Baltimore American,* May 5, 1812; *Repertory & General Advertiser,* May 15, 1812; *Spectator,* May 20, 1812). Directness in manner of speech typified nineteenth-century Quakers (*Friends Intelligencer,* p. 412; Cadbury, "Negro Membership," p. 199; conversation with Thomas E. Drake, Aug. 15, 1983).

10. *Traveller* log, May 3–4, 1812, vol. 24, Cuffe MSS. Gallatin issued a formal statement releasing Cuffe's property from Customs (Gallatin statement, attested by Edmund H. Ellery, Clerk of the Rhode Island District, vol. 6, Cuffe MSS). Obviously concerned that his reporting might be questioned, Cuffe concluded that Hutchinson "was eye and ear witness to what is afore written."

11. *Traveller* log, May 5, 1812, vol. 26, Cuffe MSS.

12. Coker and Cuffe commenced a relationship that would lead Coker to Sierra Leone eight years later. *Coker Journal,* p. 29; *Religious Remembrancer,* 8th ser., 3 (Sept. 9, 1820): 11; Bacon, *Journal,* p. 5.

13. *Traveller* log, May 7, 1812, vol. 24, Cuffe MSS; *Federal Gazette,* May 7, 1812; *American and Commercial Advertiser,* May 8, 1812.

14. *Traveller* log, May 8–11, 1812, vol. 24, Cuffe MSS; Minutes, May 25, 1811, Feb. 22, 1812, Constitution and Minutes, African School Society, 1809–35, HSD; Dillwyn to Emlens, May 6, 1812, Emlens to Dillwyn, May 5, 1812 (entry dated the 14th), vol. 5, Dillwyn MSS, LCP. Cuffe was advised by Friends in every metropolitan area he visited, suggesting that they wished blacks to benefit from transatlantic correspondence as they had (Cuffe to Allen, June 12, 1812, "African Correspondence," pp. 43–45, William Allen Papers, A&H, and vol. 21, Cuffe MSS).

15. *Traveller* log, May 9–12, 1812, vol. 24, Cuffe MSS; *Poulson's American Daily Advertiser,* May 11, 1812.

16. *Traveller* log, May 14, 1812, vol. 24, Cuffe MSS. The two most respected black societies at the time were the African Society of Mutual Relief, incorporated two years earlier, and the African Methodist Episcopal Zion Church, established at the turn of the century. Peter Williams, Jr., the city's black antislavery orator, presided over what came to be called the New York African Institution (Williams, *Oration; Mercury,* Mar. 4, 1808; Cuffe to Williams, June 13 or 14, 1816, vol. 3, Cuffe MSS; Rush and Collins, *African Methodist Episcopal Church,* pp. 9–31; Quarles, *Black Abolitionists,* p. 118).

17. *Columbian,* May 14, 1812; *Traveller* log, May 14, 16, 1812, copy of Petition to the Methodist Society, May 16, 1812, vols. 6, 24, Cuffe MSS; L. H. Eddy to John Hartshorne, May 18, 1812, Moorland-Springarn Collection, HUL. There is no record as to how the Methodist Conference dealt with Cuffe's query. Cuffe's journal provides a rare opportunity to read of his revulsion at the cruelty of chattel slavery.

18. The full title of the publication illustrates its publicity value: *A Brief*

Account of the Settlement and Present Situation of The Colony of Sierra Leone, in Africa; as Communicated by Paul Cuffe (A Man of Colour) to his Friend in New York; also, an Explanation of the Object of his Visit; and Some Advice to the People of Colour in the United States. To Which is Subjoined, An address to the people of colour from the Convention of Delegates from the Abolition Societies in the U. States.

19. *Traveller* log, May 22–23, 1812, vol. 24, Cuffe MSS. Cuffe complained to Moses Brown, who consulted with Judge Barnes and reported that the charges were legitimate (Cuffe to Brown, May 22, 1812, Cuffe to Brown and Thomas Arnold, June 6, 1812, Brown to Cuffe, June 10, 1812, 12:29, 31, Moses Brown Papers, RIHS). Thirty-two days of wharfage fees also were paid. The Westporter obviously was dissatisfied with the entire transaction (receipts, June 11, 21, 1812, Cuffe to Allen, June 12, 1812, vols. 6, 21, Cuffe MSS).

20. Insufficient records prevent a full disclosure of Cuffe's accounts at this point. Abraham Barker of New York and John James of Philadelphia both handled some sales for him. See receipts, June 6, 30, Aug. 14, 1812, Jan. 9, 1813, Abraham Barker to Cuffe, Aug. 28, 1812, vols. 6, 7, 10, Cuffe MSS. For P & A Howard's business see receipts, June 20, 1812, plus undated accounts, vol. 10, Cuffe MSS.

21. Cuffe to Sanders, Roberts, and Lockes, June 6, 1812 (Peter Howard may have hand-carried this letter to Boston), Slaughter Collection, TAL; Cuffe to Allen, June 12, 1812, "African Correspondence," pp. 43–45, William Allen Papers, A&H.

22. Cuffe to Saunders, Roberts, and Lockes, June 6, 1812, Slaughter Collection, TAL.

23. Saunders to Cuffe, June 25, 1812, and Saunders, Jarvis, and Lockes to Cuffe, Aug. 3, 1812, vol. 6, Cuffe MSS; Cuffe to "African Sierra Leone Benevolent Society," July 14, 1812, Cuffe to Lockes, July 30, 1812, NYHS.

24. Friendly Society to Allen, May 3, July 30, 1812, John Kizell to Allen, July 30, 1812, Allen to Friendly Society, Allen to Kizell, Apr. 30, 1812, pp. 11–30, William Allen Papers, A&H.

25. See African Institution, *Sixth Report,* pp. 11–28, 78–87, 114–23, 153; Allen and Clarkson to Cuffe, July 1, 1812, enclosing directors' resolutions dated Feb. 4, June 16, 1812, Allen to Cuffe, Aug. 4, 13, 1812, Allen to William Rotch, Jr., Aug. 13, 1812, Cornelius Hanbury to Cuffe, July 17, 1812, vol. 21, Cuffe MSS; Wilberforce petitions, June 24, July 10, 24, 1812, Colonial Office Sessional Papers 267/34–35, June 11, 1812, Colonial Office Sessional Papers 268/6: 287, PRO; July 6, 1812, no. 2639, William Roscoe Papers, LPL.

26. Letter-copy, Cuffe to Allen, June 12, 1812, and undated letter, vol. 21, Cuffe MSS. One of the two was written on July 15 or 30, 1812. Very few Cuffe family records have been saved other than those pertaining to business, yet it is clear that Alice Cuffe's native American roots bound her to the United States. Cuffe's financial obligations included his continuing

problems with John James. Receipts and letters verify James's mounting indebtedness to Cuffe, Cuffe's appointment of Samuel R. Fisher, Jr., as his Philadelphia lawyer, and risks the ship *Alpha* posed to Cuffe's reputation in the Quaker City (Rotch statements, May 20, 1813, Feb. 5, 1814, power of attorney, Feb. 28, 1814, Fisher to Cuffe, Mar. 26, June 28, Sept. 16, 1814, Cuffe to Fisher, Nov. 8, 1814, vols. 6, 26, Cuffe MSS).

27. E.g., *American Watchman and Delaware Republican,* Dec. 12, 16, 19, 1812; *Poulson's American Daily Advertiser,* Dec. 24, 1812; *Pennsylvania Gazette,* Dec. 16, 1812; *Mercury* [from the *Spectator*], Jan. 8, 1812. Cuffe may have left the *Liverpool Mercury*'s memoir with James Brian; hence its initial appearance in the Delaware paper.

11. WAR BRINGS FURTHER DELAYS

1. Vol. 15, Cuffe MSS; Men's Monthly Meeting, Jan. 21, Feb. 18, Apr. 15, Aug. 19, 1813, Mar. 17, 1814, Westport Monthly Meeting Records, RIHS.

2. William Rotch, Jr., to Cuffe, Jan. 27, 1813, Cuffe to Rotch, May 23, 1813, enclosing copy of Cuffe to Little, n.d., Tyson to Cuffe, May 12, 1813, Little to Cuffe, May 13, 1813, vol. 6, Cuffe MSS.

3. Cuffe to the President, Senate, and House of Representatives of the United States of America, June 16, 1813, James Madison Papers, microcopy ser. 2, p. 4, MdHS; House of Representatives Papers, HR 12A-GA.5, NA. The copy sent to Washington was not in Cuffe's handwriting; the word "free" was twice added to Cuffe's draft in the same hand: "One of these objects was to keep up an intercourse with the (free) people of colour. . . . These views having been communicated by your petitioner to the (free) people of Colour. . . ." Cuffe's Baltimore advisors must have made the final copy (Tyson to Cuffe, July 20, 1813, vol. 6, Cuffe MSS).

4. Cuffe to Lockes, Aug. 18, 1813, CHS; Allen to Cuffe, Oct. 29, 1812, vol. 5, Cuffe MSS, and "African Correspondence," pp. 52–56, William Allen Papers, A&H; Cuffe to Allen, Sept. 28, 1813, Nov. 8, 1813, "African Correspondence," pp. 94–97, 154–58, William Allen Papers, A&H.

5. Maxwell to Earl Bathurst, Nov. 24, 1812, Colonial Office Sessional Papers 267/34, Governor's Council Minutes, Jan. 5, 11, 16, Feb. 15, 1813, Colonial Office Sessional Papers 270/13, Minutes, Mar. 29, 1813, Colonial Office Sessional Papers 270/14, PRO; John Thorpe to William Allen, July 11, 1814, Maxwell Proclamation, Mar. 1, 1813, Friendly Society [Henry Warren] to Allen, Mar. 12, 30, June 20, 1813, Rules and Regulations of the Friendly Society, enclosed Mar. 12, 1814, John Kizell to Allen, Mar. 14, June 3, 1813, Kizell to Thomas Clarkson, May 30, 1813, James Wise to Allen, Mar. 15, 1813, Friendly Society [James Reid] to Allen, Nov. 10, 1813, Reinhold Butscher to Allen, July 8, 1814, John Thorpe to Allen, July 11, 1814, with Maxwell's Proclamation, Mar. 1, 1813, "African Correspondence," pp. 70–90, 93, 130–38, 140–44, William Allen Papers, A&H.

6. Corresponding numbers of Allen's *Philanthropist* attacked misleading African Institution reports (*Seventh Report,* pp. 32–33; *Eighth Report,* pp. 14–15, 17–18; *Philanthropist* 3 [no. 12, 1813]: 301–35, 4 [no. 13, 1814]: 89–91; *Edinburgh Review* 21 [July 1813]: 472–73). Evidence of the cover-up can be seen in a letter from Earl Bathurst to Governor Maxwell, Aug. 29, 1813, Colonial Office Sessional Papers 268/19, PRO.

7. Summary of a statement made to Bathurst by a deputation from the African Institution, to which a published Cuffe memoir was attached, Dec. 3, 1813, Colonial Office Sessional Papers 267/35, PRO.

8. Chetnynd(?) to Henry Goulburn, Dec. 16, 1813, Colonial Office Sessional Papers 267/37, PRO.

9. Jan. 28, 1814, Colonial Office Sessional Papers 267/41, 1551, PRO.

10. House, *Annals of Congress,* 13th Cong., 2d sess., Jan. 7, 1814, 26:569, 861–63, NA; *Niles Weekly Register,* Jan. 22, 1814.

11. Senate, *Annals,* 13th Cong., 2d sess., Jan. 10, 11, 1814, 26:570, 572, NA; printed bill, Jan. 10, 1814, Senate documents, 13th Cong., 2d sess., NA.

12. See *United States Gazette,* Jan. 12, 19, 1814, *Aurora General Advertiser,* Jan. 12, 13, 1814; *Poulson's Daily Advertiser,* Jan. 11, 13, 1814; *Baltimore Whig,* Jan. 10, 15, 1814; *Daily Advertiser,* Jan. 10, 12, 1814; *Niles Weekly Register,* Jan. 22, 1814; *American Watchman,* Jan. 19, 22, 1814; *Commercial Advertiser,* Jan. 8, 11, 13, 29, 1814; *Evening Post,* Jan. 8, 13, 28, 1814; *Columbian,* Jan. 10, 13, 15, 18, 29, 1814; *Gazette,* Jan. 10, 11, 14, 29, 1814, *Spectator,* Jan. 12, 15, Feb. 2, 1814; *Herald,* Jan. 12, 15, 29, 1814. Papers elsewhere were equally diligent: *Daily Advertiser,* Jan. 27, 29, 1814; *Baltimore Whig,* Jan. 27, 28, 29, Feb. 11, 1814; *Niles Weekly Register,* Feb. 5, 19, 1814; *American Watchman,* Feb. 2, 1814; *Poulson's American Daily Advertiser,* Jan. 29, 31, Feb. 3, 12, 1814; *United States Gazette,* Feb. 2, 1814; *Mercury,* Jan. 21, 28, Feb. 4, 18, 1814; *New England Palladium,* Jan. 14, 18, 1814; *Weekly Messenger,* Feb. 4, 1814.

13. Senate, *Annals,* 13th Cong., 2d sess., Jan. 24, 25, 27, 1814, 26:599, 501, 602, NA; House, *Annals,* 13th Cong., 2d sess., Jan. 27, 31, Feb. 9, 1814, 26:1150, 1195, 1265, NA; *American State Papers,* 1:996.

14. House, *Annals,* 13th Cong., 2d sess., Mar. 18, 1814, 27:1880–81, NA.

15. Boston's *Weekly Messenger* (Mar. 4, 1814) picked up the story from the *New York Evening Post.* The *Annals* report was carried verbatim by most newspapers in Washington, D.C., Baltimore, Wilmington, Philadelphia, New York, New Bedford, and Boston.

16. Kersey talked with Micajah Crew, John Hopkins, and Hugh Mercer to discover that persons considered free blacks were dangerous because they "associate[d] with the slaves" and stole property. Kersey found Madison advocating that freed slaves be scattered throughout the Union wherever welcomed (June 1, 1814, Kersey Journal, Jesse Kersey Papers, HCAL; Kersey, *Narrative,* pp. 74–82).

17. Cuffe to Allen, Aug. 6, 1814, "African Correspondence," pp. 152–54, William Allen Papers, A&H.

18. Truite to Cuffe, Dec. 6, 1814, Nath. G. M. Lenter to Cuffe, Feb. 13, 1814, Mercer to Cuffe, Apr. 3, July 25, 1814, vol. 6, Cuffe MSS.

19. Land transactions: Cuffe and Wainer from Robert Wilcox, Nov. 13, 1812, Cuffe from Nathanial Sowle, Dec. 11, 1812, Apr. 25, 1814, from David and Peace Sowle, Mar. 13, 1813, from John Castino, July 12, 1813, from Barnea Devol, Aug. 31, 1814, from George and Elizabeth White, June 16, 1814 (Paul and Alice Cuffe sold Nathanial Sowle's thirty-one acres, with interest, on Apr. 23, 1814), records for Westport, Mass., NBRD; see also tax receipt, Aug. 10, 1814, vol. 8, Cuffe MSS. In addition, Cuffe had an old house relocated and rebuilt by Josiah Shearman (agreement and receipt, Oct. 24, 1813, Apr. 6, 1815, vol. 25, Cuffe MSS).

20. P & A Howard's business with Cuffe netted the store $194 plus $1,429 credited by Boston's Josiah Bradlee, who sold some of the English wares imported in 1812. The sons-in-law settled debts with Cuffe in June 1814 totaling $2,377. After Peter Howard died, Alexander announced the store's closing on August 19 (random business and family documents, vols. 6, 8, 10, 21, 25, Cuffe MSS; *Mercury*, July 8, Aug. 19–Sept. 16, 1814).

21. It is probable that Cuffe was interviewed for these articles (*Mercury*, Sept. 2, 1808; Mills to Cuffe, July 10, 1815, notations for the *Messenger*, n.d., vol. 6, Cuffe MSS; Spring, *Mills*, pp. 9–16; Richards, *Mills*, pp. 35, 62).

22. More than twenty letters had arrived from Sierra Leone by October, comprising an enormously important resource for interpreting local conditions and tracing cargoes in shipment to and from the colony (Allen to Richard Reynolds, Oct. 26, 1814, in *Life of Allen*, 1:160; Friendly Society [Wise] to Allen, July 3, 9, 12, 1814, Wise to Cuffe, Apr. 3, July 3, 1814, Friendly Society [Kizell] to Allen, Feb. 14, 1814, Kizell to Allen, Feb. 14, Apr. 3, July 17, 21, 1814, Duncan Campbell, Mar. [15], July 22, 1814, John Thorpe, July 11, 1814, Stephen Gabbidon, June 12, July 27, 1814, Thorpe and Gabbidon, June 20, 1814, Leopold Butscher to Allen, July 8, 1814, Maroons to Allen, Dec. 22, 1814, "African Correspondence," pp. 108–53, 189–91, William Allen Papers, A&H; *An Act to prevent . . . Transfers of Land, on Fraudulent and Fictitious Vouchers, and Deeds of Sale*, Nov. 1, 1814, Colonial Office Sessional Papers 269/1, no. 10, Petition to Sheriff, ca. Dec. 19, 1814, Robert Purdie's Notice, Colonial Office Sessional Papers 267/40, PRO.

23. Cuffe to Lockes, Jan. 27, 1815, HCL; Forten to Cuffe, Jan. 5, Feb. 15, 1815, vol. 6, Cuffe MSS; Cuffe to Prince Saunders, Robert Roberts, and Perry Lockes, June 6, 1812, Slaughter Collection, TAL.

24. William Rathbone to Cuffe, Nov. 30, 1812, vol. 6, Cuffe MSS.

12. RENEWED OPTIMISM

1. Cuffe to Allen, Mar. 13, 1815, "African Correspondence," pp. 163–64, William Allen Papers, A&H.

2. Michael Wainer to Peleg and George Folger, Apr. 12, 1815, vol. 8, Cuffe MSS; brig *Traveller* manifest, Feb. 10, 1812, Entry of Merchandise, May 29, 1812, Outward and Inward Manifests, New Bedford Bureau of Customs, FRC.

3. The *Hero* had been whaling in the Pacific (Isaac Cory, Jr., to Cuffe, Nov. 12, 1812, vol. 6, Cuffe MSS; Cuffe to Wm. Rotch, Jr., Nov. 16, 1812, International Marine Archives, ODHS [originals in Bath Marine Museum, Bath, Maine]; Dodge, *South Seas,* pp. 30, 36). The *Alpha* affair undoubtedly damaged Cuffe's business reputation. He procrastinated, was indecisive, and may have been indifferent to James's own plight. In return, James accused Cuffe's attorney of sending him "abusive" letters, although James had done the same to Cuffe. Apparently James bought the ship from Cuffe in Oct. 1815 for $6,550 (Forten to Cuffe, Jan. 5, 1815, James to Cuffe, Jan. 17, Mar. 1, 1815, Fisher to Cuffe, Jan. 21, Feb. 9, 10, 1815, Cuffe to Fisher, Jan. 29, Mar. 2, Apr. 20, Oct. 15, 1815, sale notice, Mar. 6, 1815, William Rotch, Jr., receipts, May 20, 30, 1815, vols. 6, 25, Cuffe MSS; ship *Alpha* permanent certificate of registry, no. 352, Nov. 24, 1815, ship *Alpha* bond, Nov. 24, 1815, [partially completed], Philadelphia Bureau of Customs, record group 41, NA).

4. Mills to Cuffe, July 10, 1815, vol. 6, Cuffe MSS; Mills and Smith, *Missionary Tour,* pp. 35–44; *Panoplist, or Missionary Magazine* 11 (June 6, 1815): 170–88. Cuffe's next trip to the Boston area was in October.

5. Thomas Paul had saved the life of a wealthy Britisher visiting Boston; hence the startling bequest (Mills to Cuffe, July 10, 1815, vol. 6, Cuffe MSS).

6. Britain's African philanthropists were already fragmented (see chaps. 7, 8), but Thorpe, whom John Kizell identified as his "attorney" for grievances, greatly exacerbated the situation (Thorpe, *Letter*). Thorpe subsequently lost his post in the colony (Regent's Council, Aug. 3, 1816, Thorpe to Earl Bathurst, Oct. 26, 1816, Colonial Office Sessional Papers 267/44, PRO).

7. *Life of Allen,* 1:165. The debate continued in the Institution's *Ninth Report.* Thorpe published responses (e.g., *Reply*) through 1818.

8. Allen diary, May 16, July 9, 26, 28, 1815, in *Life of Allen,* 1:171, 175–76; *Philanthropist* 5 (no. 19, 1815): 243–61.

9. Allen to Bathurst, May 27, June 2, 15, 1815, with African Institution petition, Clarkson to Bathurst, June 22, 1815, Colonial Office Sessional Papers 267/41, PRO; Allen diary, May 4, 25, July 3, 1815, in *Life of Allen,* 1:169, 171, 174.

10. Tsar Alexander volunteered to assist "the cause of the poor Africans" in any way possible and discussed the matter at some length with Clarkson. He expressed admiration for the Society of Friends, and Allen in particular, leaving little doubt that he also knew about Cuffe (Thomas Clarkson to Richard Reynolds, Oct. 12, 14, 1814, Oct. 8, 1815, Address to Emperor of Russia and Prussia from the Committee of Suffering, June 6, 1814, Clarkson's

account of conference with the tsar, Sept. 22, 1815, 4[1]: 64, 65, 67, Clarkson Papers, LUL; Allen diary, June [?] 1814, in *Life of Allen,* 1:143; Griggs, *Clarkson,* p. 115).

11. Allen to Charles MacCarthy, Aug. 10, 1815, Allen to the Friendly Society of Sierra Leone, Aug. 11, 1815, "African Correspondence," pp. 202–21, William Allen Papers, A&H. Allen discovered that the "government was quite disposed to do all in their power to forward our views." They would have immediately given the license, "if we concluded to incur a certain risk from which they were not sure they could effectually secure us." What, for instance, would occur if a "seizing officer considered the booty of more value than his place?" Wilberforce wanted Allen to pursue the matter further with the chancellor of the exchequer (*Life of Allen,* 1:176; vol. 21, Cuffe MSS).

12. This letter of Nov. 15, 1815, was printed in African Institution, *Tenth Report,* pp. 70–71, and later in the *Boston Recorder* 2 (no. 12, Mar. 18, 1817): 45.

13. *Poulson's American Daily Advertiser* and *Mercantile Advertiser,* Sept. 22, 1815; subscribers list of Boston families, Nov. 15, 1815, Miscellaneous, 1815, MHS. Jedediah Morse awaited a reply from Wilberforce "concerning our removal to Africa," wrote Cuffe to Allen, but promised that Boston passengers would "be well recommended" (Oct. 18, 1815, "African Correspondence," pp. 184–85, William Allen Papers, A&H).

14. Brig *Traveller,* Report and Manifest, Dec. 2, 1815, New Bedford Bureau of Customs, FRC. On Dec. 2 Cuffe bonded the crew for $400. Abraham Smith, the New Bedford Postmaster to whom Cuffe paid accumulated debts, signed the bond as well (Crew List Bonds, 1808–27, New Bedford Bureau of Customs, NA; receipts, Mar.–Oct. 1815, vol. 8, Cuffe MSS). Many additional business transactions document local people who helped to prepare the brig for departure (receipts, Sept.–Dec. 1815, vols. 8–10, Cuffe MSS). The crew of seven included: first mate Alvin Phelps, Cuffe's son-in-law; William Cuffe, the captain's youngest son; Edward Cook, the brother-in-law of Paul Cuffe, Jr.; Peleg Johnson, related to either Alexander Howard's new partner, Richard Johnson, or to Samuel Johnson, who had married Cuffe's sister Lydia; Augustus Thomas, a black seaman from New Haven and the only nonfamily crew member on board; and two men from Sierra Leone (NEHGS, *Vital Records of Westport,* p. 145; NEHGS, *Vital Records of Chilmark,* p. 48; NEHGS, *Vital Records of New Bedford,* 3:100; Cuffe to Hedijah Baylies, Apr. 24, 1817, vol. 3, Cuffe MSS). The records designate Phelps and Thomas as "Black," Cook and William Cuffe as "Coloured," and Johnson as "Mulatto." No physical description exists for the two Sierra Leone men (Crew List, New Bedford Bureau of Customs, NA).

15. Cuffe's departure for Africa was announced as far west as Louisville. See Sherwood, "Paul Cuffe," p. 390.

13. ESTABLISHING AFRICAN HOMESTEADS

1. Cuffe to William Rotch, Jr., Feb. (?), 1816, vol. 3, Cuffe MSS.

2. Cuffe to Rotch, Feb. (?), 1816, Cuffe to William Allen, Feb. 6, 1816, vol. 3, Cuffe MSS.

3. Allen to MacCarthy, Aug. 10, 1815, "African Correspondence," pp. 202–10, William Allen Papers, A&H; Earl Bathurst to Governor MacCarthy, Dec. 20, 1815, Colonial Office Sessional Papers 267/42, *An Act for the better security of the Payment of the Taxes and Port Duties,* Aug. 1, 1815, Sierra Leone Acts, 1801–23, Colonial Office Sessional Papers 269/1, PRO.

4. Cuffe to Fisher, Aug. 14, 1816, vol. 3, Cuffe MSS; MacCarthy to Bathurst, June 22, 1816, Colonial Office Sessional Papers 267/42, PRO. The *Traveller* landed a cargo valued at $2,497.50, whereas the invoice at departure from New Bedford had been for $5,031.11 (*Ming's Price Current,* June 1, 1816; brig *Traveller,* Report and Manifests, New Bedford Bureau of Customs, FRC). Cuffe was the only master named in the 1816 list of importing vessels, thus emphasizing his peculiarity in the British port (List of Vessels, Feb. 7, 1817, Colonial Office Sessional Papers 267/45, PRO).

5. Governor's Council, Feb. 8, 26, 1816, Colonial Office Sessional Papers 270/14: 13–34. Crew members became willing homesteaders also. Nine families arrived aboard the *Traveller.* Senegalese Charles Columbine and Congolese Anthony Survance, with wives Judith and Elizabeth, were not listed as settlers. Officially the settlers were Samuel and Barbara Wilson; Peter, Cloe, Elizabeth, Sarah, Caroline, Clavis, and Susannah Wilcox; Robert, Ann, and Catherine Rigsby; Perry, Margaret, John, William, Maryann, and Sarah Lockes; Thomas, Judith, Judith, Thomas, Alexander, Edward, and Saralann Jarvis; William, Elizabeth, and Nancy Guinn; and Samuel, Ann, Nancy, Samuel, Sarah, and Elizabeth Ann Hughes. On Sept. 13, 1815, Samuel Hicks had petitioned the council as one who had been "in the Colony four years, having arrived in it with Captain Cuffee"; he received a "new" lot. Fellow crew member Prince Edwards had met with equal success on Nov. 3, 1815; seven months later Edwards enlarged his holdings (Governor's Council, Colonial Office Sessional Papers 270/14: 114, 121, 143, PRO).

6. *Commercial Advertiser,* June 11, 1816.

7. See Cuffe to Allen, Dec. 19, 1816, vol. 3, Cuffe MSS; Allen to Rathbone Hodgson & Co., Nov. 6, 1815, in Business Account Letter Book, 1815–20, p. 45, Rathbone Hodgson & Co. to Allen, Nov. 8, 1815, in "African Correspondence," p. 188, Richard Reynolds to Allen, Dec. 16, 1815, in Loose Letters, William Allen Papers, A&H; African Institution, *Eleventh Report,* pp. 40–41. The financial and maritime conditions under which Cuffe sailed perfectly justify George Brooks's opinion that "only an individual with considerable resources could undertake" such a risk. A U.S. merchant seeking legitimate trade would have to undertake voyages of "six to eight months," during which heavy expenses would accumulate, bills for trade items bought on credit would come due, and there would be few or no returns on the

capital tied up in the venture. He "could be bankrupt by a single venture or even by a 'saving' voyage on which there were no losses—but no profits either" (Brooks, *Yankee Traders,* p. 86).

8. Cuffe to Allen, Apr. 1, 1816, vol. 3, Cuffe MSS.

9. Quoted in Williams, *Discourse,* pp. 22–23.

10. African Institution, *Tenth Report.* The directors continued as intermediaries even after Cuffe's departure. The Colonial Office transmitted MacCarthy's acknowledgment of Cuffe's arrival to Thomas Harrison in October. Henry Goulburn told the directors that Bathurst had "recommended Mr. Cuffe to the Governor's countenance and protection," and Harrison thanked Bathurst for his services (Goulburn to Harrison, Oct. 22, 1816, Colonial Office Sessional Papers 43/54, Harrison to Goulburn, Oct. 24, Nov. 11, 1816, Colonial Office Sessional Papers CO 267/44, PRO). No mention was made of expenses incurred by Cuffe.

11. For whatever reason, William Allen's interest also waned at this point; thereafter he became involved in Prince Saunders's mission in Haiti, promoting Friend Stephen Grellet's journey there as well. During this time he lost his wife and became ill himself. He undertook two summer voyages to the European continent, where he distributed Institution reports citing Cuffe's activities, yet his numerous letters to Sierra Leone did not mention Cuffe. The *Philanthropist,* which had become an index of Allen's concerns, completely overlooked the colony in 1816 and then ceased publication until 1819 (*Life of Allen,* pp. 184, 192–202, 216–18, 228, 233–34, 246–47).

12. *Commercial Advertiser,* June 11, 1816.

13. Cuffe to Williams, June 13 or 14, 1816, vol. 3, Cuffe MSS; Williams to Cuffe, Aug. 2, 1816, no. 851, Simon Gratz Autography Letter Series, HCAL. Earlier, from New York, Cuffe had told James Forten that he hoped Philadelphians would receive "more particulars" from the settlers they had endorsed, Samuel Wilson and Anthony Survance. Although Wilson had taken ill from eating poisonous berries, and Survance had differed with Cuffe over their bill, these hardly appeared to be grounds for the alleged "many unfavorable reports" about the colony (Cuffe to Forten, May 29, 1816, Cuffe to Samuel R. Fisher, May 28, 1816, vol. 3, Cuffe MSS).

14. PERILOUS TIMES IN AMERICA

1. See Cuffe to James Brian, Jan. 16, 1817, Cuffe to Samuel J. Mills, Aug. 6, 1816, Cuffe to Samuel C. Aiken, Aug. 7, 1817, vol. 3, Cuffe MSS. See also Foster, "Urban Missionary Movement," pp. 47–53; Bourne, *Slavery,* pp. 133–34; Quarles, *Black Abolitionists,* pp. 9–14; Staudenraus, *African Colonization,* pp. 12–22.

2. Financial receipts, vols. 8, 10, 12, 23, Cuffe MSS; family matters, vol. 11, Cuffe MSS; Howard & Johnson ads, *Mercury,* Dec. 15, 1815–Dec. 27, 1816; brig *Traveller* crew list, crew list bond, July 12, 1816, sloop *Resolution*

(*of Troy*) crew list bond, July 20, 1816, New Bedford Bureau of Customs, NA; Minutes, Men's Westport Monthly Meeting, July 15–Oct. 17, 1816, RIHS.

3. *Mercury*, June 7, July 12, 26, Aug. 9, 16, Sept. 6, Oct. 18, 25, Nov. 1, 8, Dec. 13, 1816.

4. Cuffe to Mills, Aug. 6, 1816, Cuffe to Aiken, Aug. 7, 1816, vol. 3, Cuffe MSS.

5. Du Bois, *Souls*, p. 45. I am deeply indebted to Letitia Brown, who placed Cuffe within the context of Du Bois's thoughts.

6. Cuffe to Mills, Aug. 6, 1816, Cuffe to Aiken, Aug. 7, 1816, vol. 3, Cuffe MSS.

7. Cuffe to Jedediah Morse, Aug. 10, 1816, PA 43:26, HSP; Cuffe to William Harris, Aug. 10, 1816, vol. 3, Cuffe MSS; Williams to Cuffe, Aug. 2, 1816, no. 851, miscellaneous letters, HCAL.

8. Cuffe to Mills, Aug. 6, 1816, vol. 3, Cuffe MSS. Cuffe believed that on the "great day of account it will not be asked what Denomination we made a profession to be of but they who have done good and worked righteousness will be rewarded with a crown of Everlasting Life." See also sources in note 7.

9. Cuffe to Williams, n.d., Aug. 14, 30, 1816, Cuffe to Forten, Aug. 14, 1816, Cuffe to Simeon and Susannah Jackson, Oct. 20, 1816, vol. 3, Cuffe MSS. Cuffe estimated "the greater part of Boston" wished to emigrate (Cuffe to Mills, Jan. 6, 1817, vol. 3, Cuffe MSS).

10. Cuffe letters to Cooke, Survance, Thorpe, Wise, Kizell, MacCarthy, and the Sierra Leone Friendly Society, Aug. 14, 1816, Cuffe to Davis, Sept. 9, 1816, Cuffe to Wise, Sept. 15, 1816, vol. 3, Cuffe MSS.

11. Cuffe to Kizell, Aug. 14, 1816, Cuffe to Gould, Sept. 20, 1816, vol. 3, Cuffe MSS.

12. Summons, William Cuffe to Stephen Gould, Sept. 27, 1816, Paul Cuffe to Phelps, Aug. 24, 1816, vols. 3, 8, Cuffe MSS. On Aug. 22 the provocative court summons accused William of raping a certain "English woman and spinster," Prudence White. William faced a $300 fine. I have not been able to discover how the matter was resolved.

13. The civilizer found the Indians living under deplorable conditions. Although noting their apparent lack of industry and morality, deep-seated reasons emerged. Chilmark lighthouse keeper Ebenezer Skiff vehemently accused three whitemen, Simon Mayhew, William Mayhew, and Tristram Allen, of being acquisitive, land-hungry interlopers. Joel Rogers, an old friend of Cuffe's brother Jonathan, spoke equally frankly, calling the three men part of a white-"connected gang" who conspired "to impoverish us and get our land" (Joel Rogers to Cuffe, Oct. 24, 1816, Ebenezer Skiff to Cuffe, n.d., Cuffe to Pearson Freeman, Oct. 19, 1816, Cuffe to Mary Masterns, Aug. 27, 1816, Cuffe to Abner Skiff, Nov. 3, 1816, Cuffe to Skiff and

Rogers, Nov. 11, 1816, vols. 3, 11, 23, Cuffe MSS). Now, 169 years later, Wampanoags will finally have 440 acres returned on Martha's Vineyard.

14. Plans for the West Indies venture began in the late fall (Cuffe to Wm. Brandneil, Nov. 2, 1816, Cuffe to E & A Winchester, Nov. 7, 1816, Cuffe to Hicks, Jenkins & Co., Nov. 14, 1816, Cuffe to William Rotch, Jr., Nov. 28, 1816, Cuffe to Peter Williams, Jr., Dec. 1, 1816, Cuffe to Robert Braston, Dec. 12, 13, 1816, Cuffe to John Cogshall, Dec. 16, 1816, Cuffe to Stephen Grellet, Dec. 26, 1816, Crocker, Bush, & Richmond to Cuffe, July 3, 1816, Wm. Boadn to Cuffe, Dec. 5, 1816, Cuffe to Freelove Slocum, Dec. 1, 1816, vols. 1, 3, 10, Cuffe MSS).

15. Cuffe's first letter to Allen in 1816, announcing his return to the United States, is not dated. A second letter was written on Dec. 19, 1816 (vols. 1, 3, Cuffe MSS).

16. *Mercury* notices of the colonization plan appeared on Dec. 13, 27. See also *Poulson's American Daily Advertiser,* Oct. 29, Dec. 28, 1816; *Recorder,* Nov. 12, 19, 1816; *Panoplist, or Missionary Magazine* 13 (Jan. 1817): 28–30.

17. Brown, *Finley,* p. 96; Finley to Cuffe, Dec. 5, 1816, Mills to Finley, Dec. 26, 1816, Cuffe to Mills, Jan. 6, 1817, vols. 3, 11, 23, Cuffe MSS.

18. Four days after the initial meeting of the American Colonization Society on Dec. 21, 1816, the *National Intelligencer* and the *Daily National Intelligencer* carried lengthy articles with excerpts from the main speakers. Mills forwarded these to Cuffe. On Jan. 3, 1817, the *Mercury* carried an abbreviated version entitled "FREE BLACK COLONY." It included the Society's claim that it would not end American slavery; however, it concluded that such a movement "seems necessary" prior to the adoption of "the emancipation of Millions of Slaves which form the *black spots* on the disc of many of the States which are loudest in boasting their love of liberty, and sacred for the Equal Rights of Men."

19. Cuffe to Mills, Jan. 6, 1817, Cuffe to Finley, Jan. 8, 1817, vol. 3, Cuffe MSS; *Liberator,* Feb. 26, 1833. See also Garrison, *African Colonization,* pt. 2, p. 59.

20. Cuffe to Mills, Jan. 6, 1817, Cuffe to Finley, Jan. 8, 1817, vol. 3, Cuffe MSS. Cuffe's letters to Mills and Finley also showered praise on the Christian faithful.

15. COLONIZATION AND A QUIET PASSING

1. Brown, *Finley,* pp. 83–96. Jordan sets the American Colonization Society within its proper racial context by examining the trend "toward a white man's country" (*White over Black,* pp. 565–82).

2. (Georgetown) *Messenger,* Jan. 2, 1817.

3. (Georgetown) *Messenger,* Jan. 7, 14, Mar. 7, 1817.

4. The sketch of Sierra Leone commenced in the *National Intelligencer,* Jan. 9, 1817, and was comprised of letter extracts as well as a June 12, 1816,

article from the *Recorder*. The lengthy insertion reached Charleston, South Carolina, before it appeared in Cuffe's hometown (*Carolina Gazette*, Feb. 15, 1817; *Mercury*, Feb. 21, 1817).

5. Bushrod Washington's memorial to Congress was dated Jan. 14 (*Delaware Gazette*, Jan. 22, 1817; *Niles Weekly Register*, Jan. 25, 1817). News of Finley's post came in a letter to *Poulson's American Daily Advertiser*, Apr. 16, 1817.

6. Forten to Cuffe, Jan. 25, 1817, vol. 11, Cuffe MSS; *Poulson's American Daily Advertiser*, Aug. 12, 1817.

7. Forten to Cuffe, Jan. 25, 1817, Samuel J. Mills to Cuffe, July 14, 1817, vol. 11, Cuffe MSS; Finley to (?) in the *National Intelligencer*, Mar. 17, 1817. See also Brown, *Finley*, pp. 122–24.

8. The evidence forcefully bears out Katz's refreshing analysis. He concludes that the free black leadership "maintained a lively interest in colonization in general and the plans of the American Colonization Society in particular" (introduction to Garrison, *African Colonization*, pp. i–xi).

9. See reports in the *Daily National Intelligencer*, Jan. 30, Feb. 4, 5, 1817; *York Gazette and Public Advertiser*, Jan. 16, 1817; *Poulson's American Daily Advertiser*, Jan. 20, 1817; *Freeman's Journal*, Jan. 21, 1817; *United States Gazette*, Jan. 25, 1817; *Courier*, Jan. 27, 1817; *Boston Repertory*, Jan. 28, 1817.

10. Cuffe to imposter, n.d., vol. 3, Cuffe MSS. See also "John Cuffee" to Paul Cuffe, Jan. 13, 1817, vol. 11, Cuffe MSS.

11. Early references to death came in letters to Freelove Slocum, Sept. 29, 1816, S & S Jackson, Oct. 20, 1816, Thomas Wainer, Dec. 26, 1816, and James Brian, Dec. 20, 1816, vol. 3, Cuffe MSS. Despite the attack Cuffe wrote that "the African cause Still Lives in the View of my mind" (to John James, James Brian, and Samuel R. Fisher, all dated Feb. 28, 1817, and to James Forten, Mar. 1, 1817, vol. 3, Cuffe MSS).

12. Cuffe may have suffered a heart attack while working on his new saltworks (Cuffe to Gifford & Peckham, Feb. 6, Mar. 7, 1817, Crocker, Bush & Richmond to Cuffe, May 7, 1817, vols. 3, 10, Cuffe MSS). Shipping news, personal correspondence, and manifests document the brig's departure around Mar. 20 (*Mercury*, Mar. 7, July 11, 18, 1817; *Gazette and General Advertiser*, July 2, 1817; *Ming's Price Current*, July 9, 1817; receipts, vols. 2, 3, 8, 10, 11, Cuffe MSS; brig *Traveller* manifests, Mar. 13, July 17, 1817, Outward Manifests, New Bedford Bureau of Customs, FRC).

13. Samuel Mills mailed Cuffe a copy of *A View of Exertions Lately Made. . . .* It cited the *National Intelligencer* article (Dec. 24, 1816) and included the Society's constitution, Bushrod Washington's memorial to Congress, and the Slave Trade Committee's report on the memorial, in addition to the previously published *Brief Sketch of Sierra Leone* and a joint resolution to President Madison from the committee. See also Mills to Cuffe, Mar. 12, 1817, Williams to Cuffe, Mar. 22, 1817, vols. 11, 23, Cuffe MSS.

14. The partnership of Howard & Johnson dissolved on June 6, 1817. Alexander Howard's business increased; Richard Johnson's own store closed

after Sept. 1817 for a while. In 1826 Richard Johnson married Paul and Alice Cuffe's daughter Ruth Howard, Alexander's widow. Six years later he chaired a meeting of people of color in New Bedford to protest the "terror, prejudice and oppression" perpetuated by the American Colonization Society. Johnson became William Lloyd Garrison's local agent for the *Liberator* (Garrison, *African Colonization,* pt. 2, pp. 50–51; Quarles, *Black Abolitionists,* pp. 20, 181; Crapo, *New Bedford,* p. 63).

15. Forten to Cuffe, Mar. 4, July 25, 1817, Samuel R. Fisher, June 5, 1817, Thomas Ash to Cuffe, Apr. 21, 1817, vols. 6, 11, Cuffe MSS.

16. *Poulson's American Daily Advertiser* provided the final incentive to chastize the national colonization plan (Sept. 20, 1815, Aug. 1, 4, 5, 8, 9, 1817). On Mar. 18, 1817, the *Recorder* published Forten and Parrott's 1815 letter commending their "common brother, Paul Cuffee."

17. *Poulson's American Daily Advertiser,* Aug. 12, 1817; *National Advocate,* Aug. 14, 1817; Garrison, *African Colonization,* pt. 2, pp. 12–13.

18. Cuffe apparently was aware that John Kizell had recommended a U.S.-sponsored colony at Sherbro Island and that Thomas Clarkson had referred all questions about such a colony to Cuffe in Westport. Samuel Mills's visit to Cuffe's bedside represented a final opportunity for personal advice about locating the U.S.-sponsored colony (Kizell to Cuffe, Feb. 19, 1817, Mills to Cuffe, July 14, 1817, vols. 11, 21, Cuffe MSS; Thomas Clarkson to [Francis Scott Key], Mar. 18, 1817, Letters, no. 958, Thomas Clarkson Papers, RHC). See also the *Daily National Intelligencer,* Aug. 25, 1817; *Richmond Enquirer,* Aug. 29, 1817; *Recorder,* Sept. 16, 1817.

19. Information on Cuffe's death comes from many sources (John Cuffe to brothers, June 26, 1817, David Cuffe to Freelove Slocum, July 8, 1817, Stephen Gould to Cuffe, Aug. 18, 1817, John Cuffe to Freelove Slocum, Sept. 10, 1817; Rhoda Cuffe to [James Forten], Sept. 10, 1817, vols. 3, 12, 22, Cuffe MSS). See also John Heald to Thomas Rotch, Sept. 1817, Rotch-Wales Papers, SCFL; Stephen Gould to Thomas Thompson, May 20, 1822, manuscript portfolio no. 29, p. 38, FHL.

20. The Bristol County Probate Court records show that Cuffe's assets were valued at $4,119.11 in real estate and $14,022.57 in personal property (Sherwood, "Paul Cuffe," p. 378). William Rotch, Jr., and Daniel Wing were the executors of the estate (*Mercury,* Dec. 5, 1817–Jan. 9, 1818; letters, vol. 7, Cuffe MSS). The publication of Peter Williams's eulogy, an obituary by William Rotch, Jr. (which was reprinted over a period of weeks in various newspapers), and the *Commercial Advertiser*'s newest Cuffe biography commenced the historical perspective of Paul Cuffe on three continents. See Williams, *Discourse* (reprinted in England in 1818 by Hargrove Publishers); *Mercury,* Sept. 12, 1817; *Newport Mercury,* Sept. 13, 1817, *Evening Post, Columbian, National Advocate, Gazette and General Advertiser, Recorder, Repertory, New England Palladium,* all Sept. 16, 1817; *Poulson's American Daily Advertiser,* Sept. 17, 1817; *Niles Weekly Register, Delaware Gazette, American Watchman,* all

Sept. 20, 1817; *Trenton Federalist,* Sept. 22, 1817; *Richmond Enquirer,* Sept. 23, 1817; *National Intelligencer,* Sept. 24, 1817; *Savannah Republican,* Oct. 4, 1817; *Liverpool Mercury,* Oct. 31, 1817. Cuffe's newest biography appeared in the *Commercial Advertiser,* Oct. 7, 8, 9, 1817; *Spectator,* Oct. 10, 17, 1817; *Recorder,* Oct. 21, 28, 1817; *Mercury,* Oct. 24, Nov. 7, 1817; *Royal Gazette and Sierra Leone Advertiser,* June 27, July 4, 11, 18, 25, 1818.

PAUL CUFFE'S EXTENDED FAMILY

This abbreviated genealogy gives the names of late eighteenth- and early nineteenth-century family members who participated in Cuffe's important political and business ventures. Such familial connections, typically established among families of local prosperous Quaker merchants, provided Cuffe with countless benefits. These included advice from brother John, an early political activist, the aggressive household of undaunted mariners raised by sister Mary and her husband Michael Wainer, plus the aggressive merchandizing ashore by former slave sons-in-law Alexander and Peter Howard.

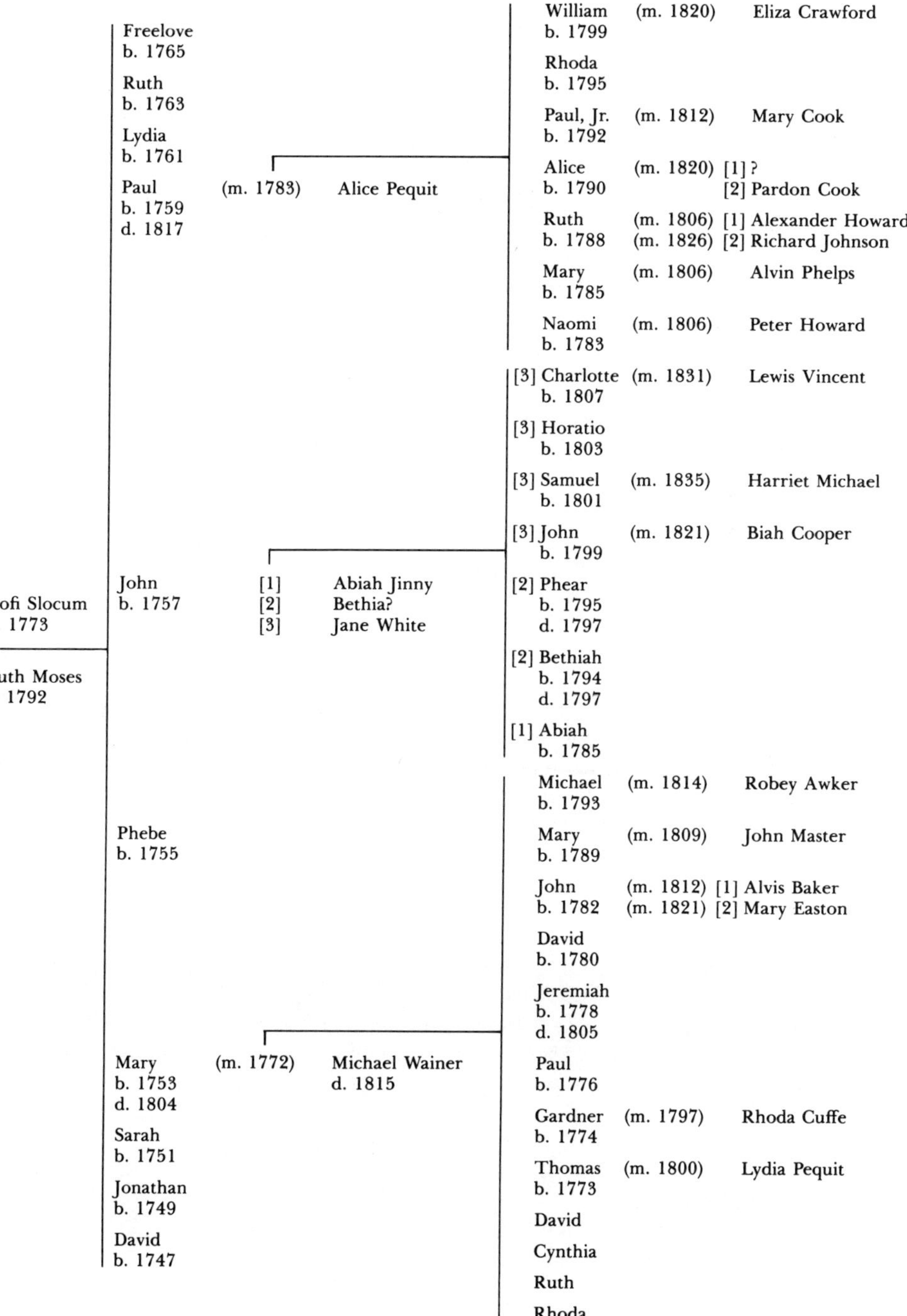

Kofi Slocum
d. 1773
Ruth Moses
d. 1792
Freelove
b. 1765
Ruth
b. 1763
Lydia
b. 1761
Paul
b. 1759
d. 1817
(m. 1783)
Alice Pequit
William
b. 1799
(m. 1820)
Eliza Crawford
Rhoda
b. 1795
Paul, Jr.
b. 1792
(m. 1812)
Mary Cook
Alice
b. 1790
(m. 1820)
[1] ?
[2] Pardon Cook
Ruth
b. 1788
(m. 1806) [1] Alexander Howard
(m. 1826) [2] Richard Johnson
Mary
b. 1785
(m. 1806)
Alvin Phelps
Naomi
b. 1783
(m. 1806)
Peter Howard
John
b. 1757
[1] Abiah Jinny
[2] Bethia?
[3] Jane White
[3] Charlotte
b. 1807
(m. 1831)
Lewis Vincent
[3] Horatio
b. 1803
[3] Samuel
b. 1801
(m. 1835)
Harriet Michael
[3] John
b. 1799
(m. 1821)
Biah Cooper
[2] Phear
b. 1795
d. 1797
[2] Bethiah
b. 1794
d. 1797
[1] Abiah
b. 1785
Phebe
b. 1755
Mary
b. 1753
d. 1804
(m. 1772)
Michael Wainer
d. 1815
Michael
b. 1793
(m. 1814)
Robey Awker
Mary
b. 1789
(m. 1809)
John Master
John
b. 1782
(m. 1812) [1] Alvis Baker
(m. 1821) [2] Mary Easton
David
b. 1780
Jeremiah
b. 1778
d. 1805
Paul
b. 1776
Gardner
b. 1774
(m. 1797)
Rhoda Cuffe
Thomas
b. 1773
(m. 1800)
Lydia Pequit
David
Cynthia
Ruth
Rhoda
Sarah
b. 1751
Jonathan
b. 1749
David
b. 1747

BIBLIOGRAPHY

I. MANUSCRIPTS AND PUBLIC RECORDS

The New Bedford Free Public Library (Mass.) is the most important among many repositories of Paul Cuffe material in this country. British government and humanitarian collections also contain valuable information, ranging from official colonial documents to William Allen's 225-page letter-copy book, "African Correspondence." The following sources were consulted in the course of researching this book.

England

Allen & Hanbury, Ltd., London (cited as A&H)—William Allen Papers, including "African Correspondence"
Church Missionary Society, London (cited as CMS)—letters of the secretary; letters and journals of missionaries
Liverpool Public Library (cited as LPL)—American Chamber of Commerce for the Port of Liverpool, Records; Roscoe Papers
Liverpool University Library (cited as LUL)—Clarkson Papers; Rathbone Papers
Methodist Missionary Society, London (cited as MMS)—Sierra Leone I Collection
Public Record Office, London (cited as PRO)—Admiralty Office Papers, 1811–12; Colonial Office Sessional Papers for Sierra Leone, 1811–17; Privy Council Papers, 1810–11
Society of Friends House Library, London (cited as FHL)—George Stacey Gibson Collection; Luke Howard Collection; manuscript portfolios nos. 17, 27, 29; Spriggs Manuscript Collection

United States

Baker Library, Harvard University, Cambridge, Mass. (cited as BL)—Bedford Marine Insurance Co. Collection
Chicago Historical Society, Ill. (cited as CHS)—miscellaneous Paul Cuffe letter

Federal Records Center, Waltham, Mass. (cited as FRC)—New Bedford Bureau of Customs Records; Newport Bureau of Customs Records

Haverford College Archives Library, Haverford, Pa. (cited as HCAL)—James Pemberton Papers; Jesse Kersey Papers; miscellaneous Paul Cuffe letters; Stephen Wanton Gould Diary; Warner Mifflin correspondence folder

Historical Society of Delaware, Wilmington (cited as HSD)—Abolition Society Papers; African School Society, Constitution and Minutes, 1809–35; Anonymous Account Book, 1807–10; James Brian Papers

Historical Society of Pennsylvania, Philadelphia (cited as HSP)—Cox, Parrish, and Wharton Papers; Emlen Papers; Logan Papers; Pemberton Papers; Pennsylvania Abolition Society Papers; Simon Gratz Autography Letter Series

Howard University Library, Washington, D.C. (cited as HUL)—Moorland-Springarn Collection

John Carter Brown Library, Brown University, Providence, R.I. (cited as JCBL)—Brown, Benson, and Ives Papers

Library Company of Philadelphia, Pa. (cited as LCP)—Dillwyn Manuscript Collection

Library of Congress, Manuscript Division, Washington, D.C. (cited as LC)—William Thornton Papers

Maryland Historical Society, Baltimore (cited as MdHS)—James Madison Papers

Massachusetts Historical Society, Boston (cited as MHS)—*Collections;* H. H. Edes Papers; Hugh Hall Papers, 1723–74; List of Indian Children to the Gospel Society of Boston; Miscellaneous, 1815; Miscellaneous Bound, 1761–65; Rotch Family Papers

Massachusetts State Archives, Boston (cited as MSA)—General Court Petitions; General Court Records and Journal of the House of Representatives, Commonwealth of Massachusetts; Revolutionary Resolves

National Archives, Washington, D.C. (cited as NA)—French Spoliation Claims; House of Representatives and Senate, 13th Congress, 2d Session, Papers; New Bedford Bureau of Customs Records; Newport Bureau of Customs Records; New York Bureau of Customs Records; Philadelphia Bureau of Customs Records

New Bedford Free Public Library, Mass. (cited as NBPL)—Paul Cuffe Manuscript Collection

New Bedford Registry of Deeds, Mass. (cited as NBRD)—documents for Dartmouth, New Bedford, and Westport

New-York Historical Society, N.Y. (cited as NYHS)—miscellaneous Paul Cuffe letters

Old Dartmouth Historical Society, New Bedford, Mass. (cited as ODHS)—International Marine Archives Collection, logs of the bark *Hero* (1806–7)

and the schooner *Ranger* (1804–5) (privately owned by Gale M. Blosser, Millbrae, Calif.); Rotch Papers, 1785–92

Peter Folger Museum, Nantucket Historical Society, Mass. (cited as PFM)—Census Records; Kezia Coffin Fanning Diary; miscellaneous Paul Cuffe letters; Nantucket Society of Friends Records

Regional History Collection and University Archives, Olin Library, Cornell University, Ithaca, N.Y. (cited as RHC)—Stephen Wanton Gould Diary; Thomas Clarkson Papers (microfilm; originals at Henry F. Huntington Library and Art Gallery, San Marino, Calif.)

Rhode Island Historical Society, Providence (cited as RIHS)—Austin Collection; Moses Brown Papers; Westport Monthly Meeting Minutes, 1797–1836

Swarthmore College Friends Historical Library, Swarthmore, Pa. (cited as SCFL)—Rotch-Wales Papers

Trevor Arnett Library, Atlanta University, Atlanta, Ga. (cited as TAL)—Slaughter Collection

William R. Perkins Library, Duke University, Durham, N.C. (cited as WPL)—William Wilberforce Papers

II. NEWSPAPERS AND PERIODICALS

The American and British media of Cuffe's day documented relevant early maritime and trading news, his voyages to Europe and Africa as a merchant and civilizer, and subsequent related events, including his obituary, which was published on three continents.

England

Edinburgh: *Edinburgh Review,* vols. 18 (Aug. 1811), 20 (July 1812), 21 (July 1813)

Liverpool: *Liverpool Mercury,* vols. 1 (1811), 7 (1817)

London: *The Christian Observer, Conducted by Members of the Established Church,* vols. 10–12; *Eclectic Review,* vols. 6–8 (1810–12); *Times;* "Memoirs of an African Captain," in *Monthly Repository of Theology and General Literature,* vol. 2, nos. 16–18 (Apr.–June 1807); *Methodist Magazine,* nos. 8–9 (1811–18); *Philanthropist, The Repository for Hints and Suggestions Calculated to Promote the Comfort and Happiness of Man,* 9 vols. (1811–23); *Universal Magazine,* vols. 17–21 (1812–14)

Sierra Leone

Freetown: *Royal Gazette and Sierra Leone Advertiser,* vol. 1, nos. 37–41 (June–July 1818)

United States

Delaware: *American Watchman; Delaware and Eastern Shore Advertiser; Delaware Gazette; Mirror of the Times*

District of Columbia: *Daily National Intelligencer; National Intelligencer*

Georgia: *Columbian Museum and Savannah Advertiser; Georgia Republican; Republican and Savannah Evening Ledger; Savannah Republican*

Maryland: *American and Commercial Advertiser; Baltimore American; Baltimore Whig; Christian Messenger; Federal Gazette and Baltimore Daily Advertiser; Federal Republican and Baltimore Telegraph; Niles Weekly Register*

Massachusetts: *Columbian Courier; Continental Journal and Weekly Advertiser;* (Boston) *Daily Advertiser;* (New Bedford) *Medley; Nantucket Gazette; New Bedford Mercury; New England Palladium; Old Colony Gazette; Panoplist and Missionary Magazine; Recorder; Weekly Messenger*

New Jersey: *Trenton Federalist*

Missouri: *Missouri Gazette*

New York: *Columbian; Commercial Advertiser; Courier; Evening Post; Gazette and General Advertiser; Herald; Ming's Price Current; National Advocate; Spectator*

Ohio: *Western Spy*

Pennsylvania: *Aurora General Advertiser; Claypoole's American Daily Advertiser; Freeman's Journal and Columbian Chronicle; Political and Commercial Register; Poulson's American Daily Advertiser; Religious Remembrancer; United States Gazette; Weekly Aurora; York Gazette*

Rhode Island: *Newport Mercury*

South Carolina: *Carolina Gazette*

Virginia: (Georgetown) *Messenger; Richmond Enquirer*

III. BOOKS AND JOURNAL ARTICLES

This listing includes all sources cited in the notes as well as many pertinent secondary sources which were consulted in the course of researching this book.

Accounts of Two Attempts: A Brief Account of the Proceedings of the Committee Appointed in the Year 1795 by the Yearly Meeting of Friends. . . . London: Phillip & Fardon, 1806.

Acts and Resolves of the Province of Massachusetts Bay. Boston: Wright & Potter Printing Co., 1922.

Adams, Henry, ed. *Documents Relating to New England Federalism, 1800–1815.* Boston: Little, Brown & Co., 1905.

African Institution of London. *Eighth Annual Report . . . March 23, 1814.* London: Ellerton & Henderson, 1814.

———. *Eleventh Report of the Directors of the African Institution.* London: Ellerton & Byworth, 1817.

———. *Fourth Report of the Directors of the African Institution . . . 28th of March, 1810.* London: George Ellerton, 1810.

———. *Seventh Annual Report . . . March 24, 1813.* London: Ellerton & Henderson, 1813.

———. *Sixth Report of the Committee of the African Institution . . . 25th of March 1812.* London: Ellerton & Henderson, 1812.

———. *Tenth Report of the Directors of the African Institution, Read at the Annual General Meeting on the 12th Day of March, 1816.* London: Ellerton & Byworth, 1816.

———. *Third Report of the Directors of the African Institution Read at the Annual General Meeting on the 25th of March, 1809.* London: Ellerton & Byworth, 1809.

Ahuma, S. R. B. *Memoirs of West African Celebrities.* Liverpool: D. Marples & Co., 1905.

Ajayi, J. F. A., and Michael Crowder, eds. *History of West Africa.* 2 vols. New York: Columbia University Press, 1972.

Ajayi, J. F. A., and Ian Espie, eds. *A Thousand Years of West African History.* Ibadan, Nigeria: Ibadan University Press, 1965.

Albion, Robert G., and Jennie B. Pope. *Sea Lanes in Wartime: The American Experience, 1775–1942.* New York: W. W. Norton & Co., 1942.

Alexander, Archibald. *A History of Colonization on the Western Coast of Africa.* Philadelphia: W. S. Martien, 1846.

Allen, Richard. *The Life, Experience, and Gospel Labors of the Rt. Rev. Richard Allen.* (1887). New York: Abingdon Press, 1960.

[Allen, William.] *William Allen, His Life and Labors.* London: Charles Gilpin, 1848.

———. *Life of William Allen, with Selections from His Correspondence.* 2 vols. Philadelphia: H. Longstreth, 1847.

Allinson, W. J. "A Brief Memoir of Paul Cuffee." *The Non-Slaveholder* 5 (Dec. 1850): 265–68.

[American Colonization Society.] *First Annual Report of the American Society for Colonizing the Free People of Colour of the United States.* Washington, D.C.: Davis & Force, 1818.

———. *Second Annual Report of the American Society for Colonizing the Free People of Colour of the United States.* Washington, D.C.: Davis & Force, 1819.

Andrews, Charles C. *The History of the New York African Free Schools.* New York: Mahlon Day, 1830.

Aptheker, Herbert. *American Negro Slave Revolts.* New York: Columbia University Press, 1943.

Armistead, Wilson. *Anthony Benezet.* London: A. W. Bennett, 1859.

Ashby, Irene M. *William Allen.* London: Edward Hicks, 1893.

Bacon, E. *Abstract of a Journal Kept by E. Bacon.* Philadelphia: Clark & Raser, 1824.

Bacon, Margaret H. *The Quiet Rebels: Story of the Quakers in America.* New York: Basic Books, 1969.

Bartlett, Irving H. *From Slave to Citizen: The Story of the Negro in Rhode Island.* Providence, R.I.: Urban League of Greater Providence, 1954.

Beals, Charles E. "William Ladd, the Apostle of Peace." *Granite Monthly* (n.s.) 7 (Sept. 1912): 273–77.

Beckwith, George C. *Eulogy on William Ladd, Late President of the American Peace Society.* Boston: Whipple & Damrell, 1841.

Bennett, Norman R., and George E. Brooks, eds. *New England Merchants in Africa: A History Through Documents, 1802–65.* Boston: Boston University Press, 1965.

Billington, Ray Allen. "James Forten: Forgotten Abolitionist." In *The Making of Black America,* ed. August Meier and Elliott Rudwick, vol. 1. (1949). New York: Atheneum Press, 1969.

———, ed. *The Journal of Charlotte Forten.* New York: Dryden Press, 1953.

Board of Trade. *New Bedford, Massachusetts: Its History, Industry, Institutions, and Attractions.* New Bedford, Mass.: Mercury Publishing Co., 1889.

Booth, Charles. *Zachary Macaulay: His Part in the Movement for the Abolition.* London: Longmans, Green & Co., 1934.

Boulding, Kenneth. "Economic Life." In *The Quaker Approach to Contemporary Problems,* ed. John K. Kavanaugh. New York: G. P. Putnam's Sons, 1953.

Bourne, George. *The Book of Slavery Irreconcilable.* Philadelphia: n.p., 1816.

Bracey, John H., August Meier, and Elliott Rudwick, eds. *Black Nationalism in America.* Indianapolis: Bobbs-Merrill Co., 1970.

———. *Afro-Americans.* Boston: Allyn-Bacon, 1972.

Bragg, George F. *Richard Allen and Absalom Jones.* Baltimore: Church Advocate Press, 1916.

Brief Account of the Settlement and Present Situation of the Colony of Sierra Leone, in Africa. New York: Samuel Wood, 1812.

Brigham, Clarence S. *History and Bibliography of American Newspapers, 1690–1820.* 2 vols. Worcester, Mass.: American Antiquarian Society, 1947.

Bristol County History. New Bedford, Mass.: n.p., n.d.

Brooks, George E., Jr. *Yankee Traders, Old Coasters, and African Middlemen.* Boston: Boston University Press, 1970.

———. "The Providence African Society's Sierra Leone Scheme, 1794–95: Prologue to the African Colonization Movement." *International Journal of African Historical Studies* 7, no. 2 (1974): 183–202.

Brown, Isaac VanArsdale. *Memoirs of the Rev. Robert Finley.* Philadelphia: John W. Moore, 1819.

Brown, Letitia W. *Free Negroes in the District of Columbia, 1790–1846.* New York: Oxford University Press, 1972.

Bullard, John M. *The Rotches.* Milford, N.H.: Cabinet Press, 1947.

Burgess, Samuel. *Address to the American Society for Colonizing the Free People of Colour of the United States.* Washington, D.C.: Davis & Force, 1818.

Butterfield, L. H., ed. *Letters of Benjamin Rush.* 2 vols. Princeton, N.J.: Princeton University Press, 1951.

Cadbury, Henry. "Negro Membership in the Society of Friends." *Journal of Negro History* 21 (Apr. 1936): 153–99.

Calvert, Monte A. "The Abolition Society of Delaware, 1801–7." *Delaware History* 10 (Oct. 1963): 295–320.

Candler, Warren A. *The Life of Thomas Coke.* Nashville: Methodist Episcopal Church, 1923.

Chapman-Huston, Desmond, and Ernest C. Cripps. *Through a City Archway: The Story of Allen and Hanbury's, 1715–1954.* London: John Murray, 1954.

Clark, Allen C. "Dr. and Mrs. William Thornton." *Records of the Columbian Historical Society* 18 (1915): 144–208.

Clarkson, Thomas. *An Essay on the Slavery and Commerce of the Human Species, Particularly the African.* London: J. Philips, 1786.

———. *The History of the Rise, Progress, and Accomplishment of the Abolition of the African Slave-Trade by the British Parliament.* 2 vols. (1808). London: Frank Cass & Co., 1968.

Coke, Thomas. *An Interesting Narrative of a Mission Sent to Sierra Leone in Africa, by the Methodists, in 1811.* London: private printing, 1812.

Coker, Daniel. *Journal of Daniel Coker.* Baltimore: Edward J. Coale, 1820.

Collins, George, and Christopher Rush. *A Short Account of the Rise and Progress of the AME Church in America.* New York: Marks, 1843.

Contee, Clarence G. "The Emergence of Du Bois as an African Nationalist." *Journal of Negro History* 54 (Jan. 1969): 48–60.

Corner, George W., ed. *The Autobiography of Benjamin Rush.* Princeton, N.J.: Princeton University Press, 1948.

Crane, Benjamin, Benjamin Hammond, and Samuel Smith. *Field Notes . . . of the Survey of Lands of the Proprietors of Dartmouth, New Bedford, Westport.* New Bedford, Mass.: New Bedford Free Public Library, 1910.

Crapo, Henry H. *The New Bedford Directory.* New Bedford, Mass.: J. C. Parmenter, 1836.

———. "Villages of Dartmouth in the British Raid of 1778." *Old Dartmouth Historical Sketches,* no. 23 (1909): 6–16.

Crooks, J. J. *Historical Records of the Royal African Corps.* Dublin: Browne & Nolan, 1925.

———. *A History of the Colony of Sierra Leone in Western Africa.* Dublin: Browne & Nolan, 1903.

Crosby, Alfred W. *America, Russia, Hemp, and Napoleon: American Trade with Russia and the Baltic, 1783–1812.* Columbus: Ohio State University Press, 1965.

Curtin, Philip D. *The Image of Africa.* Madison: University of Wisconsin Press, 1964.

[Davies, William.] *Extracts from the Journal of the Rev. William Davies, First When a Missionary at Sierra Leone, Western Africa.* Llanidloes: Wesleyan Printing Office, 1835.

Davis, David Brion. *The Problem of Slavery in the Age of Revolution, 1770–1823.* Ithaca, N.Y.: Cornell University Press, 1975.

———. *The Problem of Slavery in Western Culture.* Ithaca, N.Y.: Cornell University Press Paperbacks, 1969.

Dean, Paul. *A Discourse Delivered Before the African Society, . . . July 14, 1819.* Boston: Nathaniel Coverly, 1819.

[Delaware Abolition Society.] *The Constitution of the Delaware Society for Promoting the Abolition of Slavery.* Wilmington: R. Porter, 1816.

Dodge, Ernest S. *New England and the South Seas.* Cambridge, Mass.: Harvard University Press, 1965.

Donnan, Elizabeth. "Agitation Against the Slave Trade in Rhode Island, 1784–90." In *Persecution and Liberty: Essays in Honor of Lincoln Burr.* New York: Century Co., 1931.

———. "The New England Slave Trade after the Revolution." *New England Quarterly* 3 (Apr. 1930): 251–78.

———, ed. *Documents Illustrative of the History of the Slave Trade to America.* 4 vols. (1930–35). New York: Octagon, 1965.

Dookhan, Issac. *A Pre-Emancipation History of the West Indies.* London: Collins, 1971.

Douglass, William. *Annals of the First African Church in the United States of America.* Philadelphia: King and Baird, 1862.

Dow, George F. *Slave Ships and Slaving.* (1929). Port Washington, N.Y.: Kennikat Press, 1969.

Drake, St. Clair. "Negro Americans and the African Interest." In *American Negro Reference Book.* New York: Prentice-Hall, 1967.

Drake, Thomas E. "Elihu Coleman, Quaker Antislavery Pioneer of Nantucket." In *Byways in Quaker History.* Wallingford, Pa.: n.p., 1944.

———. *Quakers and Slavery in America.* New Haven, Conn.: Yale University Press, 1950.

Du Bois, W. E. B. *The Philadelphia Negroes, A Social Study.* (1899). New York: Schocken Books, 1967.

———. *The Souls of Black Folk.* (1903). New York: New American Library, 1969.

———. *The Suppression of the African Slave Trade to the United States of America, 1638–1870.* (1896). New York: Schocken Books, 1969.

Duignan, Peter, and Clarence Clendenen. *The United States and the African Slave Trade, 1619–1862.* Stanford, Calif.: Stanford University Press, 1963.

Dykes, Eva. *The Negro in English Romantic Thought.* Washington, D.C.: Associated Publishers, 1942.

Eaton, Leonard K. "Medicine in Philadelphia and Boston, 1805–30." *Pennsylvania Magazine of History and Biography* 75 (1951): 66–75.

Eddy, George S. Introduction to "Account Book of Benjamin Franklin Kept by Him During His First Mission to England as Provincial Agent, 1757–62." *Pennsylvania Magazine of History and Biography* 40 (1931): 97–133.

Elkins, Stanley M. *Slavery: A Problem in American Institutional and Intellectual Life.* (1959). New York: Grosset & Dunlap, 1963.

Ellis, Leonard Bolles. *The History of New Bedford and Its Vicinity, 1602–1892.* Syracuse, N.Y.: B. Mason & Co., 1892.

Elmes, James. *Thomas Clarkson: A Monograph.* London: Blackader & Co., 1969.

Elsbree, Oliver Wendell. "The Rise of the Missionary Spirit, 1790–1830." *New England Quarterly* 1, no. 3 (July 1928): 295–322.

Extraordinary Conversion and Religious Experience of Dorothy Ripley. . . . 2 vols. New York: G. and R. Waite, 1810.

Fayle, F. *The Spitalfields Genius.* London: Hodder & Stoughton, 1884.

Federal Writer's Project (Works Progress Administration). *Delaware, a Guide to the First State.* New York: Viking Press, 1938.

Fendell, P. R., ed. *Letters and Other Writings of James Madison.* 4 vols. Philadelphia: J. B. Lippincott, 1865.

Ferguson, John. *Memoir of the Life and Character of Rev. Samuel Hopkins.* Boston: Leonard W. Kimball, 1830.

Fergusson, Charles Bruce, ed. *Clarkson's Mission to America, 1791–92.* Halifax: Public Archives of Nova Scotia, 1971.

[Finley, Robert.] *A View of Exertions Lately Made for the Purpose of Colonizing the Free People of Colour.* Washington, D.C.: Jonathan Elliot, 1817.

Ford, Paul L., ed. *Writings of Thomas Jefferson.* 10 vols. New York: G. P. Putnam's Sons, 1892–99.

Forten, James. *Letters from a Man of Color on a Late Bill Before the Senate of Pennsylvania.* Philadelphia: by the author, 1813.

Foster, Charles I. "The Urban Missionary Movement, 1814–37." *Pennsylvania Magazine of History and Biography* 75 (1951): 47–53.

Fox, Earl Lee. *The American Colonization Society, 1817–40.* Baltimore: Johns Hopkins Publications, 1919.

Franklin, John Hope. *From Slavery to Freedom.* New York: Alfred A. Knopf, 1980.

Franklin, Susan B. "William Ellery, Signer of the Declaration of Independence." *Rhode Island History* 13, no. 1 (1954): 11–17.

Frazier, E. Franklin. *The Negro Church in America.* New York: Schocken Books, 1966.

Fyfe, Christopher. *A History of Sierra Leone.* London: Oxford University Press, 1962.

———. *Sierra Leone Inheritance.* London: Oxford University Press, 1964.

———. "The West African Methodists in the Nineteenth Century." *Sierra Leone Bulletin of Religion* 3, no. 1 (1961): 22–28.

Garrison, William L. *Thoughts on African Colonization,* ed. William Katz. (1832). New York: Arno Press, 1968.

George, Claude. *The Rise of British West Africa.* (1904). London: Frank Cass & Co., 1968.

Glocester, S. H. *A Discourse Delivered on the Occasion of the Death of Mr. James Forten, Sr.* Philadelphia: I. Ashmead & Co., 1843.

Greene, Lorenzo J. *The Negro in Colonial New England.* (1942). New York: Atheneum Press, 1969.

———. "The New England Negro as Seen in Advertisements for Runaway Slaves." *Journal of Negro History* 29 (Apr. 1944): 129–31.

Greene, Lorenzo J., and Carter G. Woodson. *The Negro Wage Earner.* (1930). New York: Atheneum Press, 1969.

Griggs, Earl Leslie. *Thomas Clarkson, the Friend of Slaves.* (1936). Westport, Conn.: Negro University Press, 1970.

Griggs, Earl Leslie, and Clifford Prator, eds. *Henry Christophe–Thomas Clarkson, a Correspondence.* New York: Greenwood Press, 1968.

Hallet, Robin. *The Penetration of Africa: European Exploration in North and West Africa to 1815.* New York: Frederick W. Praeger, 1965.

Harris, Sheldon H. "An American's Impression of Sierra Leone in 1811." *Journal of Negro History* 47, no. 1 (1962): 35–41.

———. *Paul Cuffe: Black America and the African Return.* New York: Simon & Schuster, 1972.

———. "Paul Cuffe's White Apprentice." *American Neptune* 23 (July 1963): 192–96.

[Harrison, George.] *Some Remarks on a Communication from William Roscoe to the Duke of Gloucester. . . .* London: George Ellerton, 1810.

Hart, Albert Bushnell. *Commonwealth History of Massachusetts.* 3 vols. New York: States History Co., 1929.

Haskell, Ruth. *The Story of Cuttyhunk.* New Bedford, Mass.: Reynolds, 1953.

Heads of Families at the First Census of the United States Taken in the Year 1790: Massachusetts. Baltimore: Genealogical Publishing Co., 1966.

Hedges, James B. *The Browns of Providence Plantations.* 2 vols. Providence, R.I.: Brown University Press, 1968.

Henderson, W. O. "The American Chamber of Commerce for the Port of Liverpool, 1801–1908." In *Transactions of the Historic Society of Lancastershire and Cheshire for the Year 1933,* vol. 85. Liverpool, England, 1935.

Historical and Biographical Encyclopedia of Delaware. Wilmington: Ardine Publishing & Engraving Co., 1882.

Hoare, Prince. *Memoirs of Granville Sharp, Esq.* London: Henry Colburn & Co., 1820.

Holder, Charles F. *The Quakers in Great Britain and America.* New York: Neuner Co., 1913.

Holsoe, Svend. "Slavery and Economic Response among the Vai." In *Slavery in Africa: Historical and Anthropological Perspectives,* ed. Suzanne Miers and Igor Kopytoff. Madison: University of Wisconsin Press, 1977.

Howard, Horatio P. *A Self-made Man: Capt. Paul Cuffee.* New Bedford, Mass.: n.p., 1913.

Hunt, Gaillard. "William Thornton and Negro Colonization." *Proceedings of the American Antiquarian Society* (n.s.) 30 (1920): 32–61.

James, Sydney V. *A People among People: Quaker Benevolence in Eighteenth-Century America.* Cambridge, Mass.: Harvard University Press, 1963.

Johnston, H. P., ed. *The Correspondence and Public Papers of John Jay.* 4 vols. New York: G. P. Putnam's Sons, 1890–93.

Jones, Elias. *Revised History of Dorchester County, Maryland.* Baltimore: Read Taylor Press, 1925.

Jones, Rufus M. *The Quakers in American Colonies.* London: Macmillan & Co., 1911.

Jordan, Winthrop D. "The Influence of the West Indies on the Origins of New England Slavery." *William and Mary Quarterly* (3d ser.) 18 (1961): 243–50.

———. *White over Black: American Attitudes Toward the Negro, 1550–1812.* Baltimore: Penguin Books, 1969.

Justice, Hilda. *Life and Ancestry of Warner Mifflin.* Philadelphia: Ferris & Leach, 1905.

[Kersey, Jesse.] *A Narrative of the Early Life, Travels, and Gospel Labors of Jesse Kersey.* Philadelphia: T. Ellwood Chapman, 1852.

Knustford, Margaret J. Trevelyan. *Life and Letters of Zachary Macaulay.* London: E. Arnold, 1900.

Kraus, Michael. "Slavery Reform in the Eighteenth Century: An Aspect of Transatlantic Intellectual Cooperation." *Pennsylvania Magazine of History and Biography* 60, no. 1 (Jan. 1936): 53–66.

Kummer, C. E., and Frederic Arnold. *The Free State of Maryland: A History of the State and Its People, 1634–1941.* Baltimore, Md.: Historical Record Association, n.d.

Lader, Lawrence. *The Bold Brahmins: New England's War Against Slavery.* New York: E. P. Dutton, 1961.

Langley, Harold D. "The Negro in the Navy and Merchant Service." *Journal of Negro History* 42 (Oct. 1967): 273–74.

Legum, Colin. *Pan-Africanism, a Short Political Guide.* London: Pall Mall Press, 1962.

Lowry, Ann B. "Quakers and the Meeting House at Apponagansett." *Old Dartmouth Historical Sketches,* no. 70 (1940): 8–12.

Lynch, Hollis R. *Edward W. Blyden, Pan-Negro Patriot.* London: Oxford University Press, 1967.

———. "Pan-Negro Nationalism in the New World Before 1862." In *The Making of Black America,* ed. August Meier and Elliott Rudwick, vol. 1. (1949). New York: Atheneum Press, 1969.

———. "Sierra Leone and Liberia in the Nineteenth Century." In *One Thousand Years of West African History,* ed. J. F. A. Ajayi and Ian Espie. Ibadan, Nigeria: Ibadan University Press, 1965.

MacCormack, Carol P. "Wono: Institutionalized Dependency in Sherbro Descent Groups." In *Slavery in Africa: Historical and Anthropological Per-*

spectives, ed. Suzanne Miers and Igor Kopytoff. Madison: University of Wisconsin Press, 1977.

Macy, Obed. *History of Nantucket.* 2d ed. Mansfield, Mass.: Macy and Pratt, 1880.

[Madison, James.] "James Madison's Attitude Toward the Negro." *Journal of Negro History* 6 (Jan. 1921): 74–102.

Marriner, Sheila. *Rathbones of Liverpool, 1845–73.* Liverpool: Liverpool University Press, 1961.

[Massachusetts Colonization Society.] *Proceedings of the Annual Meeting Held in Park St. Church, February 7, 1833.* Boston: Pierce & Parker, 1833.

Mathison, Gilbert. *Short Review of the Reports of the African Institution and the Controversy with Dr. Thorpe.* London: William Stockdale, 1816.

Mease, James. *Picture of Philadelphia.* Philadelphia: B. & T. Kite, 1811.

Meier, August, and Elliott Rudwick, eds. *The Making of Black America.* 2 vols. (1949). New York: Atheneum Press, 1969.

Mellor, George R. *British Imperial Trusteeship, 1783–1850.* London: Faber & Faber, 1951.

Memoir of Captain Paul Cuffee. Liverpool: Egerton Smith & Co., 1811.

Miers, Suzanne, and Igor Kopytoff, eds. *Slavery in Africa: Historical and Anthropological Perspectives.* Madison: University of Wisconsin Press, 1977.

Mills, Samuel J., and Daniel Smith. *Report of a Missionary Tour Through that Part of the United States which Lies West of the Alleghany Mountains. . . .* Andover, Mass.: Flagg & Gould, 1815.

Mineka, Francis E. *The Dissidence of Dissent: The Monthly Repository, 1806–38.* Chapel Hill: University of North Carolina Press, 1944.

Minton, Henry M. *Early History of Negroes in Business in Philadelphia.* Nashville: AMESS Union, 1913.

Montgomery, Elizabeth. *Reminiscences of Wilmington in Familiar Village Tales.* Philadelphia: T. K. Collins, 1851.

Moore, George H. *Notes on the History of Slavery in Massachusetts.* New York: D. Appleton & Co., 1866.

Moore, John J. *History of the African Methodist Episcopal Church in America.* New York: Teacher's Journal Office, 1884.

Morgan, William James, ed. *Naval Documents of the American Revolution.* 5 vols. Washington, D.C.: Government Printing Office, 1971.

Morison, Samuel Eliot. *The Maritime History of Massachusetts, 1783–1860.* Boston: Houghton Mifflin Co., 1961.

Morse, Jedidiah. *A Discourse Delivered at the African Meeting-House in Boston, July 14, 1808. . . .* Boston: Lincoln & Edmonds, 1808.

———. *Signs of the Times: A Sermon Preached Before the Society for Propagation of the Gospel.* Charlestown, Mass.: Samuel T. Armstrong, 1810.

Narrative of the Life of Paul Cuffe, a Pequot Indian. Vernon, N.Y.: H. N. Bill, 1839.

National Archives Microfilm Publications. *Population Schedule of the First*

Census of the United States, 1790. Washington, D.C.: General Services Administration, 1957.

———. *Population Schedule of the Second Census of the United States, 1800.* Washington, D.C.: General Services Administration, 1959.

———. *Population Schedule of the Third Census of the United States, 1810.* Washington, D.C.: General Services Administration, 1960.

Nell, William C. *Colored Patriots of the American Revolution.* Boston: Robert F. Wallcut, 1855.

New England Historic Genealogical Society. *Vital Records of Chilmark, Massachusetts to the Year 1850.* Boston, 1904.

———. *Vital Records of Dartmouth, Massachusetts to the Year 1850.* 3 vols. Boston, 1929–30.

———. *Vital Records of Nantucket, Massachusetts to the Year 1850.* 3 vols. Boston, 1925, 1927–28.

———. *Vital Records of New Bedford, Massachusetts to the Year 1850.* 3 vols. Boston, 1932, 1941.

———. *Vital Records of Westport, Massachusetts to the Year 1850.* Boston, 1918.

Park, Edward A., ed. *The Works of Samuel Hopkins, D.D. . . . with a Memoir of His Life and Character.* 3 vols. Boston: Doctrinal Tract & Book Society, 1854.

Parrish, John. *Remarks on the Slavery of the Black People.* Philadelphia: Kimber, Conrad & Co., 1806.

Pease, Alfred E., ed. *The Diaries of Edward Pease.* London: Headley Brothers, 1907.

Pease, Zephaniah W., ed. *The Diary of Samuel Rodman.* New Bedford, Mass.: Reynolds Publishing Co., 1927.

Perpetual Laws of the Commonwealth of Massachusetts from the Establishment of Its Constitution in the Year 1780 to the End of the Year 1800. Boston: I. Thomas & E. T. Andrews, 1801.

Peterson, John. *Province of Freedom: A History of Sierra Leone, 1787–1870.* Evanston, Ill.: Northwestern University Press, 1969.

Pettigrew, Thomas Joseph. *Memoirs of the Life and Writings of the Late John Coakley Lettsom.* London: Nichols, Son & Bentley, 1817.

Pinney, John W. "Captain William Ladd, the Apostle of Peace." In *Collections and Proceedings of the Main Historical Society* (2d ser.) 10 (1899): 113–37.

Porter, R. *A Directory and Register for the Year 1814 . . . of the Borough of Wilmington and Brandywine.* [Wilmington, Del.]: by the author, [1814].

Priestly, Margaret. *West African Trade and Coastal Society: A Family Study.* London: Oxford University Press, 1969.

Quarles, Benjamin. *Black Abolitionists.* New York: Oxford University Press, 1969.

———. *The Negro in the American Revolution.* Chapel Hill: University of North Carolina Press, 1961.

Ralfe, J. *The Naval Chronology of Great Britain . . . from the Commencement of the Wars in 1803 to the End of the Year 1816.* 3 vols. London: Whitmore & Fenn, 1820.

Rattray, R. S. *Ashanti.* (1923). New York: Oxford University Press, 1969.

Rhoads, F. T. "The Social Life of Yearly Meeting Work—Past and Present." In *The Friends Meeting House, Fourth and Arch Street, Philadelphia.* Philadelphia: John C. Winston, 1904.

Richards, Thomas C. *Samuel J. Mills, Missionary, Pathfinder, Pioneer, and Promoter.* Boston: Pilgrim Press, 1906.

Ricketson, Daniel. *The History of New Bedford.* New Bedford, Mass.: B. Lindsey, 1858.

Ritter, Abraham. *Philadelphia and Her Merchants.* Philadelphia: by the author, 1860.

Robinson, James. *The Philadelphia Directory for 1807.* New York: T. S. Manning, 1807.

[Rotch, William.] *Memorandum Written by William Rotch in the Eightieth Year of His Age.* Boston: Houghton Mifflin Co., 1916.

Rush, Christopher, and George Collins. *A Short Account of the Rise and Progress of the African Methodist Episcopal Church in America.* New York: W. Marks, 1843.

Salvador, George. *Paul Cuffe, the Black Yankee, 1759–1817.* New Bedford, Mass.: by the author, 1969.

Saunders, Prince. *An Address Delivered at Bethel Church, Philadelphia . . . Before the Pennsylvania Augustine Society, for the Education of People of Color.* Philadelphia: Joseph Rakestraw, 1818.

———. *Haitian Papers.* Boston: Caleb Bingham & Co., 1818.

———. *A Memoir Presented to the American Convention for Promoting the Abolition of Slavery and Improving the Condition of the African Race, Dec. 11, 1818.* Philadelphia: Dennis Heartt, 1818.

Seebohm, Benjamin. *Memoirs of the Life and Gospel Labors of Stephen Grellet.* 2 vols. Philadelphia: T. Ellwood Chapman, 1852.

Sharf, J. Thomas. *History of Delaware, 1609–1888.* 2 vols. Philadelphia: L. J. Richards & Co., 1888.

Shepperson, George. "Notes on Negro American Influences on the Emergence of African Nationalism." In *Independent Black Africa,* ed. William J. Hanna. Chicago: Rand McNally, 1964.

Sherwood, Henry Noble. "Early Negro Deportation Projects." *Mississippi Valley Historical Review* 2 (Mar. 1916): 484–508.

———. "Paul Cuffe." *Journal of Negro History* 8 (Apr. 1923): 153–229.

———. "Paul Cuffe and His Contribution to the American Colonization Society." In *Proceedings of the Mississippi Valley Historical Association for the Year 1912–13,* 4:370–402.

Slocum, Charles Elihu. *History of the Slocums, Slocumbs, and Slocombs of America.* (1882). Defiance, Ohio: by the author, 1908.

[Society of Friends.] *Accounts of Two Attempts Towards the Civilization of Some Indian Nations in North America.* London: Phillip & Fardon, 1806.

Spring, Gardiner. *Memoirs of the Rev. Samuel Mills.* New York: J. Seymour, 1820.

Stackpole, Edouard A. *The Forgotten Man of the Boston Tea Party.* n.p., 1973.

———. *Nantucket in the American Revolution.* Falmouth, Mass.: Nantucket Historical Association, 1976.

———. *The Sea-Hunters: The New England Whalemen During Two Centuries, 1635–1835.* Philadelphia: J. B. Lippincott, 1953.

———. *William Rotch of Nantucket, America's Pioneer in International Industry.* New York: Newcomen Society in North America, 1950.

Starbuck, Alexander. *History of the American Whale Fishery.* 2 vols. (1878). New York: Argosy-Antiquarian, 1964.

Staudenraus, P. J. *The African Colonization Movement, 1816–65.* New York: Columbia University Press, 1961.

Stump, Brice N. *Between the Blackwater and Nanticoke: History and Legend of Eastern Dorchester County.* MS, author's files, 1967.

Tabor, Mary K. "Social Life among the Friends of Long Ago." *Old Dartmouth Historical Sketches,* no. 21 (1908): 7–16.

Thomas, John L. *The Liberator, William Lloyd Garrison.* Boston: Little Brown & Co., 1963.

Thomas, Lamont D. "Memoirs of an African Captain." *Negro History Bulletin* 43 (Jan. 1980): 11–12.

Thompson, Mack. *Moses Brown, Reluctant Reformer.* Chapel Hill: University of North Carolina Press, 1962.

Thorpe, Frances N. *A Constitutional History of the American People, 1776–1850.* 2 vols. New York: Harper & Brothers, 1898.

Thorpe, Robert. *A View of the Present Increase of the Slave Trade, the Cause of that Increase, and Suggesting a Mode for Effecting Its Total Annihilation.* London: Longman, 1818.

———. *A Letter to William Wilberforce. . . .* London: F. G. & C. Rivington, 1815.

———. *A Reply "Point by Point" to the Special Report of the Directors of the African Institution.* London: F. C. & J. Rivington, 1815.

Tolles, Frederick B. *George Logan of Philadelphia.* New York: Oxford University Press, 1953.

———. *Quakers and the Atlantic Culture.* New York: Macmillan Co., 1960.

Totah, Khalil A., and Edward L. Macomber. *Historical Sketch for the Two-Hundredth Anniversary of Friends Meetings, Westport, Massachusetts.* New Bedford, Mass.: by the Society of Friends, 1916.

Tower, Walter S. *A History of the American Whale Fishery.* Philadelphia: University of Pennsylvania Press, 1907.

Turner, Edward R. "The First Abolition Society in the United States." *Pennsylvania Magazine of History and Biography* 36 (1912): 92–109.

Vickers, John. *Thomas Coke, Apostle of Methodism.* London: Epworth Press, 1969.

Wax, Donald D. "Quaker Merchants and the Slave Trade." *Pennsylvania Magazine of History and Biography* 86 (Apr. 1961): 144–59.

Wesley, Charles H. *Richard Allen.* Washington, D.C.: Associated Publishers, 1935.

West, Richard. *Back to Africa: A History of Sierra Leone and Liberia.* New York: Holt, Rinehart & Winston, 1970.

Wilberforce, Robert, and Samuel Wilberforce, eds. *Correspondence of William Wilberforce.* 2 vols. Philadelphia: Henry Perkins, 1846.

Wilks, Ivor. "The Mossi and Akan States, 1500–1800." In *History of West Africa,* ed. J. F. A. Ajayi and Michael Crowder, vol. 1. New York: Columbia University Press, 1965.

Williams, Gomer. *History of the Liverpool Privateers and Letters of Marques with an Account of the Liverpool Slave Trade.* London: William Heinemann, 1897.

Williams, Rev. Peter. *A Discourse Delivered on the Death of Capt. Paul Cuffe Before the New York African Institution.* New York: A. E. Young, 1817.

———. *An Oration on the Abolition of the Slave Trade, Delivered in the African Church in the City of New York, January 1, 1808.* New York: Samuel Wood, 1808.

Woodson, Carter G. *The History of the Negro Church.* Washington, D.C.: Associated Publishers, 1921.

———. "The Relations of Negroes and Indians in Massachusetts." *Journal of Negro History* 5 (Jan. 1920): 44–57.

Works Progress Administration. *Maryland, A Guide to the Oldline State.* New York: Oxford University Press, 1940.

———. *Ships Documents of Rhode Island.* Providence, R.I.: National Archives Project, 1941.

———. *Ship Registries of New Bedford.* 3 vols. Boston, 1940.

———. *Whaling Masters Voyages, 1731–1925.* New Bedford, Mass., 1938.

Worth, Henry B. "Heads of Westport and Its Founders." *Old Dartmouth Historical Sketches,* no. 21 (1908): 17–25.

Wright, James M. *The Free Negro in Maryland, 1634–1860.* New York: Columbia University Press, 1921.

———. *The Negro in Our History.* Washington, D.C.: Associated Publishers, 1922.

INDEX

INDEX

NOTE ON THE AUTHOR

Lamont D. Thomas has taught humanities for fifteen years at the high school level. He received his B.A. and M.A. at Trinity College, Hartford, Connecticut, and has studied at the University of London and briefly taught in Liberia. In 1969 he researched African literature as a curriculum consultant for Project Africa at Carnegie-Mellon University. His publications have appeared in educational and historical journals. Archival research in the United States and England over a period of several years has culminated in his first book.

BOOKS IN THE SERIES BLACKS IN THE NEW WORLD

Before the Ghetto: Black Detroit in the Nineteenth Century
David M. Katzman

Black Business in the New South: A Social History of the North Carolina Mutual Life Insurance Company *Walter B. Weare*

The Search for a Black Nationality: Black Colonization and Emigration, 1787-1863 *Floyd J. Miller*

Black Americans and the White Man's Burden, 1898-1903
Willard B. Gatewood, Jr.

Slavery and the Numbers Game: A Critique of *Time on the Cross*
Herbert G. Gutman

A Ghetto Takes Shape: Black Cleveland, 1870-1930
Kenneth L. Kusmer

Freedmen, Philanthropy, and Fraud: A History of the Freedman's Savings Bank *Carl R. Osthaus*

The Democratic Party and the Negro: Northern and National Politics, 1868-92 *Lawrence Grossman*

Black Ohio and the Color Line, 1860-1915 *David A. Gerber*

Along the Color Line: Explorations in the Black Experience
August Meier and Elliott Rudwick

Black over White: Negro Political Leadership in South Carolina during Reconstruction *Thomas Holt*

Keeping the Faith: A. Philip Randolph, Milton P. Webster, and the Brotherhood of Sleeping Car Porters, 1925-37 *William H. Harris*

Abolitionism: The Brazilian Antislavery Struggle
Joaquim Nabuco, translated and edited by Robert Conrad

Black Georgia in the Progressive Era, 1900-1920
John Dittmer

Medicine and Slavery: Health Care of Blacks in Antebellum Virginia *Todd L. Savitt*

Alley Life in Washington: Family, Community, Religion, and Folklife in the City, 1850-1970 *James Borchert*

Human Cargoes: The British Slave Trade to Spanish America, 1700-1739 *Colin A. Palmer*

Southern Black Leaders of the Reconstruction Era
Edited by Howard N. Rabinowitz

Black Leaders of the Twentieth Century
Edited by John Hope Franklin and August Meier

Slaves and Missionaries: The Disintegration of Jamaican Slave Society, 1787-1834 *Mary Turner*

Father Divine and the Struggle for Racial Equality
Robert Weisbrot

Communists in Harlem during the Depression
Mark Naison

Down from Equality: Black Chicagoans and the Public Schools, 1920-41 *Michael W. Homel*

Race and Kinship in a Midwestern Town: The Black Experience in Monroe, Michigan, 1900-1915 *James E. DeVries*

Down by the Riverside: A South Carolina Slave Community
Charles Joyner

Black Milwaukee: The Making of an Industrial Proletariat, 1915-45
Joe William Trotter, Jr.

Religious Philanthropy and Colonial Slavery: The American Correspondence of the Associates of Dr. Bray, 1717-1777
John C. Van Horne

Black History and the Historical Profession, 1915-80
August Meier and Elliott Rudwick

Rise to Be a People: A Biography of Paul Cuffe
Lamont D. Thomas

Reprint Editions

King: A Biography
David Levering Lewis Second edition

The Death and Life of Malcolm X
Peter Goldman Second edition

Race Relations in the Urban South, 1865-1890
Howard N. Rabinowitz, with a Foreword by C. Vann Woodward

Race Riot at East St. Louis, July 2, 1917
Elliott Rudwick

W. E. B. Du Bois: Voice of the Black Protest Movement
Elliott Rudwick

The Negro's Civil War: How American Negroes Felt and Acted during the War for the Union *James M. McPherson*

Lincoln and Black Freedom: A Study in Presidential Leadership
LaWanda Cox

RISE TO BE A PEOPLE

A Biography of Paul Cuffe

Lamont D. Thomas

Paul Cuffe (1759-1817) rose from humble Afro-Indian beginnings along Buzzards Bay in colonial New England to become a successful international merchant and celebrated champion of blacks and of Pan-African movements. Drawing on archival sources from Africa, England, and the United States, Thomas presents a sweeping reinterpretation of Cuffe's remarkable life in *Rise to Be a People*.

The author traces—through countless contemporary newspapers, letters, and shipping records — Cuffe's unrivaled business career as the fastest-rising black maritime merchant during the Federalist era. These and other primary sources authenticate such pioneering ventures as the commercial trade of Nova Scotian gypsum to Wilmington, Delaware; the thriving black New Bedford firm of Cuffe and Howards (cofounded with his former slave sons-in-law); the first non-slave-trading triangular scheme connecting North America, Africa, and Europe; and a black settler society in Sierra Leone cofounded specifically to challenge the economic monopoly of British merchants. For these accomplishments, Thomas argues, Cuffe should be recognized as an exemplary proponent of Western capitalism, not as a tool of economic imperialism.

Both a devout Quaker and political activist, Paul Cuffe has been hailed by noted scholar John Hope Franklin for having "identified a critical flaw in the revolutionary principles to which white Americans adhered" and by historian Letitia W. Brown as "a one-man civil rights movement." Whether sailing into